T0257706

IET SECURITY SERIES 24

Proof-of-Stake for Blockchain Networks

Call for authors: Advances in Distributed Computing and Blockchain Technologies

The objective of this book series is to enlighten researchers with the current trends in the field of blockchain technology and its integration with distributed computing and systems. Blockchains show riveting features such as decentralization, verifiability, fault tolerance, transparency, and accountability. The technology enables more secure, transparent, and traceable scenarios to assist in distributed applications. We plan to bring forward the technological aspects of blockchain technology for Internet of Things (IoTs), cloud computing, edge computing, fog computing, wireless sensor networks (WSNs), peer-to-peer (P2P) networks, mobile edge computing, and other distributed network paradigms for real-world enhanced and evolving future applications of distributed computing and systems.

Topics to be covered include: distributed computing and its applications; distributed vs. decentralized systems; tools and platforms for distributed systems; performance evaluation of distributed applications; blockchain technologies; blockchains and application domains; blockchains vs. distributed systems; cryptocurrency and distributed ledger technology; blockchain and IoT; ubiquitous computing; pervasive computing; cloud, edge, and fog computing; Internet of Things (IoT) technology; security issues in IoT; software tools and platforms for implementing blockchains in IoT networks; performance optimization of blockchain technology for distributed systems; social and ethical impacts of blockchains in distributed applications; blockchain technology and sustainability.

Proposals for international coherently integrated multi-authored or edited books, handbooks, and research monographs will be considered for this book series. We do not endorse, however, call for chapter books. The chapter authors will be invited personally and individually by the book editors. Each proposal will be reviewed by the book series editors with additional peer reviews from independent reviewers. Please contact:

- Dr Brij B. Gupta, National Institute of Technology (NIT), India; e-mail: gupta.brij@ieee.org
- Prof. Gregorio Martinez Perez, University of Murcia (UMU), Spain; e-mail: gregorio@um.es
- Dr Tu N. Nguyen, Kennesaw State University of Georgia, USA; e-mail: tu.nguyen@kennesaw.edu

Proof-of-Stake for Blockchain Networks

Fundamentals, challenges and approaches

Edited by
Cong T. Nguyen, Dinh Thai Hoang, Diep N. Nguyen,
Eryk Dutkiewicz, Loi Luu and Robert Joyce

The Institution of Engineering and Technology

Published by The Institution of Engineering and Technology, London, United Kingdom

The Institution of Engineering and Technology is registered as a Charity in England & Wales (no. 211014) and Scotland (no. SC038698).

The Institution of Engineering and Technology
Futures Place
Kings Way, Stevenage
Hertfordshire, SG1 2UA, United Kingdom

www.theiet.org

British Library Cataloguing in Publication Data
A catalogue record for this product is available from the British Library

ISBN 978-1-83953-828-5 (hardback)
ISBN 978-1-83953-829-2 (PDF)

Typeset in India by MPS Limited

Cover Image: Yuichiro Chino / Moment via Getty Images

Contents

**9 Summarizing Proof-of-Stake mechanisms and their practical
    deployments: applications, attacks, solutions, and future directions   189**
    Cong T. Nguyen, Dinh Thai Hoang, Diep N. Nguyen,
    Van-Dinh Nguyen and Eryk Dutkiewicz

About the editors

Cong T. Nguyen is a researcher and lecturer at the Institute of Fundamental and Applied Sciences and the Faculty of Information Technology, Duy Tan University, Vietnam. His research interests include blockchain technology, game theory, optimization, and operational research. He received his BS degree from Frankfurt University of Applied Sciences, Germany, MS degree from Technical University Berlin, Germany, and PhD degree from the University of Technology Sydney (UTS), Australia.

Dinh Thai Hoang is a faculty member of the School of Electrical and Data Engineering at the University of Technology Sydney, Australia. His research interests include emerging wireless communications and networking topics, especially machine-learning applications in networking, edge computing, and cybersecurity. He has received several awards, including ARC DECRA, IEEE TCSC Award, and IEEE TCI Rising Star Award. He is an editor of IEEE TWC, IEEE TMC, IEEE TCCN, IEEE TVT, and IEEE COMST.

Diep N. Nguyen is the Director of the Agile Communications and Computing Group, and the Director of Transnational Education, University of Technology Sydney (UTS), Australia. His research interests include mobile computing, computer networking, and machine-learning applications, with emphasis on systems' performance and security/privacy. He is a senior member of the IEEE, serving on Editorial Boards of the *IEEE Transactions on Mobile Computing*, *IEEE Communications Surveys & Tutorials*, and *IEEE Open Journal of the Communications Society*.

Eryk Dutkiewicz is the head of the School of Electrical and Data Engineering at the University of Technology Sydney, Australia. He has a joint professor appointment at Hokkaido University in Japan. He is also co-director of the UTS-VNU Joint Research Centres in Hanoi and in Ho Chi Minh City, Vietnam. He is a co-author of over 400 publications and 19 patent filings. His current research interests include 5G/6G communications and IoT systems and networks.

Loi Luu is founder of Caliber Ventures, a venture studio that helps build new blockchain startups with talented founders around the world. He previously founded Kyber Network, one of the earliest and popular on-chain decentralised trading protocols for cryptocurrencies, in 2017 and still serves as chairman of the board. He was selected in the Forbes 30 under 30 list for Asia, and Top 10 Innovators under 35 for Asia Pacific by MIT Technology Reviews. He earned his PhD in Computer Science from the National University of Singapore, where he worked to improve base technical layers, namely decentralisation, scalability and security for the public blockchain infrastructure.

Robert Joyce is the Head of Customer Strategy and Innovation for nbn Australia. He has 25+ years in telecommunications working for operators and vendors around the globe. Prior to joining nbn, he was Chief Technology Officer for Nokia in Australia and New Zealand, and, prior to that, Head of Radio Access Technologies for Qatar's Ooredoo Group where he oversaw the launch of the world's first 5G network in May 2018. He has published numerous academic papers on mobile communications and holds a PhD in "Self-Organising Heterogeneous Networks" from the University of Leeds, UK.

Introduction

Blockchain has recently attracted much attention from both academia and industry thanks to its advantages of transparency, decentralization, and immutability. A blockchain is a distributed database of records shared among network participants. With the help of cryptographic hash functions, digital signatures, and distributed consensus mechanisms, once a record enters the database, it cannot be altered without the consensus of the other network participants. As a result, data stored in a blockchain can be conventionally verified even in a decentralized and trustless environment, which has led to numerous blockchain applications ranging from finance, healthcare, entertainment, over to supply chain, transportation, and so on. Therefore, it is highly expected that blockchain will bring a vast array of opportunities to the development of next-generation information technologies and trigger a new round of technological innovations and industrial transformation in the context of future communication technologies.

Nodes in a blockchain network can be faulty, performing arbitrary or malicious behaviors, or possessing misinformation due to connection latency, i.e., Byzantine failures. The consensus mechanism is thus the core component of a blockchain network, which ensures that every participant agrees on the state of the network in such trustless environments. However, most of the current blockchain networks have been employing the Proof-of-Work (PoW) consensus mechanism which has serious limitations such as huge energy consumption, low transaction processing capabilities, and centralization and scalability issues. To overcome these problems, a new consensus mechanism has been developed recently, namely Proof-of-Stake (PoS), with many advantages including negligible energy consumption and especially very low consensus delay. As a result, this mechanism is expected to become a cutting-edge technology for future blockchain networks. For example, Cardano, the current biggest PoS cryptocurrency network, has a market capitalization of more than $18 billion. Moreover, Ethereum, the second most famous cryptocurrency with more than $231 billion in market capitalization, is planning to switch from PoW to PoS in September 2022. As a result, PoS is expected to gain even more attention from both the industry and academia. However, the PoS mechanism is also facing some challenges, including consensus security concerns, PoS-specific attacks, performance and scalability issues, and centralization risks.

In this regard, we introduce a new book, titled *"Proof-of-Stake for Blockchain Networks: Fundamentals, challenges and approaches,"* which will provide a comprehensive discussion and ideas on the PoS consensus mechanism. The book begins with an overview of blockchain technology and consensus mechanisms including basic concepts, network architecture, main components, and a brief introduction to other types of consensus mechanisms. The book then provides an in-depth view of diverse applications of the PoS consensus mechanism, including content caching in 6G networks, UAV networks, and mobile roaming management. Finally, we discuss important issues and their potential solutions, including trading and wealth evolution in PoS, quantum security for PoS, PoS-specific attacks, PoS performance and scalability issues, and stake pools and centralization risks in PoS blockchain networks.

Through this book, we aim to:

- Provide a fundamental overview of blockchain technology and different types of consensus mechanisms.
- Provide an in-depth view of diverse PoS applications, including content caching in 6G networks, UAV networks, and mobile roaming management.
- Discuss important issues and their potential solutions, including trading and wealth evolution in PoS, quantum security for PoS, PoS-specific attacks, PoS performance and scalability issues, and stake pools and centralization risks in PoS blockchain networks.

Chapter 1
Blockchain fundamental
Wenbo Wang[1], Shaohan Feng[2] and Zhengwei Ni[2]

Blockchain, as the fundamental technology underpinning decentralized and immutable ledgers, was originally proposed by the famous cryptocurrency project Bitcoin in 2008 [1]. Since then, extensive research has been conducted in this area, and their focus ranges in a wide spectrum from theoretical analysis of blockchain's backbone protocols [2] to its various applications, including in FinTech [3] and autonomous transaction-driven systems [4]. In simpler terms, IBM defines blockchain as "a shared, immutable ledger for recording transactions, tracking assets and building trust." From a technical perspective, the term "blockchain system" can be interpreted in two dimensions, namely, the "blockchains" which refer to a tamper-proof framework of data organization, and the "blockchain networks," which refer to a distributed system for "blockchain" data deployment and maintenance. These two interleaved aspects are driven by the development of both computer sciences and economic mechanisms and are also considered the key innovation brought forth by blockchain technologies.

The blockchain is built using an array of interconnected technologies. For on-chain data organization, blockchain protocols employ a number of established cryptographic techniques, such as asymmetric signatures and cryptographic hash functions, to establish a secure cryptographic link between blockchain users' identities and their corresponding transactions. This ensures proof of transaction authentication, thereby establishing ownership of tokenized assets. On the network level, users of a blockchain network collectively maintain an arbitrary order of transaction records by utilizing data "blocks" (i.e., data subsets) that are cryptographically linked according to their chronological order of confirmation. This cryptographic referencing technique enables the blockchain system to promptly detect any attempt at data tampering.

With regards to blockchain node/network organization, the longstanding challenge of binary agreement in state machine replication [5] is effectively addressed through consensus protocols implemented within a scalable, weakly synchronized network. This is accomplished through creatively incorporating economic incentive

[1]Faculty of Mechanical and Electrical Engineering, Kunming University of Science and Technology (KUST), China
[2]School of Information and Electronic Engineering (Sussex Artificial Intelligence Institute), Zhejiang Gongshang University, China

mechanisms into the process of global blockchain state maintenance, forming the data confirmation protocol now well-known as "block mining." This innovative approach rewards individual network participants for their contributions to establishing the order and validity of the transactions, therefore ensuring the security and decentralization of the blockchain.

Through consensus mechanisms, blockchain technology enables a logical data consistency, which further enables programmability with the distributedly executing scripts known as smart contracts.* These smart contracts serve as a decentralized intermediary not only for transaction notary and ID management but also for a wide range of applications such as general resource management [4,7]. The fully Turing-complete state machine provided by smart contracts over blockchains [8] ensures tamper-proof and decentralized execution, facilitating the development of general-purpose autonomous organizations, which creates the prosperous ecosystems for distributed applications (DApps, see [9] for an example).

This chapter aims to give a comprehensive overview of blockchains, primarily focusing on their component-protocol organization. The objective is to equip readers with the fundamental knowledge of blockchain systems, which is necessary for the discussions in subsequent chapters. The remaining sections of this chapter are structured as follows: Section 1.1 gives a layered overview of the blockchain system. Section 1.2 introduces the data organization protocol of blockchains. Section 1.3 focuses on the mechanisms of several mainstream consensus blockchain protocols. Section 1.4 introduces the basic operation mechanisms of smart contracts. The last section of this chapter presents some concluding remarks.

1.1 A structural overview of blockchain systems

Viewing from the network perspective, blockchain consists of a decentralized network of computing nodes connected via a virtual peer-to-peer (P2P) network. These nodes maintain replicated copies of the same set of digital transactions, ensuring that the information is widely distributed and redundant. The nodes in the network are designed to be trustless, meaning that they do not rely on a central authority for verification. The primary goal of a blockchain system is to enable consensus among these trustless nodes, ensuring that they can collectively agree upon a single canonical record of the set of transactions in chronological order. This canonical record, known as the blockchain, is tamper-proof, meaning that once a transaction is added to the blockchain, it becomes virtually impossible to alter or manipulate.

To achieve the functionalities mentioned earlier, a blockchain network is typically structured around four key protocol layers, each responsible for different functionalities. These layers include:

• Data and network organization layer: The protocols defined in this layer govern how data is organized, stored, and spread within the blockchain network. They

---

*The work in [6] provides a good example for the implementation of smart contract protocols.

define the structure of blocks, transaction formats, data validation mechanisms, and the rules for network communication between nodes.

- Incentivized distributed consensus layer: This layer incorporates the protocols that enable nodes in the blockchain network to reach consensus on the validity and order of transactions. The protocols are represented by the well-known mechanisms such as Proof of Work (PoW) [1], PoS [10], or other consensus algorithms that incentivize participants to validate transactions and secure consistency of data in the network.

- Layer of smart contracts and distributed virtual machines (VMs): This layer provides the protocols that allow the execution of smart contracts within a blockchain network. Smart contracts are self-executing contracts encoded on the blockchain with predefined rules and conditions. Distributed VMs (VMs) provide an environment for executing these smart contracts, paving the way for decentralized and autonomous organizations.

- Application layer based on DApps: The application layer builds upon the underlying layers and comprises of a wide range of DApps. These DApps engage with the blockchain network through human–machine interfaces, delivering diverse services and functionalities to blockchain users. The combination of these four layers allows for the creation of secure, transparent, and autonomous organizations running on blockchain technology.

It is worth noting that while some surveys may present the data organization, network organization, consensus, and incentivization protocols into separate layers (e.g., [7]), we group them into two core layers in this section mainly owing to their intertwined relationship and interdependency. We provide in Figure 1.1 a structural overview of these layers and the related ingredient technologies.

As illustrated in Figure 1.1, the protocols for data organization in blockchains offer various cryptographic functionalities to ensure secure and unique identities of nodes. These protocols also specify how records, such as transaction records and account balances, are cryptographically linked together in the blockchain on a node's local copy to maintain order and prevent tampering. The term "blockchain" originated from the practice in classical blockchain networks like Bitcoin, where digitally signed transactional records were grouped into tamper-evident batch data structures called "blocks." These blocks were then arranged in linear chronological order, creating a chain of blocks connected by tamper-evident hash pointers. However, to enhance processing efficiency, network scalability, and security, the linear framework of data organization can also be expanded to include nonlinear structures like trees and graphs of blocks (e.g., a directed acyclic graph in [11]). Similar to linear blockchains, the ordering of blocks in these structures is determined by the direction of the links between them. Regardless of the specific structure of block organization for order identification, cryptographic representation of data plays a crucial role in protecting privacy and ensuring data integrity in blockchain networks. Compared to conventional databases, it also enables more efficient storage on the blockchain while maintaining data integrity through cryptographic techniques such as hashing and digital signatures.

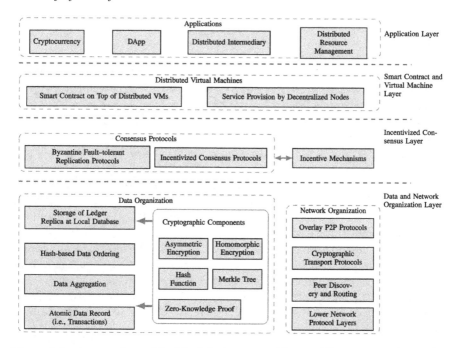

Figure 1.1   *An overview of the blockchain protocol layers. The arrows indicate the dependency between protocol components.*

In parallel to data organization protocols, network protocols are equally crucial in organizing the nodes in a blockchain system as a P2P network. These protocols enable the discovery of peers and routes (e.g., [12]), maintain connections, and ensure the encrypted transmission and synchronization of data over P2P links. Reliable data synchronization (e.g., through gossip protocol) across these connections is of utmost importance for the consensus layer, which is responsible for preserving the authenticity, consistency, and order of blockchain data throughout the network.

When it comes to distributed system design, consensus protocols play a crucial role in achieving Byzantine agreement [13] about the blockchain state within blockchain networks. These protocols ensure that nodes within the network can reach a consensus on a common update, namely, the consensus regarding the of the blockchain state with an updated blockchain header, even in the face of potential conflicting inputs and arbitrary faulty (i.e., Byzantine) behaviors exhibited by certain nodes. When implementing permissioned access-control schemes for network functionalities, blockchain networks typically adopt well-established Byzantine Fault–Tolerant (BFT) consensus protocols, such as Practical BFT (PBFT) [14], to reach consensus among a small group of authenticated nodes [15]. On the other hand, in open-access/permissionless blockchain networks, probabilistic Byzantine agreement is achieved in a decentralized manner through a combination of various techniques, including leader-election simulation based on cryptographic puzzles and monetary incentivization. Comparatively, permissioned consensus protocols rely on a semi-centralized consensus framework, which provides immediate consensus finality and high transaction-processing throughput at the cost of high messaging overhead. In contrast, permissionless consensus protocols are more suitable for blockchain networks with little control over network synchronization and node behaviors, although they may only provide probabilistic consensus finality. In blockchain networks which exhibit bounded delay and have an honest majority of nodes, permissionless consensus protocols offer significantly better support for network scalability at the expense of lower transaction processing throughput.

A reliable consensus layer further enables the deployment of a distributed VM on the smart contract layer. This layer serves as an abstraction, masking the intricacies of data organization/storage, data propagation, and consensus formation within a blockchain. It acts as an intermediary between the lower-level protocols and the applications, defining the implementation of high-level programming languages (e.g., Solidity in Ethereum [8]) for encoding smart contracts. The smart contract layer enables direct communication between the DApps and the blockchain network. These smart contracts are typically executed on a fully Turing-complete[†] machine (e.g., Ethereum virtual machines), ensuring the proper execution of general-purpose computation in a distributed manner. This allows blockchains to not only offer trusted data recording and timestamping services but also enable the functionalities of general-purpose autonomous organizations with DApps.

1.2 Data and network organization in blockchains

In terms of data structure, a blockchain can be envisioned as an ever-growing, append-only sequence [16], which prevents data deletion or modification. When it comes to data organization within the blockchain network, each node in the system maintains a local replica of the blockchain. This replica is structured hierarchically into three levels: transactions, blocks, and the blockchain itself. Each level necessitates specific cryptographic functionalities to safeguard the integrity and authenticity of the data. In what follows, a brief description will be provided with respect of these three levels, respectively.

1.2.1 Transactions and addresses

Transactions are typically created by groups of users or autonomous entities like smart contracts. Their purpose is to represent the transfer of tokens from senders to designated recipients. Transactions are the basic unit of data in a blockchain and consist of two main parts: inputs and outputs. The input of a transaction contains information about the token values being sent and the identities or addresses of the sending entities. This association guarantees that the tokens being transferred are accounted for and come from valid sources. On the other hand, the outputs determine how the

---

[†]In some existing blockchain systems, e.g., Bitcoin, the supported smart contracts could be Turing-incomplete.

input tokens will be distributed among the intended recipients (addresses). These outputs specify the new ownership of the tokens once the transaction is confirmed. To ensure the authenticity and integrity of a transaction record, cryptographic hashing and asymmetric encryption techniques are utilized. These techniques make sure that the transaction remains secure against tampering and that only authorized parties can access and modify its contents. A brief explanation of the two techniques is provided as follows.

- Cryptographic hashing: A cryptographic hash function is a mathematical process that takes any input of arbitrary length, such as a string of binary data, and maps it into a unique, fixed-length output known as the hash value or image. This transformation is achieved through cryptographic algorithms designed to ensure that even a small change in the input will produce a significantly different hash value. One important characteristic of a secure hash function, like Secure Hash Algorithm 256-bit (SHA-256), is that it is computationally infeasible to reverse-engineer or retrieve the original input from its corresponding hash value. This property is known as pre-image resistance. Furthermore, a secure hash function also exhibits the property of collision resistance. This means that the probability of two different inputs producing the same hash value is extremely low. While it is theoretically possible for two different inputs to result in a collision of the same hash value, the chances of this occurring are astronomically small. The adoption of secure hash functions aims to minimize the likelihood of collisions, making them highly reliable for ensuring data integrity and authenticity in blockchain transactions.
- Asymmetric key: In a blockchain network, every node generates a pair of keys: a private key and a corresponding public key. The private key is kept secret and known only to the owner node. It is used in conjunction with a digital signature function to create a fixed-length signature string for any given input message. The digital signature is unique to both the message and the private key used to generate it. On the other hand, the public key is openly shared with the other nodes and associated with a verification function. This function takes both the message and its claimed signature as inputs. The verification function uses the public key to verify whether the signature matches the input message and was generated using the correct private key. If the signature is valid and matches the message, the verification function returns a "true" result, indicating that the message has not been tampered with and was signed by the owner of the corresponding private key.

The participants (i.e., nodes or autonomous entities) in a blockchain network establish their identities by revealing their public keys as permanent addresses, which are represented as hashcodes of their public keys. These hashcodes are also known as pseudo-identities. They provide a way for nodes in the network to uniquely identify and interact with each other. When a transaction is created in the blockchain network, each input tuple is signed using the private key associated with the sending account, resulting in a unique digital signature. The network then is able to publicly validate the authenticity of the inputs by using the public key hashcode, the input tuple, and the digital signature as inputs to the verification function. The verification function checks whether the signature matches the input tuple and was generated using the correct private key associated with the pseudo-identities.

1.2.2   Block organization with hash pointers

In a blockchain network, a block functions as a container that holds a specific subset of transaction records. These blocks are created exclusively by those nodes actively participating in the consensus process (see later discussion for more details). The primary purpose of using a block-based data structure is to maintain the integrity of the transaction records and establish the order of them within a node's local view. To achieve this, each block includes a hash pointer data field within its structure. This hash pointer serves as a reference to the previous block in the chain, creating a link between blocks. By including this reference, the blockchain ensures that any modification to a previously confirmed block would be immediately detectable, as the resulting change would alter the hash pointer value stored in subsequent blocks.

Additionally, the block utilizes a cryptographic data structure known as the Merkle tree [17] to generate a tamper-evident representation for the transaction set contained within the block. This tree organizes the transactions in a hierarchical structure, which serves as a concise digest of all the transactions within the block. Any modification to a single transaction would result in a different root value of the tree. This property enables participants in the network to easily verify the integrity of the entire transaction set. The key component related to block data organization is described as follows:

- Hash pointer: A hash pointer to a block refers to the hashcode (hash value) obtained by applying a cryptographic hash function to the concatenation of the data fields within that block (see Figure 1.2). Apart from transaction records, these data fields include the hash pointers of the reference blocks, which indicates that the transactions contained in the reference blocks were created prior to the transactions in the current block. This mechanism of hash pointer generation ensures the chronological order and thus integrity of the blockchain. If any data within a block were to change, the hashcode representing this block would also change. Consequently, the hash pointer stored in any of its subsequent blocks no longer matches the updated hashcode, indicating that the referenced block has been tampered with.
- Merkle tree (see Figure 1.2): A Merkle tree is a data structure used to represent a collection of transactions. It takes the form of a binary tree, where each leaf node corresponds to the hashcode (hash value) of an individual transaction. Non-leaf nodes of the Merkle tree, also known as internal nodes, are labeled with the hashcode derived from concatenating the hashcodes (i.e., labels) of their two child nodes. This process continues recursively until the topmost node of the tree, namely, root hash is generated.

The root of the Merkle tree, often referred to as the Merkle digest, represents a summary of all the transactions in the tree. By storing only the Merkle root of the transactions within a block, a node can maintain locally a lightweight form of the blockchain. This means that instead of storing every transaction in its entirety,

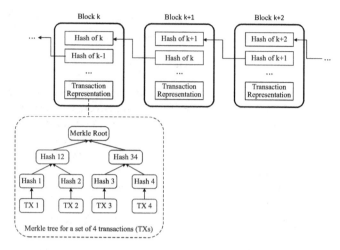

Figure 1.2   A chain of blocks, where the transactions in a single block are represented by a Merkle tree

the block only needs to store the Merkle root as a compact representation of the entire set of transactions. This lightweight storage approach allows for efficient validation and synchronization of the blockchain. Nodes can quickly verify the integrity of a block on the chain by comparing the stored Merkle root with the recalculated Merkle root based on the received transactions. If they match, it indicates that the transactions have not been tampered with. However, when utilizing this lightweight storage method, a node must retrieve complete transaction records from its peers by querying the network. This ensures that the node has access to the full details of the transactions, even though it only stores the Merkle root locally.

Within a node's local view of the blockchain, blocks are organized in a specific order based on the hash pointers that reference their predecessors or previous blocks. When there is only one predecessor block, these hash pointers create a chain-like structure, where each block is linked to the one before it in chronological order. Every blockchain includes a unique block called the "genesis block." The genesis block serves as the initial block in the chain and acts as the common ancestor for all valid blocks in the blockchain. It establishes the foundation from which subsequent blocks are built upon. The organization of blocks can vary depending on the number of hash pointers allowed to be retained by each block. We note that some blockchain implementations may allow multiple hash pointers, enabling a block to reference multiple previous blocks. This flexibility allows for more complex branching and merging of the blockchain, accommodating different consensus mechanisms and network requirements (e.g., the tree-like structure in GHOST [18]).

In addition to the Merkle digest, block header, and hash pointers, a block in the blockchain network can also contain auxiliary data fields. These additional fields serve various purposes and can include information such as timestamps, transaction fees, nonce values, or any other relevant metadata. The specific definition and usage of these auxiliary fields depend on the protocol adopted for block generation, which can vary across different blockchain implementations. Different blockchain networks and protocols have their own rules regarding block generation and the inclusion of auxiliary data fields. These rules are typically defined in a company with the consensus algorithm design, ensuring consistency and interoperability within the blockchain network.

1.2.3 Blockchain networks

In permissionless blockchains, the network protocol plays a crucial role in establishing a random topology among nodes and facilitating efficient information propagation for the synchronization of blockchain replicas. Unlike permissioned blockchains that require authentication, permissionless blockchains organize nodes as virtual overlay P2P networks without any centralized authority. To form the network topology and enable data communication, many permissionless blockchain networks leverage existing P2P protocols with slight modifications. For example, in Bitcoin-like blockchain networks, nodes rely on a predefined set of volunteer DNS servers for peer discovery and topology maintenance. These DNS servers return a random set of IP addresses belonging to bootstrapping nodes [19]. New nodes can use these addresses to initialize their list of peers, allowing them to connect to the network. Once connected, nodes in the blockchain network utilize these lists of peers to request or advertise addresses. The connection between nodes and peers is managed based on reputation using a penalty score system. If a peer sends malformed messages or behaves maliciously, the receiving node will increase the penalty score associated with that peer [20]. This penalty score serves as a measure of the peer's trustworthiness and reliability. As the penalty score increases, the receiving node may locally ban the IP address of the faulty node. This action helps maintain the integrity and security of the network by preventing malicious or unreliable nodes from participating further.

The information exchange protocol in a blockchain network is responsible for replicating the blockchain across all nodes in the network. This protocol enables the broadcast of transactions and blocks through P2P links using a gossip-like approach. In most blockchain networks, P2P links are established through persistent TCP connections. These connections are initiated after a protocol-level three-way handshake, which involves exchanging replica state and protocol/software versions of each node [21]. This handshake ensures that both nodes have compatible software versions and can communicate effectively. Once connections to peer nodes are established, another three-way handshake occurs specifically for exchanging new transactions and blocks with neighboring nodes. In this process, nodes notify their peers about received or generated transactions or blocks using hashcodes. Peers then respond with data-transfer requests specifying the hashcode of the required data. By exchanging hashcodes and responding with data-transfer requests, nodes efficiently propagate information throughout the network. This approach minimizes the amount of data that needs to be transmitted, as only the necessary information is requested based on the hashcodes.

Unlike in permissioned blockchains, nodes in a public blockchain are granted full access to core network functionalities. Furthermore, based on the functionalities they enable, nodes in a permissionless blockchain can be categorized as lightweight nodes, full nodes, and consensus nodes. Each type of node has specific responsibilities within the blockchain network:

- Lightweight nodes: Lightweight nodes, such as wallets, have limited storage capacity and only store block digests locally. They do not maintain a complete replica of the blockchain. Their primary function is to verify and propagate messages as well as maintain neighbor connections within the network. Lightweight nodes rely on other nodes, typically full nodes, to provide them with the necessary information to validate transactions and ensure the integrity of the blockchain.
- Full nodes: Full nodes maintain a complete and up-to-date replica of the blockchain. They store all transaction data, including the entire transaction history. Full nodes independently verify transactions and blocks, ensuring that they adhere to the consensus rules of the blockchain network. These nodes play a crucial role in maintaining the security and decentralization of the blockchain by validating transactions and contributing to the overall consensus process.
- Consensus nodes: Consensus nodes participate in the consensus mechanism of the blockchain network. They have the ability to publish new blocks and potentially influence the state of the blockchain. Consensus nodes can use either complete or lightweight storage, depending on the specific blockchain implementation. They are supposed to solve complex mathematical puzzles or performing other consensus algorithms to reach an agreement on the next valid block to be added to the blockchain.

Figure 1.3 provides an example of different node types in a public blockchain network. Note that consensus nodes are often referred to as "miners" in the

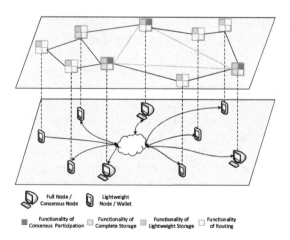

Figure 1.3   Roles of nodes in a public blockchain, where the links between consensus nodes are shown in blue in the virtual P2P network

context of blockchain consensus formation, particularly when incentive mechanisms are involved. It is important to note that the roles of nodes in a permissionless blockchain can lead to varying individual interests and thus potential conflicts. Therefore, protocol designs must take into account trustless behaviors, especially at the consensus layer, to prevent malicious participants from compromising the integrity of the blockchain. With the network protocols, it is now the responsibility of consensus mechanism design to achieve decentralized and secure operation in a blockchain.

1.3   Incentivized consensus in blockchains

The consensus layer in a blockchain aims to ensure that all nodes in the P2P network maintain a consistent view of the blockchain state, in other words, a unique identical chronological order of transactions. This problem can be likened to fault–tolerant state-machine replication, where the objective is to achieve consensus on a single, shared view of the sequence of blocks despite the occurrence of Byzantine or arbitrary failures [13]. Namely, each consensus node agrees on maintaining the same sequence of blocks. Byzantine failures encompass various types of failures that can occur within the network. These failures include malicious attacks, collusions, node mistakes, and connection errors. They can introduce inconsistencies or discrepancies in the blockchain state across different nodes.

The sequence of blocks represents the blockchain state, and transaction confirmations lead to state transitions. Transaction confirmations play a crucial role in the state replication process. As transactions are confirmed and included in blocks, they lead to state transitions within the blockchain. Each confirmed transaction contributes to the overall state of the blockchain, and achieving consensus on these state transitions is essential for maintaining a consistent blockchain state across the network. Blockchain updating protocols aim to achieve probabilistic consensus, also known as atomic broadcast, by satisfying the following properties [22]. These properties are crucial for preventing invalid or fraudulent transactions, ensuring smooth operation and no indefinite pending state update, and preventing forks or divergent views of the blockchain:

- Validity (correctness): The validity property ensures that honest nodes adopt the proposed blockchain extension if all honest nodes agree on it. In other words, if a majority of honest nodes agree on a particular block or transaction, it is considered valid and should be accepted by all honest nodes.
- Agreement (consistency): This property guarantees that when an honest node confirms a new block header, other honest nodes update their local views accordingly. It means that once a block is added to the blockchain and confirmed by an honest node, all other honest nodes should reach a consensus and include the same block in their local copies of the blockchain.
- Liveness (termination): Liveness ensures the eventual confirmation of transactions originating from honest nodes. It means that if an honest node initiates a valid

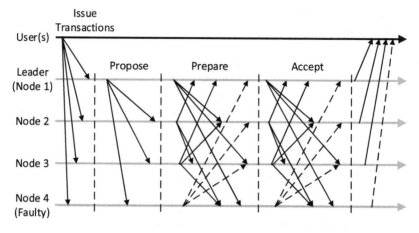

*Figure 1.4   BFT-based message pattern of three-way handshake in permissioned
blockchains*

transaction, it should eventually be included in the blockchain and confirmed by
the network.
- Total order: The total order property ensures that honest nodes accept the same
  transaction order in their local views. It means that all honest nodes should agree
  on the chronological order of transactions within the blockchain.

The consensus protocols used in blockchain networks can vary depending on the
type of network. In permissioned blockchain networks, where there is tight control
over consensus node synchronization, conventional BFT protocols are often utilized
to achieve consensus properties. An example of such a network is Ripple [23], where
synchronized servers adopt a voting mechanism to reach a consensus on the validity
and inclusion of transactions in the blockchain. For the generation of new blocks in
permissioned networks, external oracles can designate a primary node responsible for
creating the blocks. To ensure consensus among the nodes, a practical BFT (PBFT)
protocol with a three-phase commit scheme can be employed (see Figure 1.4). This
protocol, as seen in HyperLedger Fabric [15], allows the nodes to agree on the order
and content of transactions before adding them to the blockchain.

Permissionless blockchain networks, in contrast, do not have identity authentication or explicit synchronization schemes. This requires the consensus protocol
in permissionless networks to be scalable and tolerant to pseudo identities and poor
synchronization. In permissionless networks, any node can propose a state transition
by creating its own candidate block for the blockchain header. For linear blockchains,
the primary objective of the consensus protocol in these networks is to ensure that
every consensus node follows the "longest chain rule" [24]. According to this rule,
only the longest chain, organized as a linked list, is accepted as the canonical state
of the blockchain. This ensures that all nodes converge on the same version of the
blockchain.

Direct voting-based BFT protocols are not suitable for permissionless blockchain networks due to the lack of identity authentication. Instead, incentive-based consensus schemes like the PoW protocol [1] are widely adopted.

1.3.1 PoW for incentivized consensus

The PoW protocol addresses the challenges of pseudonymity, scalability, and poor synchronization in a permissionless blockchain. It offers a solution to the Byzantine generals problem by employing a cryptographic puzzle-solving racing game. From a single node's perspective, the PoW consensus protocol comprises three primary procedures: chain validation, chain comparison and extension, and PoW puzzle solution search:

- Chain validation: This procedure involves examining the structural properties of a given blockchain or candidate blockchain to ensure valid PoW solutions and no conflicts between transactions. During chain validation, nodes also verify that transactions are included in blocks only if they meet specific conditions (e.g., valid sender and receiver addresses, sufficient fees).
- Chain comparison and extension: This procedure compares the lengths of different blockchain proposals to guarantee that only the longest valid proposal is adopted by honest nodes. When a node receives a new block from its neighbor nodes, it compares the lengths of its local blockchain view and the new proposal. If the new proposal is longer, the node adds the new block to its local view and broadcasts it to other nodes. This process ensures that all honest nodes eventually reach consensus on the same longest chain.
- PoW solution searching: Briefly, the PoW solution involves exhaustively querying a cryptographic hash function to find a partial preimage that meets a predefined condition. Let $\mathcal{H}(\cdot)$ represent the hash function and x denote the binary string constructed based on the candidate block data. A specific condition usually requires that $\mathcal{H}(x)$ starts with a predetermined number of zeros.

Formally, the PoW solution can be defined as follows: find the nonce n value that, when combined with the block data in x, produces a block header hashed value bh that meets the predefined condition:

$$bh = \mathcal{H}(x \| n) \leq D(h), \tag{1.1}$$

where for some fixed length of bits L, $D(h) = 2^{L-h}$, which in binary form starts with at least h zeros.

The time complexity for solving the puzzle in (1.1) is $O(2^h)$ [25]. This ensures that the PoW solution process can be used to simulate a verifiable process of weighted random coin-tossing, where the probability of winning depends on the hashrate (rate of querying the random oracle) contributed by nodes to the network. In simpler term, each new block can be seen as being generated through a lottery-like process, where the probability of a node or node coalition winning the game, i.e., being the first to find

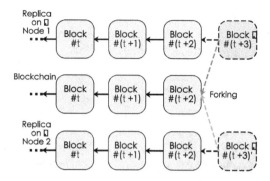

Figure 1.5   An example of temporary fork at nodes 1 and 2, where their local PoW solutions lead to different proposals of the new blockchain header

a satisfying preimage, is determined by the ratio of their computational resources to the total computational resources in the network. This probability can be expressed as:

$$\text{Pr}_i^{\text{win}} = \frac{w_i}{\sum_{j \in \mathcal{N}} w_j}, \qquad (1.2)$$

where w_i represents the computational resources contributed by node i to puzzle solving and $\mathcal{N}$ is the set of all nodes. This puzzle race game actually simulates a leader election process in the traditional protocols. However, unlike BFT, in PoW, a node accepts received block proposals based on the longest-chain rule after chain validation. Since there is no need for an all-to-all messaging phase, the message complexity of PoW is much smaller ($O(n)$) than BFT.

The property of PoW protocol consuming significant computational power leads to a competitive race, where nodes invest in high hashrate to increase their chances of solving the puzzle and winning. This serves as a deterrent against Sybil attacks, as malicious nodes faking multiple identities cannot easily possess the corresponding computational power. However, the substantial economic cost, particularly in terms of electricity consumption for hash queries, makes it impractical for nodes to consistently participate in the consensus process at a financial loss. To tackle this issue, the PoW protocol introduces incentives by probabilistically rewarding participants through a mechanism involving token supply and transaction tipping [1]. The protocol assumes that all participant nodes act in their own self-interest, ensuring that the consensus mechanism is compatible with individual interest. In other words, any node that deviates from faithfully following the protocol will suffer a financial loss.

However, as nodes can propose arbitrary blocks, temporary forks can occur in the blockchain state [24] (see Figure 1.5). To ensure convergence to a canonical state, the PoW protocol relies on the assumption that the majority of nodes follow the longest chain rule and altruistically forward information to their neighbors. However, rational nodes may lack incentives for transaction/block propagation, making it difficult to resolve blockchain forking. As a result, it has been suggested that special incentive measures should be taken into account not only in the consensus layer but also in the network protocol layer [26].

1.3.2 Proof of Stakes

To tackle the problem of consuming resource for useless puzzle solution, Proof-of-Stake (PoS) protocols have been proposed as an alternative to PoW-based leader election mechanism in the process of chain extension. These protocols, discussed in papers such as [10,27], remove the PoW puzzle-solving structure and instead simulate a verifiable random function based on the stake distribution among the consensus nodes in the network. In a PoS protocol, the selection of a node to create a new block and extend the chain is not based on the share of computational power but rather on the ownership or stake of these digital tokens. The more tokens a node possesses, the higher its chances of being selected as the validator for the next block. This approach ensures that those who hold a larger stake in the network have a greater influence over the consensus process.

A typical random leader election algorithm, known as follow-the-coin as proposed by [27], exemplifies how PoS works. The algorithm uses the concept of digital tokens (i.e., coins) as the minimum unit of value in the blockchain. Each token is assigned an index between 0 and the total number of available coins. In a simplified PoS protocol, the current header block is used to seed the follow-the-coin algorithm and select a random validation leader for generating the next header block. To achieve this, the hash function $\mathcal{H}(\cdot)$ is queried with the current header block of the chain, and the output hashcode is used as the random token index to initialize the leader searching process. The algorithm then outputs a token index and traces back to the minting block associated with the selected token. The node that created the block or currently holds that token is then designated as the leader to generate the new block. In this procedure, the probability that a node i owning a total amount of state s_i is elected as the leader among consensus node set $\mathcal{N}$ is

$$\mathrm{Pr}_i^{\mathrm{win}} = \frac{s_i}{\sum_{j \in \mathcal{N}} s_j}, \tag{1.3}$$

which thus takes a similar form of (1.2) for winner determination in PoW. To enable public verification of the block, the validation leader is required to include its signature in the new block, replacing the nonce field used in PoW-based blockchains.

PoS does not rely on the puzzle solution competition to simulate the random generating process of the leader node for proposing new blocks. Instead, it relies on asymmetric key-based signing and verification. Therefore, this process is often referred to as "virtual mining" because now the block mining nodes do not consume any computation or other resources. This leads to the desired feature that forking no longer occurs when all nodes are honest. Compared to PoW, PoS preserves the longest-chain rule but uses a different approach to simulate the verifiable random function for block leader generation. This allows for the same techniques used to analyze Byzantine agreements in PoW-based blockchains to be applied to quantitatively analyze PoS protocols.

Another popular category of PoS can be found in Ethereum [28], where stake-holders work as the peer nodes in a BFT protocol. Validating nodes can broadcast vote messages to determine which block in the blockchain should be finalized. Unlike traditional identity-based voting, the validator's vote is tied to the stake that they hold rather than their identity. More specifically, to join the block validation committee, a node needs to deposit an amount of stakes to gain the proportional voting power in the committee. The Ethereum PoS protocol ensures deterministic liveness (as opposed to the probabilistic liveness of PoW) and accountable safety. It can tolerate Byzantine nodes controlling up to 1/3 of the total voting power weighted by stake in the network. The practical protocol implemented in Ethereum is known as Casper [28], which emphasizes the BFT-based mechanism for finalizing the chain with verified checkpoint blocks at every fixed interval of blocks.

Based on the standard PoW mechanism, a number of improved protocols have been developed, aiming at enhancing the security level of the consensus protocol. For instance, the random generator used in the standard follow-the-coin protocol is expected to produce unbiased and unpredictable random index of coins. However, when taking the blockchain header block as the seed of the hash function, it is possible for the current block-generation leader to test several possible new blocks containing different transactions to increase its chance of being elected again in the next epoch. This vulnerability is known as the grinding attack [10]. Instead of using the header block, the hash function can be seeded using the timestamp [29] or some already-confirmed block that is a certain number of blocks deep in the chain [30] to prevent nodes from taking advantage of such a vulnerability.

1.4   Smart contracts and DApps

Protocols in the consensus layer ensure that each normal node in the blockchain network eventually aligns itself with the canonical state of the blockchain. In most of existing blockchain platforms, this enables a Turing-complete distributed virtual state machine. As a result, when executing locally a set of scripts/codes that are associated with the transactions in the blockchain and are guaranteed to only lead to deterministic state transitions,[‡] a normal node is able to compare its local execution results with those agreed upon by the other nodes as part of the blockchain state update. Then, following the principle of BFT consensus, the node is able to validate the local execution results.

A smart contract is the byte codes that define the aforementioned state transition logic. It is written and compiled in a specific programming language (e.g., Solidity for Ethereum, depending on the blockchain platform in concern), and then published on the blockchain in the form of a transaction by the publisher node. For instance, in Ethereum [31], once deployed, a smart contract is stored on the chain and assigned a unique address. Then, a smart contract owns an account in a similar way to an

---

[‡]Deterministic state-transition ensures that the same inputs will always produce the same outputs, leading to consistent (thus verifiable) results across all nodes.

on-chain node. Compared to the addresses of on-chain nodes (see Section 1.2.1), the address of a smart contract is obtained by inputting the public key of the publisher and a nonce into the cryptographic hash function. To achieve this, the publisher needs to submit a transaction containing the byte codes and all necessary parameters, along with certain transaction fees needed for incentivizing distributed script execution. At this stage, the initial parameters define the initial state of the smart contract.

A deployed smart contract can be executed in either a one-to-many or many-to-many form, depending on the involved participants or stakeholders. In the one-to-many scenarios, a designated node in the network, typically the smart contract publisher, initiates the smart contract execution by sending a transaction to the address representing that smart contract. Subsequently, the smart contract execution automatically proceeds once the other participants fulfill the execution condition by sending their transactions, respectively. For each participant, the transaction to be sent as an input to the smart contract should specify the functions in the smart contract that are to be utilized and their associated parameters. As long as the pre-defined conditions in the smart contract are satisfied, the smart contract is executed. In the many-to-many cases, it is possible for multiple participants to initiate the smart contract execution by sending their respective transactions. Similar to the one-to-many scenario, all other participants need to meet the conditions defined in the smart contract before the execution of the smart contract can take place.

During the smart contract execution, a series of transactions may be generated. In contrast to transactions created by nodes, transactions generated by a smart contract are signed using the private key of the smart contract publisher. These transactions are then confirmed as components of the newly generated blocks in the consensus formation process. Prior to transaction confirmation, these transactions remain pending in the transaction pool of the blockchain for validation. At this stage, any normal node (typically, a consensus node) interested in validating these transactions can locally execute the smart contract and compare the outputs with the pending transactions in the pool. The smart contract, or more precisely, the consensus nodes executing the smart contract, will periodically check if any condition that triggers the state transition is satisfied. Consequently, any transaction output by the smart contract is added to the pool of transactions for validation. Furthermore, once the output transactions are confirmed and added to the blockchain, the initial state of the smart contract may be updated if the execution of the smart contract changed its internal variables.

With the help of the smart contract layer, the implementation of decentralized applications no longer requires consideration of the underlying protocol details of the blockchain. In the context of a specific blockchain platform, a DApp is typically comprised of a collection of smart contracts, each corresponding to a unique microservice. It is important to note that the smart contracts should not be considered to be confined to the management of only virtual on-chain resources, such as node identity registration and digitized asset (token) distribution. At the application level, a DApp can readily associate a wide range of physical-world resources, including sensor-generated data in IoTs and operational resources in a cyber-physical system (just to mention a few example), with the transactions on the blockchain. Recently a number of technical surveys [4,32–34] have outlined the potential strengths of smart-contract-based DApps across various domains, ranging from distributed resource allocation to digital twins. Interested readers are encouraged to explore these references for further details, as they serve as a convenient starting point for deeper investigation.

1.5 Conclusion

In this chapter, we have provided a comprehensive overview of the fundamental knowledge regarding blockchains. We have summarized the four crucial protocol layers that are essential for blockchain implementation. Specifically, we have introduced the fundamentals of the data organization and network organization protocols in blockchains. Furthermore, by combining incentive mechanisms and consensus mechanisms, we have presented two major protocols, namely, PoW and Proof-of-Stake, to illustrate the fundamental mechanisms of incentivized consensus protocols in permissionless blockchains. Finally, we have provided a high-level overview of the smart contract layer as well as the decentralized applications of blockchains.

References

[1]   Nakamoto S. Bitcoin: a peer-to-peer electronic cash system. Self-published Paper. 2008 May. Available from: https://bitcoin.org/bitcoin.pdf.

[2]   Bonneau J, Miller A, Clark J, *et al.* SoK: research perspectives and challenges for bitcoin and cryptocurrencies. In: *2015 IEEE Symposium on Security and Privacy.* San Jose, CA; 2015. p. 104–121.

[3]   Sangwan RS, Kassab M, and Capitolo C. Architectural considerations for blockchain based systems for financial transactions. *Procedia Computer Science.* 2020;168:265–271. "Complex Adaptive Systems", Malvern, PA, November 13–15, 2019.

[4]   Yue K, Zhang Y, Chen Y, *et al.* A survey of decentralizing applications via blockchain: the 5G and beyond perspective. *IEEE Communications Surveys & Tutorials.* 2021;23(4):2191–2217.

[5]   Raynal M. Communication and agreement abstractions for fault-tolerant asynchronous distributed systems. *Synthesis Lectures on Distributed Computing Theory.* 2010;1(1):1–273.

[6]   Kosba A, Miller A, Shi E, *et al.* Hawk: the blockchain model of cryptography and privacy-preserving smart contracts. In: *2016 IEEE Symposium on Security and Privacy (SP).* San Jose, CA; 2016. p. 839–858.

[7]   Wang X, Ren X, Qiu C, *et al.* Integrating edge intelligence and blockchain: what, why, and how. *IEEE Communications Surveys & Tutorials.* 2022; 24(4):2193–2229.

[8]   Atzei N, Bartoletti M, and Cimoli T. A survey of attacks on ethereum smart contracts (SoK). In: *Principles of Security and Trust: 6th International Conference, POST 2017, Held as Part of the European Joint Conferences on Theory and Practice of Software.* Uppsala, Sweden; 2017. p. 164–186.

[9]   Chatzopoulos D, Ahmadi M, Kosta S, *et al.* FlopCoin: a cryptocurrency for computation offloading. *IEEE Transactions on Mobile Computing.* 2018;17(5):1062–1075.

[10] Kiayias A, Russell A, David B, *et al.* Ouroboros: a provably secure proof-of-stake blockchain protocol. In: *Advances in Cryptology – CRYPTO 2017: 37th Annual International Cryptology Conference.* Santa Barbara, CA; 2017. p. 357–388.

[11] Popov S. *The Tangle Version 1.4.3.* IOTA Foundation; 2018.

[12] Maymounkov P and Mazières D. Kademlia: a peer-to-peer information system based on the XOR metric. In: *Peer-to-Peer Systems: First International Workshop.* Cambridge, MA; 2002. p. 53–65.

[13] Schneider FB. Implementing fault-tolerant services using the state machine approach: a tutorial. *ACM Computing Surveys.* 1990;22(4):299–319.

[14] Castro M and Liskov B. Practical Byzantine fault tolerance and proactive recovery. *ACM Transactions on Computer Systems.* 2002;20(4):398–461.

[15] Cachin C. Architecture of the hyperledger blockchain fabric. In: *Workshop on Distributed Cryptocurrencies and Consensus Ledgers (DCCL 2016).* Chicago, IL; 2016.

[16] Garay J, Kiayias A, and Leonardos N. The Bitcoin backbone protocol: analysis and applications. In: *Advances in Cryptology – EUROCRYPT 2015: 34th Annual International Conference on the Theory and Applications of Cryptographic Techniques, Part II.* Sofia, Bulgaria; 2015. p. 281–310.

[17] Merkle RC. A digital signature based on a conventional encryption function. In: Pomerance C, editor. *Advances in Cryptology – CRYPTO '87: Conference on the Theory and Applications of Cryptographic Techniques.* Santa Barbara, CA; 1987. p. 369–378.

[18] Sapirshtein A, Sompolinsky Y, and Zohar A. Optimal selfish mining strategies in bitcoin. In: *Financial Cryptography and Data Security: 20th International Conference, Revised Selected Papers.* Christ Church, Barbados; 2017. p. 515–532.

[19] Decker C and Wattenhofer R. Information propagation in the Bitcoin network. In: *Proceedings of IEEE International Conference on Peer-to-Peer Computing.* Trento, Italy; 2013. p. 1–10.

[20] Biryukov A, Khovratovich D, and Pustogarov I. Deanonymisation of clients in bitcoin P2P network. In: *Proceedings of the 2014 ACM SIGSAC Conference on Computer and Communications Security. CCS '14.* Scottsdale, AZ; 2014. p. 15–29.

[21] Gencer AE, Basu S, Eyal I, *et al.* Decentralization in Bitcoin and Ethereum Networks; 2018. arXiv preprint arXiv:180103998.

[22] Cachin C, Kursawe K, Petzold F, *et al.* Secure and efficient asynchronous broadcast protocols. In: *Advances in Cryptology – CRYPTO 2001: 21st Annual International Cryptology Conference.* Santa Barbara, CA: Springer Berlin Heidelberg; 2001. p. 524–541.

[23] Schwartz D, Youngs N, and Britto A. *The Ripple Protocol Consensus Algorithm*, vol. 5. Ripple Labs Inc White Paper; 2014.

[24] Tschorsch F and Scheuermann B. Bitcoin and beyond: a technical survey on decentralized digital currencies. *IEEE Communications Surveys Tutorials*. 2016;18(3):2084–2123.

[25] Debus J. *Consensus Methods in Blockchain Systems*. Frankfurt School of Finance & Management, Blockchain Center; 2017.

[26] Wu J, Guo S, Huang H, *et al*. Information and communications technologies for sustainable development goals: state-of-the-art, needs and perspectives. *IEEE Communications Surveys Tutorials*. 2018;20(3):2389–2406.

[27] Bentov I, Gabizon A, and Mizrahi A. Cryptocurrencies without proof of work. In: *International Conference on Financial Cryptography and Data Security*. Christ Church, Barbados; 2016. p. 142–157.

[28] Buterin V and Griffith V. Casper the Friendly Finality Gadget; 2017. arXiv preprint arXiv:171009437.

[29] Bentov I, Pass R, and Shi E. Snow white: provably secure proofs of stake. *IACR Cryptology ePrint Archive*. 2016;2016:919.

[30] Bentov I, Lee C, Mizrahi A, *et al*. Proof of activity: extending bitcoin's proof of work via proof of stake (extended abstract). *ACM SIGMETRICS Performance Evaluation Review*. 2014;42(3):34–37.

[31] Wood G. Ethereum: a secure decentralised generalised transaction ledger (EIP-150 Revision). *Ethereum Project Yellow Paper*, vol. 151. 2017.

[32] Cao B, Wang Z, Zhang L, *et al*. Blockchain systems, technologies, and applications: a methodology perspective. *IEEE Communications Surveys & Tutorials*. 2023;25(1):353–385.

[33] Wang X, Ren X, Qiu C, *et al*. Integrating edge intelligence and blockchain: what, why, and how. *IEEE Communications Surveys & Tutorials*. 2022;24(4): 2193–385.

[34] Yaqoob I, Salah K, Uddin M, *et al*. Blockchain for digital twin: recent advances and future research challenges. *IEEE Network*. 2020;34(5):290–298.

Chapter 2
Consensus mechanisms
Bahareh Lashkari[1] and Petr Musilek[1]

With the launch of the Bitcoin blockchain in 2009, the Proof-of-Work (PoW) consensus, additionally referred to as the Nakamoto consensus, was introduced. In essence, it is a leader election algorithm with an explicit and arbitrary waiting interval between consecutive leader elections. By uniformly slowing down proposals for all participants, the premise behind PoW in a blockchain is to fulfill the following desires. It enables participants to reach a uniform consensus and increases the cost of sybil attacks, strengthening the reliability of the blockchain. However, it has become increasingly difficult to maintain consensus among network nodes as the network grows. As a result, energy requirements for consistent operation of the PoW consensus caused major concerns and became the focus of extensive research.

Since their inception, consensus algorithms have gone through a series of adaptations and improvements to guarantee the consistent operation of their corresponding distributed ledger. This has led to the emergence of various consensus protocols over the last decades. The need for trustworthy consensus protocols has grown significantly as a result of the widespread adoption of distributed ledger technology in various application areas, including financial institutions. For use cases involving strict financial regulations, the safety measures of the pioneer consensus algorithms, such as proof of work, fail to operate effectively. As a result, consensus algorithms that are detached from the traditional proof of work began to emerge. Therefore, a number of consensus protocols have been introduced with varying degrees of self-enforcing principles and incentive structures. Consensus protocols like Ripple originated as a result of this breakthrough.

This chapter explores the most recent developments in consensus protocols since Paxos. It starts with an introduction to consensus mechanisms and their classification in Section 2.1. Subsequent sections explore consensus algorithms within each category, providing a comparative analysis. In each section, we present Tables 2.1–2.4 to illustrate the scalability, finality, and communication models of each class of consensus. Additionally, an analysis of quantum consensus mechanisms, categorized by their underlying techniques and quantum system, is provided in Table 2.2.5. Finally, in Section 2.4, we conclude the chapter.

[1] Department of Electrical and Computer Engineering, University of Alberta, Canada

Table 2.1   Proof compliant hybrid alternative consensus mechanism

Consensus	Scalability	Finality	Communication model
Minotaur [4]	Low	Probabilistic	Partially synchronous
Green-PoW [5]	High	Deterministic	Asynchronous
HDPoA [6]	High	Deterministic	Synchronous

Table 2.2   BFT compliant hybrid alternative consensus mechanism

Consensus	Scalability	Finality	Communication model
EB-BFT [7]	High	Probabilistic	Synchronous
FPoR [8]	High	Deterministic	Asynchronous
SG-PBFT [9]	High	Deterministic	Asynchronous
Mosaic [14]	High	Deterministic	Synchronous
DPNPBFT [15]	High	–	Synchronous
PPoR [16]	High	Deterministic	Synchronous

Table 2.3   Cross-compliant hybrid alternative consensus mechanism

Consensus	Scalability	Finality	Communication model
PoEC [19]	High	–	Synchronous
HiCoOB [20]	High	Deterministic	Synchronous
HCM [21]	High	Deterministic	–
RAFT+ [22]	High	–	Synchronous

Table 2.4   Quantum-free pure alternative consensus mechanisms

Consensus	Scalability	Finality	Communication model
PoAj [23]	High	–	–
Teegraph [24]	High	Probabilistic	Asynchronous
RVC [25]	High	–	Synchronous
Proof of Chance [26]	High	–	Partially synchronous
ACCORD [27]	High	Deterministic	Partially synchronous
PoR [28]	High	Probabilistic	–
Proof of Sense [29]	High	Probabilistic	–

Table 2.5   Comparison of quantum consensus mechanisms

Consensus	Underlying method	Quantum system	Class
QDPoS [37]	Vote-based entanglement	Digital Signature	Hybrid cross compliant
QZKP [38]	Entanglement	Zero knowledge proof	Pure quantum-based
QT [39]	Teleportation entanglement	Zero knowledge proof	Pure quantum-based
QEDPoS [40]	Entanglement	Quantum signature	Hybrid cross compliant
PQTS [41]	NPhard problem	Threshold signature	Pure quantum-based
QAA [42]	Entanglement	Code-based	Pure quantum-based
VQRN [43]	LWE (Learning with errors)	Digital signature	Pure quantum-based
PQSC [44]	Quadratic equations	Multi-variate	Pure quantum-based
MQE-PoW [45]	MQ problem	Multi-variate	Hybrid cross compliant
QEMR [32]	Homomorphic encryption entanglement	Quantum signature/ quantum identity authentication	Pure quantum-based
QSYAC [34]	Toeplitz signature	Hash based	Hybrid cross compliant
LPoW [46]	Hermite SVP problem	Lattice based	Hybrid cross compliant
GHZ-QDBA [47]	GHZ entanglement	Quantum signature	Hybrid cross compliant
QPoA [48]	QRNG	Identity-based Quantum signature	Hybrid cross compliant
CGBS [49]	Boson-sampling	BQP	Hybrid cross compliant

2.1   Introduction

The primary component of a blockchain as a distributed and decentralized network is consensus. Blockchain owes its versatility to consensus algorithms which are founded on the premise that secure updates must be carried out on the distributed ledger at frequent intervals. To this end, state machine replication is among the strategies to ensure that shared states are in place and functioning in accordance with the established state transition guidelines. As the state is distributed across a number of network replicas, the outputs from the state's execution will ultimately turn out the same. As a result, replicas must communicate with one another and use a consensus process to reach an agreement on potential state alterations. Consensus determines which node in the network is entitled to append the preceding block to the chain. This preserves the accuracy and reliability of the data by allowing users to reach an agreement on the order of the transactions.

Depending on the specific configuration of the network, the consensus algorithm employed within a distributed network may be resilient to failures and fraudulent attacks. However, establishing consensus in a distributed system becomes difficult as it needs a consensus mechanism that preserves characteristics such as adversity toler-ance, failure resilience, and network partitioning. Additionally, it needs to incorporate safety precautions like regulating the activity of malicious nodes through the adop-tion of rules like synchrony or message broadcast. As a result, the prominence of a consensus mechanism is dependent on its capacity to maintain three crucial network properties while preserving a global state agreement. Consensus has to ensure the network's safety, liveness, and fault tolerance; as a result, these qualities are assessed to determine how well it performs.

Paxos took the early steps towards developing a fault–tolerant methodology con-sidering the implications of the inconsistent system provisioning. As the very first consensus algorithm, Paxos enables a network of distributed nodes to reach an agree-ment on the result of a single update through asynchronous message-passing. The distributed nodes consist of proposers, acceptors, and learners who, respectively, suggest, choose, and learn a single value. Paxos presumptively has a group of coor-dinators. In general, the same processes serve in both the coordinator and acceptor positions. As depicted in Figure 2.1, every round has a predetermined coordinator who receives the proposal and starts contacting potential acceptors. Acceptors who receive the participation request will forward the round number and the correspond-ing round values. As a result, the coordinator is able to select a value using what is contained in the responses, then distribute it to acceptors to vote. Acceptors will vote and broadcast their votes to all learners in each round. Learners will learn the received values only if the majority of votes are aligned.

The preliminary consensus algorithm employed by the blockchain was PoW, which refers to the practice of verifying transactions through nodes and leveraging brute-force computing power. In the case of Bitcoin, there is a designated mining rate of 10 min, and the network as a whole is capable of processing a total of seven trans-actions per second. The interval over which a new block is appended to the blockchain

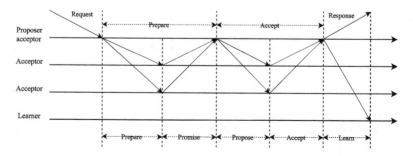

Figure 2.1   Communication model of Paxos

has to be kept consistent in order to ensure the effectiveness of PoW blockchain networks. As a result, the complexity of the cryptographic puzzle used to generate the validating hash adjusts to the hash-rate in order to uphold a predetermined mining rate. As illustrated in Figure 2.2, the new transactions keep track of all previously verified transactions, resulting in larger blocks that make it particularly more challenging to tackle these cryptographic puzzles. Therefore, the PoW offers financial value while consuming significant amounts of energy.

For use cases involving strict financial regulations, the safety measures of the pioneer consensus algorithms, such as PoW, fail to operate effectively. As a result, consensus algorithms that are detached from the traditional PoW began to emerge. Therefore, a number of consensus protocols have been introduced with varying degrees of self-enforcing principles and incentive structures. Consensus protocols like Ripple originated as a result of this breakthrough. Numerous thorough studies have examined these algorithms along with a comparative analysis of their application domains [1,2]. This chapter recapitulates our previous analysis [3] and reviews the most recent advances in the surveyed algorithms. An updated classification is presented in Figure 2.3.

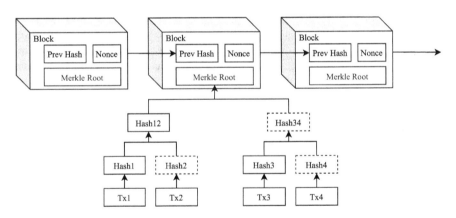

Figure 2.2   PoW mechanism

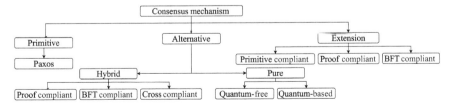

Figure 2.3   Classification of consensus mechanisms

This classification places the conventional consensus protocols in the first class, with Paxos serving as the primitive fault tolerance mechanism. Accordingly, if a consensus mechanism does not belong to primitives, it is classified as either proof compliant, Byzantine fault tolerance (BFT) compliant, primitive compliant, or cross-compliant. Any variant of Paxos that has been suggested as an extension to this consensus and implements the protocol's primary characteristics are identified as primitive compliant mechanisms. Since the invention of distributed ledgers, proof protocols have been embedded alongside blockchains due to their effectiveness in strengthening the reliability and privacy of decentralized networks. Hence, proof compliances are either modifications to proof protocols that take the fundamental elements of the protocol and try to improve the algorithm, or they are substitutes that have been presented as novel proof mechanisms.

As a result, cross-compliant refers to proof protocols that have been embedded into the configuration of other cryptographic primitives. BFT-compliant class includes the BFT algorithm and its variations. An algorithm from this class is either suggested as an addition to current BFT methods or as a substitute that incorporates the positive aspects of BFT protocols and improves upon them to minimize the drawbacks. Otherwise, it is regarded as an alternative that encompasses various BFT protocols and serves as a hybrid alternative that remains BFT-compliant. Protocols that put forward a novel consensus without maintaining the characteristics of formerly proposed mechanisms to overcome the current shortcomings are known as pure alternatives. This work expands the definition of pure protocols to include quantum-based and quantum-free algorithms. The following sections are devoted to analysing the most recent developments in each category of consensus mechanism.

2.2   Alternative consensus mechanisms

2.2.1   *Proof compliant hybrid alternatives*

2.2.1.1   Minotaur

Multi-resource blockchain consensus [4] is a fungible solution that integrates both the PoW and PoS. To ensure equal distribution across work and stake, Minotaur functions in intervals while frequently updating its available computational capacity. Minotaur claims to be capable of managing more work fluctuations while generalizing to a wide variety of resources. In essence, Minotaur is an extended chain protocol with a virtual stake that serves as the schedule for the block-proposer. The mining power of the protocol demonstrated concrete proof supporting the suitability of the approach in real-life scenarios.

2.2.1.2   Green-PoW

As an alternative approach to the classic PoW, Green-PoW [5] employs exclusive miners for the second round to reduce the classic mining centralization. The miners of the first round do not get to contribute in the second round. The miner of the initial round must wait one round before returning to the mining pool, which may compromise fairness. However, Green-PoW claims that making such a design decision is crucial to achieving the desired reduction in energy consumption as well as minimizing the impact of attack and mining centralization. As a result, the energy expenditure of the mining is used to select the subset of miners for the following round. Hence, a subset of miners controls the majority of the network where each miner has an equal share of the hashing powers resulting in 50% energy reductions. In addition, reducing the number of unaware miners using the exclusive miners also reduces the fork rate allowing GreenPoW to improve the security of the protocol.

2.2.1.3 HDPoA

HDPoA [6] is essentially a variation of PoA integrating PoW as an extra layer of security, cutting the verification period to one block. In the traditional PoA model, the network administrator must permit nodes to join the network. HDPoA develops a strategy of distributing the mining process among network nodes that allows governing 51% of the network's hash power to increase the security of the network. The quantity of confirmation blocks needed by the network to guarantee transaction finality is also decreased. However, HDPoA is optimized for deployment on public blockchain platforms where nodes are free to enter or leave the network whenever they see fit. Accordingly, performance analysis of the protocol suggests the applicability of HPDoA in IoT.

2.2.2 *BFT compliant hybrid alternatives*

2.2.2.1 EB-BFT

Elastic-batched BFT (EB-BFT) [7] allows a degree of elasticity to interchange the participant nodes and adjust the quantity of transactions based on their corresponding volume and availability of physical capacity. The quantity of eligible consensus nodes is actively modified by the EB-BFT protocol, which initially detects low-performance nodes and prevents them from taking part in consensus. The dynamic design of EB-BFT enables rapid and reliable transaction commitment and preserves the fault tolerance ratio at 1/3 while accelerating the consensus processing time.

2.2.2.2 FPoR

Fair Proof of Reputation (FPoR) [8] consensus incorporates reward and punishment mechanisms, committee-based consensus, PBFT, and reputation. FPoR claims to balance scalability, decentralization, safety, and equitable participation, which can be extended to both permissioned and permissionless distributed ledgers. FPoR is using collateral to avoid disruption and any other malicious practices. Unlike other consensus mechanisms, it incorporates collateral to establish a baseline credibility score that will affect the likelihood that consensus nodes will be chosen for a consensus group. To encourage consensus nodes to operate with integrity, FPoR combines an incentive and penalty system. While penalties are imposed on the collateral or reputation score, rewards may be granted in the form of a block or reputation.

2.2.2.3 SG-PBFT

Score Grouping PBFT (SG-PBFT) [9] is a reliable and distributed consensus protocol designed for Internet of Vehicles (IoV) applications. The protocol's decentralized arrangement decreases the load on the primary server and minimizes the possibility of single-node attacks. SG-PBFT streamlines PBFT [10] and employs a score-based system to increase the efficiency of the protocol. The consensus time only increases by about 27% for every 1000 additional nodes compared to PBFT, with significantly lower communication overhead than the traditional PBFT and CPBFT [11]. To mitigate the risk of data manipulation, vehicles are required to perform pseudo identification, hashing, and digital signatures. As a result, for malicious nodes to forge the signature or identity of another node, the user's private key is required. The design of the algorithm is flexible and can be implemented in a wide range of application domains.

2.2.2.4 Mosaic

Raft [12] and PBFT [13] are the inspiration behind the development of Mosaic [14] as a novel consensus based on random number generation for enterprise blockchains. Mosaic offers decent scalability with linear complexity in reaching consensus making it proportional to network size. Mosaic breaks down elapsed time leader election and block production phase, with the leader election requiring more intricate communications. Additionally, nodes with greater computing capacity are allocated more network traffic to process; hence, the network load can be balanced as effectively as possible. In comparison to Raft, Mosaic imposes more overhead at the expense of scalability and an equal and unbiased leader election process.

2.2.2.5 DPNPBFT

PBFT and PBFT variant consensus protocols mainly prioritize minimizing communication complexity at the expense of security or fault tolerance. As a result, DPNPBFT [15] is proposed as a Dual-Primary-Node variation of PBFT to optimize the performance of the protocol. The principle of power division is used by DPNPBFT to choose dual master nodes. In order to prevent over-centralization of the system with two master nodes, they monitor and maintain each other. Despite the design complications of DPNPBFT, the protocol is primarily optimized for settings with higher node adoption rates while maintaining a minimal communication complexity and consistent TPS of 1700. The Dual master node architecture adopted by DPNPBFT ensures a 49% fault tolerance rate and is best suited for large-scale internet of things applications.

2.2.2.6 PDBFT-based PoR (PPoR)

PPoR [16] is proposed as an integration of PBFT and PoR to address the deficiencies of blockchain-enabled trading (BET) [17] systems and enhance the energy exchange procedure among EVs. PPoR proceeds with selecting leaders by assessing the highest reputation value associated with EVs. Higher reputation EVs may serve as validators and be compensated based on how much they contribute to mining; hence, reputation value is used to determine the incentive of the EVs. Additionally, PPoR claims that the use of MLMF Stackelberg's two-stage game will maximize the profits of both consumer and seller [18]. The game-based incentive mechanism maintains the security of the network by penalizing disruptive behaviors and recognizing cooperative nodes by granting financial incentives or mining values. According to the simulation results, the suggested approach enhances throughput, transaction latency, and utility optimization in V2V transactions while ensuring the safety and scalability of transactions in the IoEV.

2.2.3 Cross compliant hybrid alternative consensus mechanism

2.2.3.1 PoEC

Proof of Endorse Contracts (PoEC) [19] is proposed as a cross-blockchain consensus built around intelligent contracts to address the governance requirements of different application domains. It enables the transmission of consensus decisions from the supervisory blockchain to the corresponding smart contract within the supervised blockchain. Subsequently, miners in the supervised blockchain are responsible for creating and validating a new block in accordance with the smart contract's current status. As a scalable cross-chain consensus protocol, PoEC allows interaction with supervised blockchains without modifying the existing consensus as illustrated in Figure 2.4. Different signatures are incorporated into the contracts in order to guarantee the security of cross-chain communications. PoEC claims to be cost-effective by allowing the controlled chain to engage in the chain regulation procedure without any changes to the primary consensus. PoEC lays the groundwork for the application of machine learning in facilitating the easy operation of the supervised blockchain.

2.2.3.2 HiCoOB

Hierarchical Concurrent Optimistic Blockchain Consensus (HiCoOB) [20] is a novel consensus protocol that encompasses a deterministic global consensus and an optimistic local consensus. Separate administrators orchestrate the local and the global consensus, allowing for their concurrent execution and lowering the burden on the

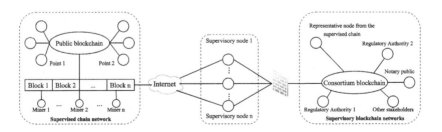

Figure 2.4 POEC's architecture

local administrator. HiCoOB synchronizes the local and the global consensus to mitigate the double spending caused by interdependent transactions. HiCoOB claims to outperform the current systems in throughput by 87%, drastically cutting down on local transaction delays with ten times less overhead in message communications. In addition to taking longer than the local consensus, the global consensus is deterministic and cannot be changed after approval. Due to the fact that local consensus governs just one cluster and is executed faster than the global consensus, several local consensuses can be launched within each round of global consensus.

2.2.3.3 HCM

Hybrid Consensus Mechanism (HCM) [21] is a novel consensus mechanism integrating the features of Delegated Proof of Stake (DPoS) to select the validators, Practical Byzantine Fault Tolerance (PBFT) to reach consensus, and Proof of Elapsed Time (PoET) for random selection of the leaders and refrain from power concentration across the network. Additionally, HCM offers a dynamic delegation and sharding method to improve the fairness and scalability of the network. As DPOS suggests, validators are picked in accordance to their reputation, stake, performance, and compliance with the protocol guidelines. Peer-to-peer messaging is used by validators to transmit messages, endorse the legitimacy of transactions, and determine their sequence. To ensure resistance to potentially fraudulent behavior, the dynamic delegation mechanism in HCM was developed. The dynamic delegation mechanism ensures fairness and prevents validators from having excessive control over the consensus. HCM has the capacity to make substantial improvements to consensus mechanisms and can be employed as a standalone blockchain network or as a software layer on top of an already-existing blockchain.

2.2.3.4 RAFT+

RAFT+ [22], a deep Q-Network (DQN) based consensus mechanism, is introduced as an alternative to RAFT to facilitate the adoption of blockchain technology in resource-constrained IoT environments. The DQN algorithm is implemented for effective leader selection and integrates reinforcement learning with deep neural networks as well as an experience recall method to remove any connections among inputs. By allowing various IoT endpoints to participate in the consensus, the structure of RAFT+ attempts to reduce the disparities between the participants. For the purpose of being able to work with limited resources, control the consensus across IoT end-points, and select leaders in a variety of circumstances, DQN is adopted as the leader selection scheme. In order to determine the selection criteria for the leader, RAFT+ first acquires the computing capabilities of each end device and prototypes the communication environment. Next, a central node (typically a base station in the blockchain network) is picked to obtain the selection criteria and choose the leader. The leader then bundles data in the form of transactions to generate a new block and execute consensus. DQN leader selection demonstrates improvements in fault tolerance while preventing network fragmentations. Furthermore, the experimenters demonstrate a 10%–21% reduction in mean block generation latency in RAFT+ compared to the original RAFT.

2.2.4 Quantum-free pure alternatives

2.2.4.1 Proof of Adjourn (PoAj)

Proof of Adjourn [23] is a cutting edge consensus protocol that offers robust resistance regardless of the hashing power of the adversary. Compared to conventional proof-based consensus mechanisms such as PoW, PoAj is a viable strategy to address extended processing times of large transactions. Figure 2.5 depicts the operational phases of PoAj. The suggested method offers a solid response against both existing and identified attacks as well as upcoming, unidentified attacks. This is predicated on a number of procedures that require oversight of a substantial portion of the hashing power.

2.2.4.2 Teegraph

Teegraph [24] is a novel consensus algorithm based on a trusted execution environment and Directed Acyclic Graph (DAG). It enables extremely effective data exchange among IoT devices without the need for a central intermediary. TEE is typically an isolated environment that facilitates secure application execution and is commonly used to optimize the performance of Blockchain systems. TEE allows every node to have access to the consensus degree of every transaction in real-time.

2.2.4.3 RVC

RVC [25] is a reputation and voting-based consensus mechanism that employs a reputation evaluation procedure instead of intricate hash computing for determining block proposers it takes into account both blockchain consensus and edge computing behavior. In order to stop malicious nodes from taking part in consensus, a historical reputation algorithm is employed by RVC that can identify and remove nodes that exhibit malicious interactions. RVC demonstrated competent results in terms of efficiency, security, and scalability; however, its ability to perform is limited by the increased number of nodes. Therefore, a block storage mechanism must be developed for complex IoT applications.

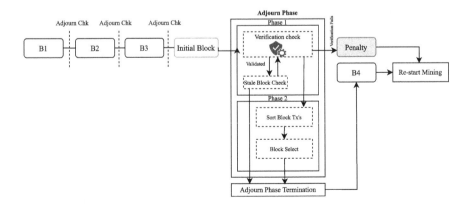

Figure 2.5   PoAj's design

2.2.4.4 Proof of Chance

PoCh [26] is a simple distributed algorithm that can be used with industrial Internet of Things (IIoT)-style dynamic network models. PoCh can keep dynamic networks from destabilizing as a result of node movements and corresponding environmental changes. For each consensus round, PoCh selects a miner and randomized terms to be continuously updated without node intervention. As a result, no weights are bound to the nodes, which makes proof of chance a lightweight and energy-effective protocol. PoCh offers strong security against 51%, double spending, and DDoS, while compared to the Proof of Stake (PoS) protocol, more than 40% of nodes must be operational for PoCh to reach consensus.

2.2.4.5 ACCORD

ACCORD [27] is a quorum-based consensus mechanism that consists of an asynchronous procedure for determining the quorum followed by a block generation mechanism and a distributed arbitration mechanism. The block generation is executed by the quorum in order to avoid oversights in the presence of authentic quorums. The distributed arbitration ensures the fairness of the protocol through the election of miners with a roughly comparable frequency and is capable of handling a large number of nodes. Hence, the miner selection does not require network synchronization, making the protocol partially synchronous. ACCORD claims to continue operating even during significant network disruptions and is also able to withstand attempts to manipulate the miner selection protocol. ACCORD was originally developed for healthcare blockchain but can be adopted by distributed ledger systems with comparable requirements.

2.2.4.6 Proof of retrievability

Proof of retrievability [28] is a novel consensus mechanism based on a deduplication algorithm designed for distributed storage. The method's data integrity assessment protocol ensures that all storage nodes effectively retain the data they commit to storing. Additionally, the protocol's built-in deduplication method allows for improved data auditing, substantially decreasing the need for data storage. The proposed method also employs ring signatures to guarantee user anonymity. By including additional users in the file signature procedure, it is possible to develop file unlinkability and shield user-outsourced data from brute-force attacks and privacy breaches. The proposed approach can prevent communication overhead and resolve the problems associated with the current distributed storage in blockchain platforms by using verifiable computation in place of a trust mechanism.

2.2.4.7 Proof of Sense

Proof of Sense [29] is proposed as the underlying consensus mechanism for blockchain-based dynamic spectrum access (DSA) systems. Proof of Sense tackles unauthorized spectrum access through examination of sensed spectrum data and employs Shamir's secret sharing approach [30] for the key sharing mechanism. Using threshold systems, Shamir presented the notion of secret sharing based on polynomial interpolation. Shamir's theory is employed in proof of sense to regulate the obstacles of key retrieval. The secret key, known as the random cryptographic key (RCK), must be located by miners in order to receive the mining reward and create the next block. The RCK recovery potential, which is the ratio of confirmed RCK recoveries to the total amount of RCK transmissions, determines how well Proof of Sense performs. Hence, instead of relying on cryptographic calculations, Proof of sense relies on spectrum sensing.

2.2.5 Quantum-based pure alternatives

The majority of the currently implemented public-key cryptographic systems are threatened by the strength of quantum computers and quantum algorithms. Due to their heavy reliance on public-key digital signatures and their application in data transmission, nearly all current blockchain deployments are particularly suscepti-ble to quantum computer attacks. With the development of the quantum Internet, it is now simpler to envision the communication of quantum nodes in a distributed environment. Distributed quantum systems have emerged as a result of this devel-opment. Accordingly, the integration of quantum Internet and quantum-distributed systems induces the emergence of quantum blockchain, featuring quantum comput-ers as nodes and quantum internet as the communication layer. However, this pure quantum configuration is only one facet of quantum blockchain. The further aspect is the presence of conventional blockchains in the post-quantum age. Due to their capacity to bypass conventional cryptography, quantum computers have the potential to negatively affect the security of blockchains and consensus.

As emphasized by Fedorov *et al.* [31], blockchain technology, as we currently recognize it, could fail if quantum technologies are not incorporated. Establishing the quantum blockchain's consensus algorithm is a key component of the quantum blockchain principle, which combines blockchain technology and quantum technol-ogy [32]. In the 1970s, the idea of integrating quantum technology and information theory first emerged. At the time, a conceptual framework for quantum computing was put forth by Paul Benioff, and Richard Feynman made a claim that classical com-puters are not capable of carrying out computations involving quantum events. Due to the inherent constraints of classical computing, quantum mechanics computations that were formerly unattainable are now feasible on computers that operate based on quantum theories and replicate quantum events.

Quantum consensus is what drives a quantum network composed of qubits to migrate to a symmetric state. As quantum computing advances, challenges of the clas-sical computing world are being examined from a quantum perspective to determine if any conventional algorithms can be enhanced. Moreover, exploring the conven-tional distributed consensus within the context of quantum structure paves the way for addressing challenges that are otherwise intractable in classical networks. The rest of this chapter examines consensus in quantum-distributed systems as well as how quantum computing affects consensus in conventional distributed systems.

The non-classical features offered by quantum resources have been extensively used in the development of innovative privacy-preserving communication models. Several quantum algorithms have recently been developed that use entanglement and coherence as quantum resources to reach Byzantine Agreement (BA). The BA problem can only be addressed if every participant of the consensus has a private list that is properly tied to its peers' private lists but remains concealed from them. As a result, complications with BA consensus can be downgraded to addressing a network's private list sharing. The quantum BA methods may accommodate up to half faulty users in the network if the BA requirements are loosened to allow the choice of all loyal parties aborting. Therefore, unlike conventional approaches, these methods can achieve consensus within a network, even in the presence of a single malfunctioning node. To prevent fraudulent nodes in the networks, the majority of blockchains at the moment use the classic BA-based PBFT algorithm or its variants. Quantum Byzantine Agreement (QBA) methods are intriguing use cases for blockchain consensus because they permit reduced communication complexity and greater fault tolerance than PBFT [33].

As a result of becoming substantial data-intensive in the presence of numerous fraudulent nodes, Kiktenko *et al.* have discovered that the traditional Byzantine agreement protocol has serious drawbacks for quantum-secured blockchain (QB). As a result, more research on an effective consensus protocol is needed [34]. Even in the presence of numerous defective nodes in the system, quantum synchronization can overcome the barrier and reach a consensus. The three-qubit entangled Aharonov state, a Quantum Key Distribution (QKD) protocol, the four-qubit singlet state, or the single-qubit protocol is all potential quantum methods to the detectable byzantine agreement [35].

The early steps toward quantum consensus were initiated by Xin Sun *et al.* proposing a voting protocol based on quantum blockchain [36]. The notion behind the proposed protocol is based on the premise that every pair of nodes (agents) is connected by an explicitly authorized quantum channel and a partially authenticated classical channel. QKD systems allow each pair of nodes to acquire a set of secret keys that are subsequently employed for message authentication. New transactions are initiated by the nodes that are minted to add new data to the chain. Consequently, the transaction's classical data are transmitted through classical channels while the corresponding quantum data is delivered over quantum channels. Every miner makes an assessment concerning the update's legitimacy after examining the transaction's alignment with their local copy. The update is then submitted to a QBA protocol, with the goal of reaching a consensus on its version and admissibility. If a minimum of half of the miners acknowledge that the update is valid, it is subsequently included in each node's copies of the database.

Table 2.5 provides an overview of the post-quantum systems and methods used in the quantum consensus algorithms.

2.2.5.1   QDPoS

Despite the fact that a number of quantum blockchain schemes have been developed, their performance is inadequate as they fail to comply with application requirements primarily because they lack a compatible consensus mechanism. Consensus algorithms like PoW and PoS are ineffective in the context of quantum blockchain because nodes with strong quantum computers hold greater computing capacity than the rest of the network. As a result, quantum delegated proof of stake (QDPoS) consensus algorithm is developed to assist in effective adaptation to the complications of the quantum era [37]. QDPoS incorporates quantum voting to promptly decentralize the quantum blockchain system where quantum states become interconnected to form the chain. Additionally, to guarantee the integrity of transactions, a quantum digital signature and a QDPoS consensus built on the theory of quantum mechanics are employed. Consequently, the quantity of quantum public keys determines the security of the used quantum digital signature.

2.2.5.2 Quantum zero knowledge proof

Quantum zero knowledge is a novel consensus mechanism built on the irreversibility of quantum quantification as well as the quantum zero-knowledge proof [38]. In comparison with conventional methods, the proposed consensus requires less energy and offers lower latency and greater throughput since it does not demand an abundance of computing resources. This consensus eliminates the conventional mathematical challenges that miners encountered saving a significant amount of processing time and energy. In addition, because the quantum consensus algorithm relies on quantum communication methods, its security is detached from the resources and processing power of the adversaries. Since the proposed consensus does not rely on hash functions either, it can tolerate security defects like 51% attack.

2.2.5.3 Quantum Teleportation

Quantum Teleportation [39] is a consensus algorithm that incorporates quantum mechanisms and relies on quantum measurements. Consequently, the proposed consensus inherits the security properties of quantum cryptography. Quantum teleportation is one of the major applications of quantum entanglement. According to the theory underlying quantum teleportations, a single anonymous quantum state can be divided and transmitted through classical and quantum channels as separate fragments of classical and quantum data. The time needed for quantum teleportation is remarkably brief and mostly comprises the duration needed to set up quantum gates and transmit classical information. Hence, compared to conventional consensus algorithms, quantum teleportation requires far less computing power, which results in decreased power consumption, a faster response time, and greater throughput.

2.2.5.4 Quantum entanglement and DPoS

This is a novel quantum consensus that integrates DPoS and quantum entanglement and introduces a Bell-state-based quantum authentication mechanism [40]. The consensus enables all users to develop verifiable quantum information using quantum signatures which can be shared in quantum networks and validated by other nodes in the network. Subsequently, other nodes engage in fair consensus competition to claim new quantum blocks, which will be connected to quantum entanglement. Finally, via quantum channels, each node integrates this new quantum block to the respective quantum blockchains. According to the analysis results of this study, the proposed consensus can withstand certain attacks, such as man-in-the-middle, double spending, and state estimation. Additionally, the integration of DPoS has had a significant impact on this scheme's transaction finality and energy usage.

2.2.5.5   Post-quantum threshold signature

This consensus is based on a threshold signature with an NP-hard nature that relies on quadratic equations and has been shown to withstand both quantum computer and conventional attacks [41]. Signature is used by the users and the private keys are generated by the group manager and distributed securely among the users. Respectively, the public keys are generated by the group manager through the private keys. With this method, consensus is only reached if the new block is signed with the quantum threshold signature by a minimum of one and a half nodes. The signature can only be verified by the group manager, who can then determine who signed it. The analysis of the proposed consensus mechanism reveals that it is significantly more efficient and secure than existing solutions. Finally, there are numerous application domains for post-quantum threshold signatures and consensus algorithms, including Internet of Things.

2.2.5.6   QAA

The advent of quantum computing undermines the conventional symmetric encryption and hash encryption used in blockchain. Hence, quantum attack algorithm (QAA) relies on stochasticity, immutability, and ambiguity of quantum measurement. This allows the proposed mechanism to discard extensive mathematical computations and preserve a significant amount of computing resources. The proposed mechanism enhances the communication efficiency across entities without dependence on intricate mathematical proofs. In addition, the proposed design does not allow adversaries to interpret ciphertext using quantum state. The consensus based on quantum attack mechanism stipulates three prerequisites from entities before commencing the communication. Each entity must ensure that their signatures cannot be forged or revoked. Also, every individual possessing the public key may validate the message's credibility at any point during the communication. The quantum measurement and quantum non-cloning principles adopted by the consensus allow the protocol to withstand security defects such as 51% and quantum attacks [42].

2.2.5.7   VQRN

This consensus is mainly based on verifiable quantum random numbers (VQRN) which is a common way of introducing entropy to non-proof-based consensus mechanisms [43]. In order to improve the randomness, fairness, and effectiveness of the protocol, the proposed consensus chooses the block proposer and block verification committees for every round through verifiable quantum random numbers. In addition to ensuring random election, this also stops adversaries from incorporating too many private keys and thereby increasing their election likelihood. Hence, regardless of network partitioning, the framework is capable of resolving active forks. Besides being resilient to collusion and adversary models, the protocol necessitates minimal computation for each user, preventing unnecessary power expenditure.

2.2.5.8 PQSC

Post-quantum for smart city (PQSC) [44] is a PoW-based consensus mechanism that relies on multivariate quadratic equations. As a substitute for the SHA256 hashing system, the proposed post-quantum consensus algorithm uses an Np-hard problem. The Gröbner basis solution algorithm [50] is used by miners to resolve the seed-based random quadratic multivariate equations. Additionally, instead of using a preset pattern, it employs a dynamic difficulty adjustment algorithm (DAA) [51] to modify the complexity of computations for blocks. All these features reinforce memory mining while also ensuring quantum safety in the context of smart city applications. With the identity-based rainbow post-quantum signature incorporated into the transaction process, the proposed consensus claims to have the lightest transaction ever established.

2.2.5.9 MQE-PoW

Multivariate quadratic equation (MQE) based PoW [45] is a quantum variant of PoW which centers around the difficulty of solving a collection of randomly generated quadratic equations over the Galois Field (GF), which is the finite field of two elements [52]. As opposed to hash-based mining, the MQ-based mining actually incentives any advancements made towards solving an NP-hard problem. The proposed MQ-based PoW is more resilient against quantum attacks as the consensus needs a larger number of qubits to find the solution while an entirely fresh batch of quadratic functions is loaded. The security principle that underlies multivariate public key cryptosystems is the difficulty of the MQ problem. As a result of the random MQ's NP-hardness, the proposed consensus algorithm is able to exhibit features such as intrinsic hardness, customizable difficulty, and verifiability.

2.2.5.10 QEMR

Quantum electronic medical record protocol (QEMR) is intended to facilitate the validation of newly acquired diagnostic data in a quantum blockchain-based QB-IMD system for processing medical data [32]. To minimize the security threats associated with digital signatures and to strengthen the blockchain's durability against quantum attacks, the algorithm employs quantum signatures and quantum identity authentication. The combined effect of quantum signature and quantum communication technology makes all new blocks credible and exempt from breaches by fraudulent eavesdroppers. It has been established through empirical analysis and experimental simulations that the QEMR algorithm is resilient to threats like intercept-resend and signature forgery.

2.2.5.11 QSYAC

Quantum-secured YAC (QSYAC) [34] is an adaptation of the original YAC in which the public-key signature is replaced by the Toeplitz Group Signature (TGS) [53]. The proposed consensus mechanism is a vote-based algorithm that integrates YAC (Yet Another Consensus) [54] and an unconditionally secure signature (USS). Teoplitz hashing is used in USS to create signatures and counteract quantum attacks. The signature method incorporates a QKD [55] process for transmitting the keys and strings, making the entire process quantum safe. The resulting TGS substitutes for the public-key signature implemented in the original YAC protocol, leading to the development of the QSYAC protocol.

2.2.5.12   LPoW

The notion behind this consensus is developing a novel consensus protocol that minimizes the distinct advantages of quantum computers over classical ones with rapid validation. Thus, the proposed consensus is built upon Hermite-SVP as the underlying NP-hard problem [56]. The Lattice-Based Proof-of-Work (LPoW) variables can be optimized to change the difficulty. As a result, expanding the lattice's dimension changes the amount of computing power needed to solve the consensus algorithm. Hermit-SVP is the preferred method because it's difficult to solve and simple to verify. Heuristic lattice sieves offer the highest quantum complexity and are used to solve the SVP problem. However, the exponential memory expenses associated with sieving is a drawback that could result in the obstruction of memory access times [46].

2.2.5.13   GHZ-QDBA

This consensus mechanism is a quantum detectable Byzantine agreement based on Greenberger–Horne–Zeilinger (GHZ) [47]. QBA and quantum cryptography have both been demonstrated to benefit from the GHZ state, which is an entangled state of at least three qubits. The proposed consensus mechanism determines the reliability of nodes by distributing the entanglement resources among various nodes, counting on the nonlocality of the GHZ state. The GHZ state requires significantly less time for setup compared to other multiparticle entangled states, broadening its applicability. Hence, the proposed scheme outperforms the existing quantum DBA in terms of scalability and efficiency as the size of the network increases. The proposed protocol asserts an efficient fault tolerance in the presence of $n-2$ fraudulent nodes. However, it has not undergone sufficient examinations to back up this claim.

2.2.5.14   QPoA

Quantum Proof of Authority (QPoA) [48] is a novel consensus developed for the Quantum-secure blockchain (QSB) framework. In QPoA, validating nodes are rearranged using a quantum random number generator (QRNG) and the Knuth algorithm which also prevents centralized attacks and conceals the primary node's identity. In addition, it replaces the classic voting procedure with a quantum voting scheme to improve the security of block generation. For the leader node election process, QPoA relies on a quantum voting protocol and QRNG. It also uses a dynamic updating procedure to preserve node authorities. For casting votes on the prospective block, QPoA uses a CDSQC-based quantum voting system featuring a permutation of qubits [57]. If a proposed block receives positive input from a majority of the validating nodes, it will be approved and inserted into the blockchain. Unlike QDPoS, QPoA determines the leader node from the validating nodes using a stochastic algorithm with QRNG, which completely masks the identity of the leader node and safeguards the distributed ledger from centralized breaches that could lead to a single point of failure.

2.2.5.15 CGBS

This is a quantum proof of work variant consensus mechanism based on coarse-grained boson-sampling (CGBS) [49]. The proof of work mechanism is intended to accommodate two forms of binning, one for validation and the other to reward miners. The first binning can be precisely computed with classical computers, whereas the latter is lacking an established classical computation but contains a viable quantum estimation. Once a given block is successfully mined, the result from both binning distributions is appended to the blockchain, implying that only one part can be verified efficiently by classical computers. As a result, nodes that employ boson-sampling are encouraged to validate the earlier blocks. Users execute boson-sampling with input states based on current block information and commit their measurements to the network. Following that, CGBS procedures are established to incentivize the miners and authenticate their measurements. The proposed method works for significant acceleration and conservation of energy over traditional hardware computation. Furthermore, the quantum benefit has a compounding impact; once more quantum miners join the network, the complexity of the issue increases to preserve uniform block mining time necessitating additional incentives for quantum miners' participation.

2.3 Extension consensus mechanisms

2.3.1 *Primitive compliant extensions*

2.3.1.1 Relaxed-Paxos

Relaxed-Paxos [58] reminisces Paxos' strategy of reaching consensus and revisiting Flexible-Paxos. Relaxed-Paxos claims that the infamous quorum intersection can be securely weakened using write-once registers. A write-once register is a constant variable that, once defined, can never be changed, hence, preserving the validity of each read. Accordingly, Relaxed-Paxos has been reconfigured defining a four-rule abstract structure to which an algorithm must adhere to reach consensus. Rule 1 implies that solely the values that have been decided upon are generated by proposers as outputs. In addition, it enables the proposer to securely progress into phase two prior to getting confirmation from a majority of acceptors in phase one. Second rule permits only the proposed input values to be written to registers. In addition, Relaxed Paxos permits a proposer to propose an input value if it is certain that none of the values it had previously learned can be ruled. In comparison, Paxos only allows a proposer to submit their input value in phase two if it is unaware of the values in the initial phase. Rules 3 and 4 collectively ensure that no two quorums are entitled to distinct values. Relaxed-Paxos claims implementing this abstraction compromises Paxos's constraints on quorum intersections.

2.3.1.2 ZPaxos

ZPaxos [59] is an enhanced version of XPaxos featuring two of its primary characteristics, including synchronous group fault detection and a recovery protocol. However,
ZPaxos uses a leaderless synchronous group to reach consensus in a single round.
Figure 2.6 depicts how the protocol operates for a system of five replicas, three of
which are in the synchronous core bundle (replicas 1, 2, and 3). This allows for both
addition and elimination of nodes in the presence of a Byzantine replica without
interfering with the throughput. The protocol claims that throughput and latency are
enhanced under both Byzantine and crash failures, with fewer communication rounds
and quicker commits.

2.3.1.3 Heterogenous Paxos

Heterogenous Paxos [60] preserves the Paxos three-message communication model
and has been proposed as an alternative to Byzantine Paxos. Heterogeneous Paxos
claims to be the first-ever consensus that uses heterogeneous learners and acceptors,
intended for cross-domain and latency-sensitive applications. Offering validity and
agreement in a fully asynchronous arrangement enables various learners to make
decisions in various circumstances. Further development of heterogeneous Paxos
is possible to support varying configurations, increased bandwidth, and reduced
computational overhead.

2.3.1.4 Layered Paxos

Layered Paxos [61] offers a framework for hierarchical structures within which
processes can be broken down into distinct elements. The primary communication network involves two communication channels. One for high-latency interaction among
processes in a specific component and another for quick communication among processes across varied components. Layered Paxos is intended to improve the overall
consensus throughput of a system that adheres to the fundamental Paxos principles concerning safety and liveliness. Layered Paxos may offer up to five times the
throughput of Paxos using rapid inter-component communication. Additionally, it
can achieve hierarchical consensus and withstand delegate crashes using a Raft-like
leader election.

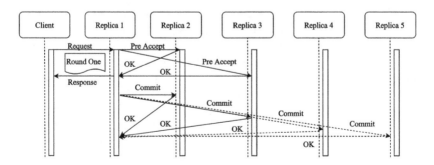

Figure 2.6   Communication model of ZPaxos

2.3.1.5 PigPaxos

Pig and piggybacking have proven to be effective in strongly consistent replication protocols to handle in-protocol communication aggregation and eliminate the leader bottleneck. Pig safeguards both the leader and the relay nodes from forming hotspots by asynchronously switching the relay nodes between replication operations. The leader can only communicate with a restricted set of relay nodes using this overlay communication structure. This allows PigPaxos [62] to offer a throughput increase of more than three times over Paxos and EPaxos with no significant latency overhead. Moreover, the PigPaxos aggregation method is easily adaptable across multiple Paxos implementations and is currently being used with distributed databases like CockroachDB.

2.3.2 *Proof compliant extensions*

2.3.2.1 PoE

Proof of Evolution (PoE) [63] is a novel consensus that preserves the safety hallmarks of PoW while utilizing a vast majority of the computational resources used for mining to run genetic algorithms that users may submit. PoE is correlated with Proof of Search (PoS), which is an improved variation of PoW to address problems with mining optimization. PoS encourages miners to submit their remarks on a relevant issue which is similar to PoE fostering cooperation among miners. PoE allows collaboration among miners so they can communicate their global optimum solutions and append that to their populations. This allows miners to develop and evolve their solutions. Hence, the overall quality of the solutions can be improved as a result of this communication.

2.3.2.2 LaKSA

Large-scale Known-committee Stakebased Agreement (LaKSA) [64] is a variation of PoS that reduces node communications through lightweight committee voting, offering a more simple, secure, and scalable proposal. Additionally, it reduces the adverse implications of long approval periods and high reward deviation. Through LaKSA, the idea of probabilistic safety is expanded, demonstrating the capacity for refined security in proof-of-stake protocols. Despite the simple design, LaKSA offers significant reliability, scalability, and security and can be further developed into a more adaptive and dynamic mechanism against adversaries.

2.3.2.3 DPoAC

Delegated proof of accessibility (DPoAC) [65] is predicated on proof-of-stake's random selection, secret sharing, and interplanetary file system (IPFS) [66]. The process of consensus can be deconstructed into two main steps. A secret is developed and assigned to shares over the first step by a super node that is selected arbitrarily. Each share is encrypted and retained across multiple IPFS nodes in the network. Since block creation access will be granted to the winning nodes, each node tries to communicate with the shareholders and recreate the secret. In the subsequent phase, PoS with random selection is implemented to determine the proper hash value and generate a block with valid transactions. The proposed approach allows nodes with limited computing power and stakes to compete for block generation, resulting in a more equitable distribution of block generation rights. Additionally, IPFS integration into DPoAC offers peer-to-peer decentralization and reliable data exchange and retrieval.

2.3.2.4   PF-PoFL

Platform-free proof of federated learning (PF-PoFL) [67] is proposed as an energy-recycling consensus that makes efficient use of the computing power that has been wasted on unnecessary PoW puzzles to carry out federated learning operations. As depicted in Figure 2.7, PF-PoFL promotes fully decentralized analysis of models and incentive distribution, and incorporates a user-level differential privacy training algorithm, for strict confidentiality guarantees and protects miners from implicit privacy breaches. Adversaries are prevented from replicating FL models because just the hashes of trained FL models become available in the federated mining procedures. Additionally, credit-based incentives are included in PF-PoFL to encourage miners' authentic participation and enhance the performance of the consensus. However, because of the unreliable environment and the self-serving characteristics of the miners, there may be potential safety risks and performance issues.

2.3.2.5   HADPoS

The heat attenuation-based delegated proof of stake consensus (HADPoS) [68] is proposed to address DPoS's deficiencies, such as centralization. The heat attenuation method lightly penalizes nodes that preserve high rankings for an extended period. This lowers the occurrence of giant monopolies and increases the level of network decentralization, ensuring each node has the chance to serve as a witness. The consensus also introduces the notion of benefit distribution to ensure the nodes participating in the voting process are compensated. Additionally, HADPoS implements the delegated proof of stake with nodes behavior and borda count (DPoSB). This allows the proposed scheme to allocate the authority with greater reliability and prevent malicious nodes from turning into witness nodes. The HADPOS experimental results

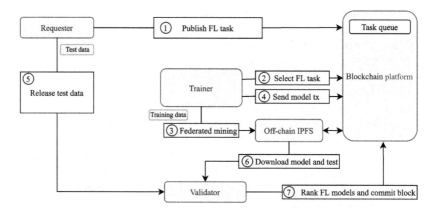

Figure 2.7   Entities and workflow of PF-PoFL

Table 2.6   Extension consensus mechanisms

Consensus	Scalability	Finality	Communication model
Relaxed-Paxos [58]	High	Deterministic	Asynchronous
ZPaxos [59]	–	Deterministic	Synchronous
Heterogenous Paxos [60]	–	Deterministic	Partially synchronous
Layered Paxos [61]	High	Deterministic	Asynchronous
PigPaxos [62]	High	Deterministic	Partially synchronous
PoE [63]	Low	Probabilistic	–
LaKSA [64]	High	Probabilistic	Partially synchronous
DPoAC [65]	High	Probabilistic	–
PF-PoFL [67]	High	Deterministic	Synchronous
HADPoS [68]	High	Probabilistic	–

reveal the node's capacity to directly influence the consensus using a heat attenuation scheme that further establishes the viability of this approach.

2.4   Conclusions

Blockchain relies heavily on consensus to establish a reliable ecosystem across a distributed network. This chapter begins to explore the primitive consensus mechanisms and how they contributed to the emergence of novel protocols. This signifies that nearly all consensus algorithms make references to the core principles outlined in Paxos in some capacity. While many experts are working to enhance the existing protocol to be more sustainable, fault–tolerant, and quantum-resistant, others emphasize the development of distinguished protocol variants that work most efficiently with particular use cases. Consequently, this chapter revisits the latest advances in consensus development and classifies them based on their fundamental components and underlying algorithms. According to the classification presented in this chapter, consensus mechanisms in certain categories often possess comparable characteristics in terms of performance, challenges, and issues. The classification also explains the common adoption of certain algorithms across specific application domain through their underlying architecture. For instance, communication across chains necessitates meeting important prerequisites, including robust consensus and block finality. These are the regulatory considerations upon which BFT-compliant extensions are based, allowing them to be consistent with business use cases. In another inference, both pure-alternative and hybrid-alternative consensus categories are more prevalent as they offer cross-industry and post-quantum solutions. Pure alternatives tend to be employed in application scenarios where rapid transaction processing and low energy expenditure are the primary concerns.

The development and application of quantum consensus mechanisms are clearly on the rise as the latest quantum computing advancements convey a significant threat to cryptography systems. The primary idea is that quantum features can improve the classical consensus and overcome issues that were previously believed to be intractable in a classical consensus environment. Quantum computing offers enormous parallel computing capacity that can be applied to decipher the mathematical underpinnings of simple cryptography. The transition from classical to quantum computing promotes interoperability through quantum properties of qubits without compromising BFT. Quantum algorithms go beyond rapid computations and serve as deterministic responses to conventionally non-deterministic challenges such as anonymous leader election in the presence of Byzantine conditions. Therefore, post-quantum cryptography is of vital importance today.

The precedent quantum consensus algorithms are discussed in this chapter, in connection to the underlying quantum mechanisms. Pertinent to this matter, Jose *et al.* [69], also observed that the majority of the algorithms in this class have made an effort to redesign the classic PoW algorithm. The classification approach [3], however, suggested that developers appeared to favor pure quantum-based algorithms. Additionally, when compared to their conventional counterparts, quantum consensus features higher fault tolerance, lower scalability, and more comprehensible decentralization [33]. This is while there is controversy about entangled qubits, which may not provide any advantage over traditional protocols. As in the case of Helm's protocol [70], the impact of qubits can be just as effectively replicated with pre-shared randomness. Therefore, quantum entanglement is not the only replacement for inter-process communication. As a result, lattice-based approaches are preferred among quantum consensus mechanisms, according to the comparison of quantum methods. Higher efficiency and resource-saving measures can be credited for this. Quantum-safe digital signatures can be used an additional layer to make distributed ledgers resistant to quantum entanglement. Hence, the lattice framework can be used to generate lightweight post quantum signature schemes compared to other schemes [69].

To conclude, existing research suggests that a quantum distributed ledger could improve not only existing intra-network interactions, but also interoperability models. Since quantum properties are promising solutions to optimise speed, scalability, and security, there are vested profits for further investigations on quantum distributed ledgers and their properties, including consensus mechanisms.

References

[1]   Xiao Y, Zhang N, Lou W, *et al.* A survey of distributed consensus protocols for blockchain networks. *IEEE Communications Surveys & Tutorials.* 2020;22(2):1432–1465.

[2]   Alsunaidi SJ and Alhaidari FA. A survey of consensus algorithms for blockchain technology. In: *2019 International Conference on Computer and Information Sciences (ICCIS)*. IEEE; 2019. p. 1–6.

[3]   Lashkari B and Musilek P. A comprehensive review of blockchain consensus mechanisms. *IEEE Access.* 2021;9:43620–43652.

[4]   Fitzi M, Wang X, Kannan S, *et al*. Minotaur: multi-resource blockchain consensus. In: *Proceedings of the 2022 ACM SIGSAC Conference on Computer and Communications Security*; 2022. p. 1095–1108.

[5]   Lasla N, Al-Sahan L, Abdallah M, *et al*. Green-PoW: an energy-efficient blockchain Proof-of-Work consensus algorithm. *Computer Networks*. 2022; 214:109118.

[6]   Alrubei S, Ball E, and Rigelsford J. HDPoA: honesty-based distributed proof of authority via scalable work consensus protocol for IoT-blockchain applications. *Computer Networks*. 2022;217:109337.

[7]   Zhang B, Kong L, Li Q, *et al*. EB-BFT: an elastic batched BFT consensus protocol in blockchain. *Future Generation Computer Systems*. 2023;139: 267–279.

[8]   Zhang T and Huang Z. FPoR: fair proof-of-reputation consensus for blockchain. *ICT Express*. 2023;9(1):45–50.

[9]   Xu G, Bai H, Xing J, *et al*. SG-PBFT: a secure and highly efficient distributed blockchain PBFT consensus algorithm for intelligent Internet of Vehicles. *Journal of Parallel and Distributed Computing*. 2022;164:1–11.

[10]   Zhang L and Li Q. Research on consensus efficiency based on practical byzantine fault tolerance. In: *2018 10th International Conference on Modelling, Identification and Control (ICMIC)*. IEEE; 2018. p. 1–6.

[11]   Wang Y, Song Z, and Cheng T. Improvement research of PBFT consensus algorithm based on credit. In: *Blockchain and Trustworthy Systems: First International Conference, BlockSys 2019*, Guangzhou, China, December 7–8, 2019, Proceedings 1. Springer; 2020. p. 47–59.

[12]   Ongaro D and Ousterhout J. In search of an understandable consensus algorithm. In: *2014 USENIX Annual Technical Conference (USENIX ATC 14)*; 2014. p. 305–319.

[13]   Castro M and Liskov B. Practical byzantine fault tolerance. In: *OsDI*, vol. 99; 1999. p. 173–186.

[14]   Sun Z, Chiu WY, and Meng W. Mosaic—a blockchain consensus algorithm based on random number generation. In: *2022 IEEE International Conference on Blockchain (Blockchain)*. IEEE; 2022. p. 105–114.

[15]   Na Y, Wen Z, Fang J, *et al*. A derivative PBFT blockchain consensus algorithm with dual primary nodes based on separation of powers-DPNPBFT. *IEEE Access*. 2022;10:76114–76124.

[16]   Abishu HN, Seid AM, Yacob YH, *et al*. Consensus mechanism for blockchain-enabled vehicle-to-vehicle energy trading in the internet of electric vehicles. *IEEE Transactions on Vehicular Technology*. 2021;71(1):946–960.

[17]   Ashfaq T, Javaid N, Javed MU, *et al*. Secure energy trading for electric vehicles using consortium blockchain and k-nearest neighbor. In: *2020 International Wireless Communications and Mobile Computing (IWCMC)*. IEEE; 2020. p. 2235–2239.

[18]   Tran TD and Le LB. Resource allocation for multi-tenant network slicing: a multi-leader multi-follower stackelberg game approach. *IEEE Transactions on Vehicular Technology*. 2020;69(8):8886–8899.

[19]   Cheng J, Zhang Y, Yuan Y, *et al*. PoEC: a cross-blockchain consensus mechanism for governing blockchain by blockchain. *Computers, Materials & Continua*. 2022;73(1):1385–1402.

[20]   Abdella J, Tari Z, Mahmud R, *et al*. HiCoOB: hierarchical concurrent optimistic blockchain consensus protocol for peer-to-peer energy trading systems. *IEEE Transactions on Smart Grid*. 2022;14(5):3927–3943.

[21]   Kumar Jha A. Hybrid Consensus Mechanism (HCM): Achieving Efficient and Secure Consensus in Blockchain Networks; 2023. Available at SSRN 4413290.

[22]   Liu Z, Hou L, Zheng K, *et al*. A DQN-based consensus mechanism for blockchain in IoT networks. *IEEE Internet of Things Journal*. 2021;9(14): 11962–11973.

[23]   Sayeed S and Marco-Gisbert H. Proof of adjourn (poaj): a novel approach to mitigate blockchain attacks. *Applied Sciences*. 2020;10(18):6607.

[24]   Fu X, Wang H, Shi P, *et al*. Teegraph: a blockchain consensus algorithm based on TEE and DAG for data sharing in IoT. *Journal of Systems Architecture*. 2022;122:102344.

[25]   Liao Z and Cheng S. RVC: a reputation and voting based blockchain consensus mechanism for edge computing-enabled IoT systems. *Journal of Network and Computer Applications*. 2023;209:103510.

[26]   Kara M, Laouid A, Hammoudeh M, *et al*. Proof of chance: a lightweight consensus algorithm for the Internet of Things. *IEEE Transactions on Industrial Informatics*. 2022;18(11):8336–8345.

[27]   Bashar GD, Holmes J, and Dagher GG. ACCORD: a scalable multileader consensus protocol for healthcare blockchain. *IEEE Transactions on Information Forensics and Security*. 2022;17:2990–3005.

[28]   Zhou W, Wang H, Mohiuddin G, *et al*. Consensus mechanism of blockchain based on PoR with data deduplication. *Intelligent Automation & Soft Computing*. 2022;34(3).

[29]   Fernando P, Dadallage K, Gamage T, *et al*. Proof of sense: a novel consensus mechanism for spectrum misuse detection. *IEEE Transactions on Industrial Informatics*. 2022;18(12):9206–9216.

[30]   Shamir A. How to share a secret. *Communications of the ACM*. 1979;22(11): 612–613.

[31]   Fedorov AK, Kiktenko EO, and Lvovsky AI. *Quantum Computers Put Blockchain Security at Risk*. Nature Publishing Group UK, London; 2018.

[32]   Qu Z, Meng Y, Liu B, *et al*. QB-IMD: a secure medical data processing system with privacy protection based on quantum blockchain for IoMT. *IEEE Internet of Things Journal*. 2023.

[33]   Ullah MA, Setiawan JW, ur Rehman J, *et al*. On the robustness of quantum algorithms for blockchain consensus. *Sensors*. 2022;22(7):2716.

[34]   Sun X, Sopek M, Wang Q, *et al*. Towards quantum-secured permissioned blockchain: signature, consensus, and logic. *Entropy*. 2019;21(9):887.

[35]   Cui W, Dou T, and Yan S. Threats and opportunities: blockchain meets quantum computation. In: *2020 39th Chinese Control Conference (CCC)*. IEEE; 2020. p. 5822–5824.

[36] Sun X, Wang Q, Kulicki P, *et al*. A simple voting protocol on quantum blockchain. *International Journal of Theoretical Physics*. 2019;58:275–281.

[37] Li Q, Wu J, Quan J, *et al*. Efficient quantum blockchain with a consensus mechanism QDPoS. *IEEE Transactions on Information Forensics and Security*. 2022;17:3264–3276.

[38] Wen XJ, Chen YZ, Fan XC, *et al*. Blockchain consensus mechanism based on quantum zero-knowledge proof. *Optics & Laser Technology*. 2022;147:107693.

[39] Wen X, Chen Y, Zhang W, *et al*. Blockchain consensus mechanism based on quantum teleportation. *Mathematics*. 2022;10(14):2385.

[40] Gao YL, Chen XB, Xu G, *et al*. A novel quantum blockchain scheme base on quantum entanglement and DPoS. *Quantum Information Processing*. 2020;19:1–15.

[41] Yi H, Li Y, Wang M, *et al*. An efficient blockchain consensus algorithm based on post-quantum threshold signature. *Big Data Research*. 2021;26:100268.

[42] Wang H and Yu J. A blockchain consensus protocol based on quantum attack algorithm. *Computational Intelligence and Neuroscience*. 2022;2022.

[43] Wang P, Chen W, Lin S, *et al*. Consensus algorithm based on verifiable quantum random numbers. *International Journal of Intelligent Systems*. 2022;37(10):6857–6876.

[44] Chen J, Gan W, Hu M, *et al*. On the construction of a post-quantum blockchain for smart city. *Journal of Information Security and Applications*. 2021;58:102780.

[45] Ding J. A new proof of work for blockchain based on random multivariate quadratic equations. In: *Applied Cryptography and Network Security Workshops: ACNS 2019 Satellite Workshops*, SiMLA, Cloud S&P, AIBlock, and AIoTS, Bogota, Colombia, June 5–7, 2019, Proceedings 17. Springer; 2019. p. 97–107.

[46] Behnia R, Postlethwaite EW, Ozmen MO, *et al*. Lattice-based proof-of-work for post-quantum blockchains. In: *International Workshop on Data Privacy Management*. Springer; 2021. p. 310–318.

[47] Qu Z, Zhang Z, Liu B, *et al*. Quantum detectable Byzantine agreement for distributed data trust management in blockchain. *Information Sciences*. 2023;637:118909.

[48] Liu A, Chen XB, Xu S, *et al*. A secure scheme based on a hybrid of classical-quantum communications protocols for managing classical blockchains. *Entropy*. 2023;25(5):811.

[49] Singh D, Fu B, Muraleedharan G, *et al*. Proof-of-work consensus by quantum sampling; 2023. arXiv preprint arXiv:230519865.

[50] Faugere JC. A new efficient algorithm for computing Gröbner bases (F4). *Journal of Pure and Applied Algebra*. 1999;139(1–3):61–88.

[51] Nakamoto S. Bitcoin: a peer-to-peer electronic cash system. *Decentralized Business Review*. 2008. Available at http://bitcoin.org/bitcoin.pdf.

[52] Garey MR and Johnson DS. Computers and Intractability: A Guide to the Theory of NP-completeness, Freeman; 1979. https://books.google.com.vn/books/about/Computers_and_Intractability.html?id=fjxGAQAAIAAJ&redir_esc=y.

[53]   Amiri R, Abidin A, Wallden P, *et al*. Efficient unconditionally secure signatures using universal hashing. In: *Applied Cryptography and Network Security: 16th International Conference, ACNS 2018*, Leuven, Belgium, July 2–4, 2018, Proceedings 16. Springer; 2018. p. 143–162.

[54]   Muratov F, Lebedev A, Iushkevich N, *et al*. YAC: BFT consensus algorithm for blockchain; 2018. arXiv preprint arXiv:180900554.

[55]   Tajima A, Kondoh T, Ochi T, *et al*. Quantum key distribution network for multiple applications. *Quantum Science and Technology*. 2017;2(3):034003.

[56]   Aggarwal D, Brennen GK, Lee T, *et al*. Quantum attacks on Bitcoin, and how to protect against them; 2017. arXiv preprint arXiv:171010377.

[57]   Thapliyal K, Sharma RD, and Pathak A. Protocols for quantum binary voting. *International Journal of Quantum Information*. 2017;15(01):1750007.

[58]   Howard H and Mortier R. Relaxed Paxos: quorum intersection revisited (again). In: *Proceedings of the 9th Workshop on Principles and Practice of Consistency for Distributed Data*; 2022. p. 16–23.

[59]   Amarasekara D and Ranasinghe D. ZPaxos: an asynchronous BFT Paxos with a leaderless synchronous group. In: *2022 21st International Symposium on Parallel and Distributed Computing (ISPDC)*. IEEE; 2022. p. 114–120.

[60]   Sheff I, Wang X, van Renesse R, *et al*. Heterogeneous paxos. In: *OPODIS: International Conference on Principles of Distributed Systems*. 2020; 2021.

[61]   Nagawiecki A and Patterson S. Layered Paxos: A Hierarchical Approach to Consensus. Rensselaer Polytechnic Institute. 2021.

[62]   Charapko A, Ailijiang A, and Demirbas M. Pigpaxos: Devouring the communication bottlenecks in distributed consensus. In: Proceedings of the 2021 International Conference on Management of Data; 2021. p. 235–247.

[63]   Bizzaro F, Conti M, and Pini MS. Proof of evolution: leveraging blockchain mining for a cooperative execution of genetic algorithms. In: 2020 IEEE International Conference on Blockchain (Blockchain). IEEE; 2020. p. 450–455.

[64]   Reijsbergen D, Szalachowski P, Ke J, *et al*. LaKSA: A probabilistic proof-of-stake protocol. arXiv preprint arXiv:200601427. 2020.

[65]   Kaur M, Gupta S, Kumar D, *et al*. Delegated proof of accessibility (dpoac): A novel consensus protocol for blockchain systems. Mathematics. 2022;10(13):2336.

[66]   Chen Y, Li H, Li K, *et al*. An improved P2P file system scheme based on IPFS and Blockchain. In: 2017 IEEE International Conference on Big Data (Big Data). IEEE; 2017. p. 2652–2657.

[67]   Wang Y, Peng H, Su Z, *et al*. A platform-free proof of federated learning consensus mechanism for sustainable blockchains. IEEE Journal on Selected Areas in Communications. 2022;40(12):3305–3324.

[68]   You C, Qin Y, Chen Q, *et al*. HADPoS: Improvement of DPoS Consensus Mechanism Based on Heat Attenuation. IT Professional. 2023;25(1):40–51.

[69]   Jose JM, and Panchami V. A Survey on Consensus Algorithms in Blockchain Based on Post Quantum Cryptosystems. In: 2022 5th International Conference on Computational Intelligence and Networks (CINE). IEEE; 2022. p. 1–6.

[70]   Helm LK. Quantum distributed consensus. In: PODC; 2008. p. 445.

Chapter 3
Basic Proof-of-Stake consensus mechanisms
Yang Xiao[1] and Wenhai Sun[2]

Proof-of-Stake (PoS) emerged from the Bitcoin community in 2012 as an alternative consensus mechanism to Proof-of-Work (PoW) to deal with the latter's high computational cost. The general principle of PoS is that a participant's expected reward should be proportional to its "stake" in the system's operation, usually evaluated by the number of native tokens deposited for consensus participation. For a stakeholder, the generation of new tokens is akin to the interest generation of deposit accounts in traditional finance. From the economic perspective, PoS associates a stakeholder's (called "minter" or "validator") economic return to its staked tokens, shifting a participant's cost into the blockchain's native monetary system, in the form of the opportunity cost of unused coins [1]. This effectively shifts participants away from PoW's brute-force competition in computing power.

In the early PoS proposals, the idea was to align the chance of winning a block generation game with a stakeholder's coin ownership, relieving participants from brute-force PoW mining. Nakamoto's longest-chain rule and block rewards-based incentive mechanism were preserved. However, due to the absence of real mining, early PoS schemes were commonly prone to unique attacks enabled by the costless simulation of the PoS chain's history. Later PoS schemes began to explore wider concepts of stakes, including consensus committee membership and voting power, as well as more deterministic block finalization rules in lieu of the longest-chain rule, such as the committee-based and BFT-based PoS varieties which we will introduce in later chapters.

In this chapter, we will cover the basic principles of PoS with a focus on the early PoS schemes to lay the foundations for more recent (and arguably more advanced) PoS schemes covered in later chapters. In Section 3.1, we provide a brief history of PoS development in the early days. Then we detail two representative PoS schemes, namely Peercoin, Proof-of-Activity, and Nxt in Sections 3.2, 3.3, and 3.4, respectively. We introduce the common security and fairness problems of PoS schemes in Section 3.5, including those caused by stake centralization and costless simulation. We briefly discuss other types of PoS schemes in Section 3.6 and finally conclude the chapter in 3.7.

[1]Department of Computer Science, University of Kentucky, USA
[2]Department of Computer and Information Technology, Purdue University, USA

3.1   PoS as a PoW replacement

PoW blockchains have been known for their computation-heavy block generation (i.e., "mining") process, which expects all participants, i.e., the miners, to brute-force a hash puzzle until a valid pre-image is found. As a PoW blockchain attracts more miners, the hash puzzle's difficulty increases to keep a constant block generation rate. This translates into enormous electricity and environmental costs for a global network that contains tens of thousands of miners. As of October 2023, Bitcoin, the first and currently the largest PoW blockchain, consumes approximately 120 TWh of electricity annually,* more than many countries.

To bring down the energy consumption of blockchain operation, PoS as an alternative consensus mechanism was first introduced in a Bitcointalk forum post in 2011 [2]. The general idea is that instead of weighting a vote on the transaction history by the share of computing power (as is done in PoW), weighting a vote by the share of coins owned (i.e., *stakes*) would achieve the same purpose. In the context of blockchain security, PoS-based consensus would rely on the honest parties owning the majority of stake value instead of the majority of computing power to counter the double-spending attack; the longest chain, which represents the only valid transaction history, would contain the most PoS staking effort instead of PoW mining effort. The PoS miners should receive block rewards proportional to their stake value. Economically speaking, PoS moves a miner's cost from outside the system (computing hardware and electricity) to inside the system (opportunity cost of unused capital) [1,3]. Though conceptually appealing, replacing PoW with PoS for Bitcoin mining faced security and operational challenges, including the centralization risk and the nothing-at-stake problem (which invites bribery attacks, long-range attacks, and stake-grinding attacks). We will discuss them in Section 3.5.

One of the first implementations of PoS was developed by King and Nadal in 2012 in their cryptocurrency project Peercoin [4], which provided a partial solution to the above challenges. In the next 2 years, various PoS-based blockchain projects emerged, represented by Nxt in 2013 and Blackcoin in 2014. These early PoS proposals were often known as **chain-based PoS** as they emulated Bitcoin's backbone protocol in that all network participants compete to become the next block generator [5] so as to keep the longest chain as the main chain. They also share the same transaction/block structure and propagation mechanism that is based on peer-to-peer gossiping. The PoS principle is realized by associating the chance of winning a block competition with stake value rather than raw computing power. However, they differ in how to realize the PoS block competition as well as valuation of stakes, which turn out to have subtle security impacts.

In the remainder of this chapter, we focus on the basic chain-based PoS schemes. While chain-based PoS is no longer the mainstream of PoS, it holds the elegance of not significantly diverging from Bitcoin's original design, and some of its principles and lessons have shed light on later PoS schemes. To differentiate from the **miner**

---

*Bitcoin Energy Consumption Index: https://digiconomist.net/bitcoin-energy-consumption

that commonly refers to a PoW miner of Bitcoin-like blockchains, unless specially noted, we use **minter** or **validator** to represent the entity that participates in a PoS consensus process.

3.2 Peercoin

Peercoin was the first public cryptocurrency system to implement the PoS idea. It was originally called PPCoin in King and Nadal's whitepaper [4] and later rebranded into its current name. We will use Peercoin throughout this chapter for consistency.

At its core, Peercoin employs a hybrid PoW/PoS mechanism for creating blocks and minting new coins. The purpose of PoW mining is to inject the initial coins into circulation so that they can be used as capital for later PoS mining. This saves an initial public offering (IPO) for coins which would be performed through a centralization process.[†] The PoS mining process makes use of the existing coins [more specifically, unspent transaction output (UTXO)] as the stakes. In this way, both PoW and PoS mining contribute to the generation of new peercoins and one can choose to participate in either process.

To realize the above goal, the Peercoin blockchain accepts two types of blocks— PoW blocks and PoS blocks. A PoW block is generated similarly to its Bitcoin counterpart, i.e., miners use their raw computing power to solve a hash puzzle, and the winning miner gets paid by new coins from the *coinbase* transaction. In comparison, the generation of a PoS block involves finding a valid PoS *kernel*, which, alongside all stake inputs, constitutes a *coinstake* transaction that pays new coins to the minter. Specifically, the *coinstake* transaction takes one of the minter's UTXOs as input and outputs the UTXO amount plus new coins to itself. Since 2013, the PoS blocks have constituted the vast majority of new blocks in the Peercoin blockchain [6].

Next, we explain how Peercoin's PoS minting works with the kernel mechanism and the block generation. The detailed implementation can be found in Peercoin's source code [7]. A simplified workflow is shown in Figure 3.1. Finding a valid kernel requires solving hash puzzles like PoW mining but with different computation requirements. For every UTXO, a minter finds a valid kernel if the following hash puzzle is solved:

$$Hash(preTxCtx, modifier, clock) < target \times coin\_age \qquad (3.1)$$

where *preTxCtx* includes some information (block timestamp, transaction timestamp, etc.) about the previous transaction to which the current UTXO belongs. *modifier* is designed to prevent a minter from pre-computing future PoS kernels. It is recomputed at a fixed time interval instead of every block, which makes it difficult for a malicious minter to gain control of additional bits in *modifier* [8]. To realize this, *clock* takes the current UNIX time that ticks every second. *target* is the hashing difficulty target similar to PoW's. Lastly but most relevant to the purpose of PoS, *coin_age* represents stake value—the coin amount in the UTXO times how long it remains unused.

[†]The Peercoin whitepaper [4] does not rule out the IPO option for future PoS blockchains where a pure PoS system is desired from the beginning.

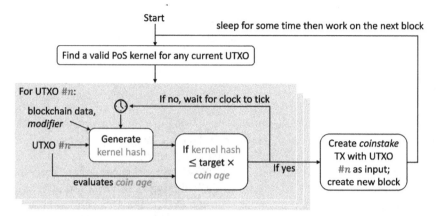

Figure 3.1   Peercoin's PoS block generation process performed by each minter. After creating the new block, the block is broadcast to the network similarly to that in Bitcoin.

Eq. (3.1) implies that within a certain time frame of a fixed difficulty target, the chance of finding a valid PoS kernel is proportional to the combined coin age of all UTXOs a minter owns, since the hash puzzle can be tried independently for each UTXO. Any valid puzzle solution can serve as the kernel for the coinstake transaction. It is worth noting that the above process avoids the competition in raw computing power, due to the limited search space for the kernel—no random nonce or transaction root that can be manipulated. As a result, a PoS minter can expect a doubled time to find a valid kernel if they decide to use half the coin age worth of UTXOs for kernel generation. In practical deployment, Peercoin requires the coin age of a UTXO to start accumulating after 30 days and stops at 90 days. Holding it for more than 90 days does not further increase the coin age value. On the one hand, the coin age accumulation scheme is designed to encourage the participation of those with small funds so that they are given an inflated chance to generate a PoS block after a long unsuccessful period. On the other hand, the 90-day limit is designed to prevent a malicious minter from accumulating an overwhelming coin age value at some future point.

When it comes to consensus security, all Peercoin minters work to extend the longest chain, similar to Bitcoin. Under the assumption that the majority of coin ages are controlled by honest minters at any point, the longest chain should have consumed the most coin age in its PoS blocks. Therefore, Peercoin has been branded for using PoW for initial coin distribution and PoS for underpinning the blockchain's consensus security [9].

While widely recognized as the first successful PoS blockchain, Peercoin has faced criticism from the beginning. First, the kernel hashing mechanism in its initial version was at risk of nothing-at-stake attacks and stake-grinding attacks. The block timestamp rule and stake modifier did not prevent an attacker from precomputing future PoS kernels. In response, Peercoin has updated the stake modifier several times to increase the difficulty of kernel precomputation [10]. Once it becomes a block generator, the attacker can produce multiple candidate blocks in the hope of increasing the attacker's chance of winning future blocks [11], leveling up the risk of a 51% attack. In response, Peercoin has updated its modifier definition several times to prohibit precomputing future PoS kernels. We will discuss the two attacks in more detail in Section 3.5.2 and later chapters. Second, the coin age mechanism still faces criticism for its vulnerability to potential abuses. Specifically, it is possible for an attacker with less than 50% of all coins to accumulate more than half of all coin age and perform a double-spending attack. It also encourages honest but greedy nodes to sleep until the 90-day cap to stake in. For this reason, similar PoS schemes like Blackcoin [12] and Nxt [13] (to introduce in Section 3.4) tend to use the face value of coins rather than coin age for stake evaluation.

3.3 Proof-of-Activity

Proof of Activity (PoA)[‡] is a hybrid PoW/PoS consensus algorithm that extends from the Bitcoin protocol. It was first proposed by the Litecoin creator Charlie Lee in 2012 via a Bitcointalk post [15] (the same forum where the original PoS idea emerged). Later, the complete PoA idea was presented by Bentov *et al.* [16], which we use for formal reference. It bears many similarities with *committee-based PoS*, which we will discuss in Section 3.6. PoA was used in cryptocurrencies Decred and Espers in 2016.

Different from Peercoin's hybrid scheme where the PoW blocks and PoS blocks are mined separately for different purposes, PoA's blocks are mined by the combined use of PoW and PoS, both contributing to the blockchain's ledger security. Specifically, the consensus process on a PoA block has two stages. In the first stage, miners compete to solve a PoW puzzle to create an empty block header (i.e., containing necessary information about the miner and the previous block hash, but no transaction root) and broadcast it to the network. In the second stage, a group of validators is randomly selected for validating and confirming the full block. A validator's chance of being selected is proportional to its owned currency amount. When the block is finalized in the blockchain, the selected validators as well as the PoW miner will share the block reward. The block generation process of PoA is shown in Figure 3.2.

Now we describe how the validators in the second stage are selected; this is where PoS comes into the scene. The selection process crucially relies on the *Follow-The-Satoshi* (FTS) mechanism, which is used to trace the movement of an atomic piece of the mined cryptocurrency (i.e., satoshi in Bitcoin) across user wallets by tracing the path of the recipient's public keys across transactions.[§] Given a certain satoshi index (between zero and the total number of satoshis mined), FTS outputs the public key of the user who currently owns that satoshi. Now back to PoA's validator

---

[‡]"PoA" may also refer to Proof of Authority, a consensus technique used by permissioned blockchains to determine authorized participants [14]. We use it to represent proof of activity in this book.
[§]This public key tracing is enabled by Bitcoin's UTXO model, where a transaction sender must include the public key of the recipient in a transaction.

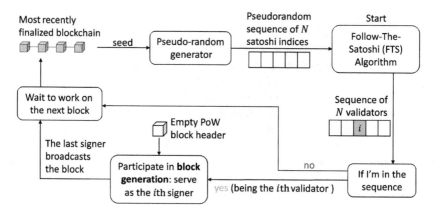

Figure 3.2   *PoA's block generation process performed by each minter. The FTS-based validator selection process embodies the PoS principle. The generation of the empty PoW block header is not shown in this figure.*

selection problem. Given a pseudorandom sequence of N satoshi indices, FTS will output a sequence of N validators. The chance of a validator being included in this sequence is proportional to its owned token amount, embodying the PoS principle. Lastly, the pseudorandom sequence of satoshi indices is generated by each validator independently based on common knowledge of the empty block header and the previous block's hash. As a result, the FTS-based selection result is self-discoverable; the chosen validator automatically knows in what order should it provide a validation signature.

Compared to pure PoW, pure PoS, and Peercoin's hybrid scheme, PoA provides an additional layer of security against the 51% attack. An attacker would need to possess both 51% or more of the total mining power in the network and 51% or more of the coins staked in the network [17]. This is because PoA requires miners to prove their ownership of a certain amount of coins before they can start mining. Therefore, if an attacker wanted to amass enough mining power to execute a 51% attack, they would also need to acquire a significant number of coins to stake on the network.

In 2016, the PoA authors proposed a new PoS scheme called Chains of Activity (CoA) [18] partially based on PoA. Rather than a Bitcoin extension, CoA falls into the class of committee-based PoS schemes, along with the Ouroboros PoS protocol that we will introduce in later chapters. In a nutshell, such schemes require that for every new batch of blocks, a pre-determined committee of validators shall take turns to propose and finalize a block.

3.4   Nxt

Nxt is another chain-based PoS blockchain that gained wide attention. It resembles Peercoin in many aspects as both rely on an owner's coin balance to derive the stake value and use a PoW-like hashing puzzle to generate PoS blocks. In this section, we

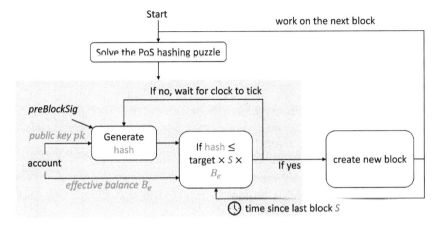

Figure 3.3   Nxt's PoS block generation process performed by each minter

focus on the major differences between Nxt and Peercoin. Readers are referred to the Nxt whitepaper [13] for more technical details.

Compared to Peercoin's hybrid PoS/PoW approach, Nxt is a pure PoS blockchain. No PoW mining is needed for generating blocks or new coins. Nxt performed the initial token offering in November 2013—a total of 1 billion Nxt tokens were created at the genesis block—no new Nxt tokens have been generated ever since. As a result, Nxt's block rewards only come from fees paid from the included transactions. This design has two purposes. First, it makes the profitability of staking directly related to the stakeholder's transaction validation effort, incentivizing the stakeholder to include as many transactions as possible in the new block, since it is the only way to accumulate wealth. Second, limiting the total supply of Nxt tokens at the beginning makes the currency system deflationary by default, which theoretically better preserves the token value.

Besides the difference in handling initial coin supply, Nxt and Peercoin have major differences in how they perform the PoS block competition and how they evaluate stakes. To differentiate from Peercoin's "minting" process, Nxt calls the discovery of a valid PoS block header *forging*, and each PoS block contender is called a *forger*. Nxt's forging process requires solving the following hashing puzzle:

$$Hash(preBlockSig, pk) < target \times S \times B_e \qquad (3.2)$$

where *preBlockSig* is the generation signature of the previous block and *pk* is the forger account's public key. *target* is the difficulty target, S is the time since the last block (in seconds), and B_e is the "effective balance," defined as the tokens that have been stationary in the forger's account for 1440 blocks.

At first glance, the term $S \cdot B_e$ in (3.2) looks similar to Peercoin's coin age, as the latter is also the product of coin value and time value. The difference is that B_e counts the entire account balance, instead of just one UXTO as in Peercoin. Also, S is the same for every forger and always starts from zero when a new block cycle begins. This means that the stake value only appreciates within one block cycle and reset to the base value once the block cycle ends. In comparison, Peercoin appreciates stake value (i.e., coin age) continuously throughout block cycles until the 90-day cap. As a result, at any time, the hashing difficulty per token owned is universal for all Nxt forgers. This provides a level ground for all forgers to participate and there is no advantage of stake hoarding (i.e., stay away from forging and resume at a future time). It also provides a better defense against nothing-at-stake and stake-grinding attacks, since the hash input—*preBlockSig* and *pk*—is determined for every block cycle, and *pk* uniquely resolves to the account with B_e effective balance.

Despite Nxt's improved security and fairness, there is one catch. The hashing puzzle in (3.2) should only be attempted at certain discrete time intervals, e.g., 1 minute, to prevent nothing-at-stake attacks. This serves a similar goal to the clock input in Peercoin's hashing puzzle. How to maintain a global clock that verifiably ticks per interval is still a challenge for Nxt [19].

3.5   Challenges for PoS consensus mechanisms

3.5.1   Centralization

PoS is subject to the centralization of staking power. Just like a Bitcoin miner may increase its success rate of solving the PoS puzzle by acquiring more computing resources, a PoS minter/validator may also increase its success rate by amassing more stakes through external coin purchases. When a few colluding minters hold the majority amount of the total token value, the 51% attack risk will also signify. Similar to PoW mining pools, PoS staking pools allow individual participants to pool their tokens in order to receive more stable staking income. Popular PoS blockchains such as Ethereum may have mandatory staking amounts that surpass the tokens owned by an average user. The presence of PoS staking pools can potentially add to the risk of a 51% attack, reminiscent of the 51% attack in PoW mining. From the practical perspective, opinions vary on whether PoS mining is more subject to centralization than PoW mining. On the one hand, stake pooling may require less coordination effort since tokens are more easily aggregated them computing hardware. On the other hand, PoW miners may be able to buy efficient hardware at scale with lower cost, giving larger miners a nonlinear advantage over smaller players.

The centralization of staking has been evident in the Ethereum blockchain since its transition into full PoS ("The Merge") in September 2022. As of October 2023, the largest Ethereum staking pool, Lido [20], controls 76% of all liquid staked Ether,[||] which is slightly over 28% of all staked Ether [22]. Stake centralization is also complicated by the varying demands of token liquidity. Unlike PoW, not all tokens can be used for the PoS process since they need to be used to make normal transactions. During periods of high staking rewards and low circulation demand, unstaked Ether

---

[||]Unlike normal Ether stake that is locked during PoS participation, liquid staked Ether can be traded or used freely while earning staking rewards [21]. It may be priced differently and has its own token symbol.

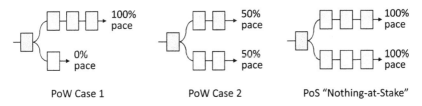

Figure 3.4   PoS's nothing-at-stake problem illustrated. A PoS minter can work on two branches with full effort simultaneously; a PoS miner has to distribute effort among the branches.

may flock into the staking pools. With only 23% of all circulating Ether staked as of October 2023, any major inflow of unstaked Ether could drastically change the power ratios of the existing staking pools.

3.5.2   Costless simulation and the nothing-at-stake problem

Freeing blockchain participants from competition in raw computing power is the core motivation for replacing PoW with PoS. This design principle also incurs the nothing-at-stake problem, as well as the more general **costless simulation** concern. Costless simulation means any player can simulate any segment of blockchain history (including the imminent future) at the cost of no real work, which may give attackers shortcuts in growing an alternative blockchain and committing the 51% attack [3].

The **nothing-at-stake** problem is the first known costless simulation problem. It refers to that a PoS node can generate conflicting blocks on all possible forks (of the same blockchain height) without risking their stake. This problem was identified in the Bitcoin talk forum not long after the emergence of the original PoS idea. In Peercoin and Nxt, for example, PoS minters can choose to perform the hash puzzle for all competing branches should a blockchain fork happen (called "multi-bet"), since it does not require extra physical resources as in PoW mining; what is only lost is the opportunity cost for winning the next PoS block. As is shown in Figure 3.4, a PoS minter can advance both branches at the full pace while a PoW miner has to distribute their effort among the branches. If all rational PoS minters choose to multi-bet, the network will see a significant rise in forks that reduce the difficulty for double-spending attacks. To combat the nothing-at-stake problem, PoS can be augmented with a punishment ("slashing") mechanism such as forfeiting multi-bettors' stakes, which is currently deployed in Ethereum's PoS mechanism, Casper FFG [23].

Costless simulation also gives rise to other types of attacks. We discuss them in Sections 3.5.3, 3.5.4, and 3.5.5 shortly.

3.5.3   Bribery attack

Bribery attack, also known as posterior corruption, was originally an attack targeting Bitcoin-alike PoW blockchains [24]. It requires the attacker to "rent" (i.e., "bribe") a majority portion of mining power from the miners for a short period to extend a fork that rewrites a recent segment of blockchain history. The bribed miners are compensated with rents ("out-of-band") or bribe transactions in the finalized fork ("in-band"). In PoS blockchains, bribery attacks can be similarly carried out by colluding stakeholders who had a majority portion of the total stake value at some point. The costless simulation property of PoS also makes it easier for the colluding parties to predict the potential compensation and allows the attacker to target far back in the ledger history. As a special case, stakeholders who once held significant stake values at some point could be bribed to work on an alternative history provided by the attacker from that point in the hope of regaining their spent wealth [3]. To counter bribery attacks, a PoS blockchain may enforce certain punishment rules on those engaged in bribery or a quick checkpointing mechanism to add finality to recent ledger history.

3.5.4   Long-range attack

Long-range attack is another risk associated with costless simulation. Compared to bribery attackers who attempt to rewrite recent history, a long-range attacker attempts to rewrite the blockchain history starting from the early history of the ledger, when there were only a few PoS participants involved in the competition which simplifies the collusion [11]. By starting at the early point, the colluding PoS participants can claim the majority of block rewards once the alternative ledger becomes the longest chain. Long-range attacks are infeasible on PoW blockchains due to the sheer volume of PoW computation needed even at the early stage [25]. For blockchains with no block rewards, i.e., solely relying on transaction fees to compensate validators, a specific type of long-range attack known as **stake-bleeding attack** is still possible [26]. It allows the colluding parties to claim the majority of transaction fees from an early point. It is worth noting that the attacker has the motivation to perform a long-range attack even if there is a stake punishment mechanism in place (e.g., slashing rules) since the attack's success would rewrite the blockchain history and thus invalidate previously correct blocks.

While a successful long-range attack against major blockchains has never been observed, it still needs to be prevented for maximum security consideration. One approach is to adopt a deterministic checkpointing mechanism so that any history before a certain number of checkpoints cannot be modified. This, however, requires a trusted authority to publish finalized checkpoints. Without a trusted authority, it is also possible to checkpoint into a trustworthy public blockchain, such as Bitcoin, as is demonstrated in [27] where Bitcoin's recent Taproot upgrade [28] can enable such checkpoints efficiently.

3.5.5   Stake-grinding attack

In chain-based PoS, stake grinding refers to a class of attacks in which minters use computational resources to bias the PoS competition to their advantage [29]. Stake grinding attacks are partially enabled by costless simulation—pre-computing future PoS or post-computing past PoS is easy—as well as a loose requirement on PoS's randomness sources. In the first version of Peercoin for example, when a minter wins the PoS competition and is about to propose the new block, it may try out different versions of the full block (e.g., by tweaking the transaction timestamp) to find out the version that increases the minter's chance of winning the PoS competition of subsequent blocks.

To counter stake-grinding attacks, later versions of Peercoin provide more strict rules on the randomness input, hence, the "modifier" field as we have seen in (3.1). Nxt chooses to forego self-selected randomness in the hash puzzle and opt for a deterministic PoS ash input [11] as we have seen in (3.2). More recent schemes that adopt the committee-based PoS model (e.g., Ouroboros and Algorand) adopt the multiparty computation paradigm for all candidates to derive unbiased randomness and use it for PoS-based committee elections.

3.5.6 The subjectivity problem

Subjectivity in blockchain refers to the need for subjective information to agree on the current state of blockchain [30]. For PoS blockchains that do not use the longest-chain rule for finalizing the main chain, there lack of transparent and objective information (like the longest chain) for a newcomer to catch up with the latest ledger. Take BFT-based PoS for example (to introduce in Section 3.6), the newcomer needs to pull possible versions of the main chain from existing validators and recount the votes for each block. It is possible to retrieve multiple equally valid chains which can be hard to decide upon. In response, the current PoS-based Ethereum consensus protocol Gasper (the combination of Casper FFG [23] and Greedy Heaviest Observer SubTree (GHOST) for main chain selection), all honest validators need to maintain uniform *weak subjectivity checkpoints* in addition to the blockchain itself. The checkpoints have only limited reversibility and can provide an authentic view of the main chain.

3.6 Alternative PoS designs and classification

Starting in 2014, new PoS blockchain proposals gradually shifted away from the chain-based model. Instead of randomly sampling all participants (chance weighted by stake) for the next block's generator, these new models tend to be equipped with a more structured design of the staking process as well as the finalization of the blockchain ledger. This paradigm shift coincided with the emerging criticism of early blockchain systems which tended to have ad hoc designed consensus protocols; established wisdom from distributed systems and cryptography could be used to design more secure and formally verifiable protocols [31]. Among them, three types of PoS exist—committee-based PoS, delegated PoS, and BFT-based PoS, as shown in Figure 3.5. They are not mutually exclusive due to the mixed use of certain mechanisms, such as committee-election and BFT consensus-based blockchain finalization. Here we discuss their main design principles briefly while readers are referred to [3] for a discussion on the performance and security properties of each type. Lastly, we will also discuss PoS sidechains, when the PoS mechanism is not used for main chain consensus.

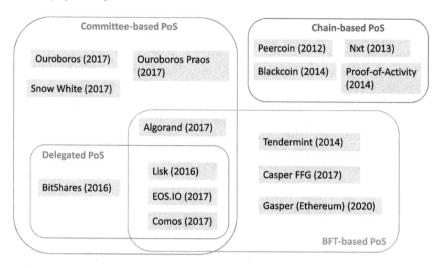

Figure 3.5   *Different types of PoS consensus protocols and representative*
implementations

3.6.1   Committee-based PoS

Instead of having all network users validate transactions and participate in the consensus process, committee-based PoS requires only a selected committee of validators to participate in consensus and curating the blockchain ledger. The sampling of the validator committee conforms to the PoS principle—those with a higher staked token value are more likely to be chosen. This process usually requires a certain randomness source for each validator candidate to derive the same list of validators for the next consensus epoch. For example, a verifiable random function (VRF) [32] allows each candidate to independently check if it gets selected. Afterward, the committee may start proposing new blocks in an orderly manner, such as by round-robin, due to the limited committee size. Notable committee-based PoS schemes include the Ouroboros [33] (used by the cryptocurrency Cardano), Ouroboros Praos [34], and Snow White [35] which we will discuss in later chapters.

Committee-based PoS does not limit the methods for reaching consensus on a unified blockchain. It can either keep using Nakamoto's longest-chain rule or switch to BFT-style consensus with periodic checkpoints. As we will introduce later in this section, Delegated PoS (DPoS) is a special type of committee-based PoS where the staking process resembles a socialized voting process.

3.6.2   BFT-based PoS

Committee-based PoS also coincided with the renewed interest in Byzantine Fault Tolerant (BFT) consensus and State Machine Replication (SMR) schemes [36] in the blockchain community. BFT consensus, in its simplest form, allows a group of nodes to agree on a common value given that a certain portion of nodes behave arbitrarily (i.e., suffering from Byzantine fault). BFT-SMR extends BFT consensus into supporting the consensus on a common sequence of actions and has been extensively studied by the distributed systems community [37–40]. It typically requires a fixed, end-to-end-connected network of nodes to engage in intensive mutual communication and local computation to keep a replicated state machine. The BFT consensus outputs are deterministic often with the help of a checkpointing mechanism, meaning that the blockchain history behind the most checkpoint is 100% irreversible. This is in stark comparison to Nakamoto's longest-chain rule that only provides probabilistic finality [3]. The small validator committee of committee-based PoS also makes it well-positioned to use BFT consensus. More recent BFT-SMR schemes have been targeting.

In this regard, BFT-based PoS protocols tend to separate block proposing from BFT consensus-based block finalization, where block proposal can be done either by anyone who wins the PoS lottery (akin to chain-based PoS) or by a committee in an orderly manner. The BFT consensus part ensures there can be only one block finalized for each block height despite multiple block proposals. Well-known BFT-based PoS schemes include Tendermint [41], Algorand [42], and Casper FFG [23]. They tend to employ a BFT protocol tailored to the blockchain network's participation and communication models. It is worth noting that a BFT-based PoS scheme can also be a committee-based PoS scheme, where the PoS principle is applied to electing a community. For example, Algorand relies on cryptographic sortition, a stake-weighted VRF algorithm, to determine the block-proposing committee on an epoch basis. The committee proposes candidate blocks and performs a Byzantine agreement protocol (a form of BFT consensus) to finalize one block for each block height. In comparison, Casper FFG applies the PoS principle in the block finalization process where each validator's vote on a candidate block is weighted by the validator's stake. We will introduce these BFT-based PoS schemes in later chapters.

3.6.3   Delegated PoS

Delegated PoS (DPoS) is a way of socialized committee election that employs the PoS principle. It requires a token owner (called "delegator") to periodically delegate its token value to a candidate validator. Each candidate validator can actively promote itself (e.g., with added services) and attract token-weighted votes from global token owners. The total delegated token value, instead of self-owned tokens, is used for the election process. A higher delegated token value gives a higher chance of being elected as a validator. The top N candidate validators measured by stake value received are elected to be the consensus committee which will be responsible for transaction validation and blockchain consensus until the next election round. Popular blockchain platforms employing a DPoS mechanism include BitShares 2.0 [43], Steemit [44], EOS.IO [45], Lisk [46], and Cosmos [47]. It is worth noting that DPoS conceptually does not specify the mechanisms beyond PoS-based committee election and DPoS schemes may overlap with BFT-based PoS for blockchain generation and finalization. For example, when the committee is elected, they can employ a round-robin block-proposing mechanism and BFT consensus (such as in EOS.IO and Cosmos) to process transactions and finalize blocks efficiently.

More recently, **Nominated PoS (NPoS)** has attracted interest as has been used by Polkadot [48]. NPoS is a special type of DPoS in that a token owner (called "nominator") chooses a group of validators (16 for Polkadot) it fairly trusts and all validators in the group evenly share the nominator's placed stake. Unlike in DPoS where the elected validators are solely responsible for the blockchain consensus, the nominators in NPoS are subject to loss of stake if they nominate a bad validator [49].

3.6.4 PoS sidechains

A sidechain is an affiliated blockchain that works alongside a target main blockchain, such as Ethereum, to enable the transfer of assets, data, or smart contracts between the main chain and the other standalone blockchains [50]. A sidechain is designed to be interoperable with the main chain but also operates with some degree of independence. For example, it may adopt its own consensus protocols while relying on the security of the main blockchain for certain functions, like the finality of transactions.

A good example of PoS sidechain is Polygon. Polygon PoS sidechain, or called Heimdall layer, is a key component of the Polygon network, where a set of proof-of-stake nodes (i.e., validators) are running in parallel to the Ethereum mainnet to monitor the set of staking contracts deployed on the Ethereum, and commit the Polygon Network checkpoints to the Ethereum [51]. This PoS sidechain provides essential functions to the objective of Polygon to scale up Ethereum and allows for faster and more cost-effective transactions. This alleviates congestion and improves the overall scalability of the Ethereum ecosystem.

In the Polygon PoS sidechain, validators are responsible for validating all the blocks since the last checkpoint, Creating a Merkle tree of the block hashes, and Publishing the Merkle root hash to the Ethereum. A subset of validators will also be further selected to act as block producers to create blocks and broadcast the blocks on the network. The proposer is also selected from the validators to perform other key functions, such as collecting signatures for checkpoints and committing the checkpoints on the Ethereum. Therefore, validators are important to the security and stability of the Polygon sidechain system.

Polygon sidechain leverages the PoS mechanism to manage the status of validators, block producers, and proposers. Specifically, the PoS function is accomplished by implementing a set of staking management contracts on Ethereum. In order to become a validator, MATIC tokens need to be deposited to the staking contracts on the Ethereum mainnet. The staking contracts also allow the validator to earn staking rewards for performing transaction verification on the Polygon network and save checkpoints on the Ethereum mainnet. The stake ratio of the validators in the pool also decides on the responsibility of creating blocks and proposing checkpoints. It is mentioned that the PoS can also mitigate the data unavailability problem for the Polygon sidechain.

3.7 Conclusion

In this chapter, we have discussed the basic PoS principles, from how it works as a PoW alternative to its economic implication, as well as several widely recognized chain-based PoS schemes: Peercoin, PoA, and Nxt. Among them, Peercoin was the first public blockchain to implement the PoS idea using coin age to evaluate stake weight; PoA leverages the Follow-The-Satoshi (FTS) mechanism to select a group of validators based on stake weight who will jointly sign a new block; Nxt improves Peercoin by abandoning coin age and refreshing the stake value for every new block cycle. These chain-based PoS schemes inherit Bitcoin's networking functions and blockchain finalization rules after block generation, including peer-to-peer block propagation and the longest-chain rule. We also highlighted the challenges of chain-based PoS related to costless simulation, such as the nothing-at-stake problem, bribery attack, long-range attack, and stake-grinding attack. Lastly, we provided an overview of alternative PoS mechanisms which have been the trend in the last several years.

Chain-based PoS blockchains are no longer the trend in the PoS landscape. Among the three previously introduced chain-based PoS blockchains, Peercoin is the only one actively traded as of October 2023, with a market capitalization far less than major cryptocurrencies. However, these pioneering schemes have offered valuable lessons on the staking mechanism design as well as security risks for later PoS schemes and the broader blockchain community.

References

[1] Poelstra A. Distributed consensus from proof of stake is impossible. Self-Published Paper. 2014.

[2] Quantum Mechanic. Proof of Stake Instead of Proof of Work; 2011. Bitcoin Forum. https://bitcointalk.org/index.php?topic=27787.0.

[3] Xiao Y, Zhang N, Lou W, *et al.* A survey of distributed consensus protocols for blockchain networks. *IEEE Communications Surveys & Tutorials.* 2020;22(2):1432–1465.

[4] King S and Nadal S. Ppcoin: Peer-to-Peer Crypto-currency with Proof-of-Stake. self-Published Paper, August 2012; no. 19.

[5] Yaga D, Mell P, Roby N, *et al.* Blockchain technology overview; 2019. arXiv preprint arXiv:190611078.

[6] Anderson L, Holz R, Ponomarev A, *et al.* New kids on the block: an analysis of modern blockchains; 2016. arXiv preprint arXiv:160606530.

[7] Peercoin kernel.cpp. https://github.com/peercoin/peercoin/blob/master/src/kernel.cpp [Accessed: 10/28/2023].

[8] Peercoin Official Development Repo – kernel.cpp. https://github.com/ peercoin/peercoin/blob/master/src/kernel.cpp [Accessed: 4/15/2023].

[9] Peercoin Foundation. Peercoin – The Pioneer of Proof of Stake; 2023. https://www.peercoin.net/.

[10]   Peercoin Foundation. Peercoin kernel.cpp; 2023. https://github.com/ peer-coin/peercoin/blob/master/src/kernel.cpp.

[11]   Andreina S, Bohli JM, Karame GO, *et al.* Pots: a secure proof of tee-stake for permissionless blockchains. *IEEE Transactions on Services Computing.* 2020;15(4):2173–2187.

[12]   Vasin P. Blackcoin's proof-of-stake protocol v2; 2014. https://blackcoin.co/ blackcoin-pos-protocol-v2-whitepaper.pdf.

[13]   Nxt community. Nxt Whitepaper; 2016. https://nxtdocs.jelurida.com/ Nxt_Whitepaper.

[14]   De Angelis S, Aniello L, Baldoni R, *et al.* PBFT vs proof-of-authority: applying the CAP theorem to permissioned blockchain, *2nd Italian Conference on Cyber Security, ITASEC 2018*, Milan, Italy, February 6th–9th; 2018.

[15]   Charles Lee. Proof of Activity Proposal; 2012. Bitcoin Forum. https://bitcointalk.org/index.php?topic=102355.0.

[16]   Bentov I, Lee C, Mizrahi A, *et al.* Proof of activity: extending bitcoin's proof of work via proof of stake [extended abstract] y. *ACM SIGMETRICS Performance Evaluation Review.* 2014;42(3):34–37.

[17]   Proof-of-Activity (PoA). https://golden.com/wiki/Proof-of-activity_(PoA)-BWK8BAG [Accessed: 4/6/2023].

[18]   Bentov I, Gabizon A, and Mizrahi A. Cryptocurrencies without proof of work. In: *International Conference on Financial Cryptography and Data Security.* New York, NY: Springer; 2016. p. 142–157.

[19]   Popov S. A probabilistic analysis of the nxt forging algorithm. *Ledger.* 2016;1:69–83.

[20]   Lido – Liquidity for staked tokens. https://lido.fi/ [Accessed: 10/27/2023].

[21]   What is stETH?. https://help.lido.fi/en/articles/5230610-what-is-steth [Accessed: 10/27/2023].

[22]   Obol Labs. Ethereum Staking Ecosystem. https://dune.com/obol_labs/eth-staking-ecosystem?ref=bankless.ghost.io [Accessed: 10/27/2023].

[23]   Buterin V and Griffith V. Casper the friendly finality gadget; 2017. arXiv preprint arXiv:171009437.

[24]   Bonneau J. Why buy when you can rent? Bribery attacks on bitcoin-style consensus. In: *International Conference on Financial Cryptography and Data Security.* New York, NY: Springer; 2016. p. 19–26.

[25]   Deirmentzoglou E, Papakyriakopoulos G, and Patsakis C. A survey on long-range attacks for proof of stake protocols. *IEEE Access.* 2019;7: 28712–28725.

[26]   Gaži P, Kiayias A, and Russell A. Stake-bleeding attacks on proof-of-stake blockchains. In: *2018 Crypto Valley Conference on Blockchain Technology (CVCBT).* IEEE; 2018. p. 85–92.

[27]   Azouvi S and Vukolić M. Pikachu: securing pos blockchains from long-range attacks by checkpointing into bitcoin pow using taproot. In: *Proceedings of the 2022 ACM Workshop on Developments in Consensus*; 2022. p. 53–65.

[28]   Wuille P, Nick J, and Towns A. BIP 342 – validation of Taproot Scripts. https://github.com/bitcoin/bips/blob/master/bip-0342.mediawiki [Accessed: 10/25/2023].

[29] Buterin V. Proof of Stake FAQ. https://vitalik.ca/general/2017/12/31/pos_faq. html [Accessed: 10/29/2023].

[30] Weak Subjectivity. https://ethereum.org/en/developers/docs/consensus-mechanisms/pos/weak-subjectivity/ [Accessed: 10/29/2023].

[31] Cachin C and Vukolić M. Blockchains consensus protocols in the wild; 2017. arXiv preprint arXiv:170701873.

[32] Micali S, Rabin M, and Vadhan S. Verifiable random functions. In: *40th Annual Symposium on Foundations of Computer Science* (Cat. no. 99CB37039). IEEE; 1999. p. 120–130.

[33] Kiayias A, Russell A, David B, *et al.* Ouroboros: a provably secure proof-of-stake blockchain protocol. In: *Annual International Cryptology Conference.* New York, NY: Springer; 2017. p. 357–388.

[34] David B, Gaži P, Kiayias A, *et al.* Ouroboros praos: an adaptively-secure, semi-synchronous proof-of-stake blockchain. In: *Advances in Cryptology–EUROCRYPT 2018: 37th Annual International Conference on the Theory and Applications of Cryptographic Techniques*, Tel Aviv, Israel, April 29–May 3, 2018 Proceedings, Part II 37. New York, NY: Springer; 2018. p. 66–98.

[35] Daian P, Pass R, and Shi E. Snow white: robustly reconfigurable consensus and applications to provably secure proof of stake. In: *Financial Cryptography and Data Security: 23rd International Conference*, FC 2019, Frigate Bay, St. Kitts and Nevis, February 18–22, 2019, Revised Selected Papers 23. New York, NY: Springer; 2019. p. 23–41.

[36] Schneider FB. Implementing fault-tolerant services using the state machine approach: a tutorial. *ACM Computing Surveys (CSUR)*. 1990;22(4): 299–319.

[37] Chandra TD and Toueg S. Unreliable failure detectors for reliable distributed systems. *Journal of the ACM* (JACM). 1996;43(2):225–267.

[38] Castro M and Liskov B. Practical Byzantine fault tolerance. In: *OSDI*, vol. 99; 1999. p. 173–186.

[39] Kotla R, Alvisi L, Dahlin M, *et al.* Zyzzyva: speculative byzantine fault tolerance. In: *Proceedings of Twenty-First ACM SIGOPS Symposium on Operating Systems Principles*; 2007. p. 45–58.

[40] Attiya H and Welch J. *Distributed Computing: Fundamentals, Simulations, and Advanced Topics*, vol. 19. New York, NY: John Wiley & Sons; 2004.

[41] Kwon J. Tendermint: Consensus Without Mining. Technical Report. Ithaca, NY: Cornell University. Retrieved May 2014;18:2017.

[42] Gilad Y, Hemo R, Micali S, *et al.* Algorand: scaling Byzantine agreements for cryptocurrencies. In: *Proceedings of the 26th Symposium on Operating Systems Principles*; 2017. p. 51–68.

[43] BitShares Blockchain Foundation. BitShares Documentation. https://how. bitshares.works/en/master/ [Accessed: 4/11/2023].

[44] Steemit Inc.; 2018. https://steem.com/steem-whitepaper.pdf.

[45] IO E. EOS.IO Technical White Paper v2; 2018. Available from: https://github. com/EOSIO/Documentation/blob/master/TechnicalWhitePaper.md.

[46] Delegated Proof of Stake Consensus for LSK Token; 2022. https://lisk.com/ blog/posts/delegated-proof-stake-consensus-lsk-token [Accessed: 4/12/2023].

[47]   Kwon J and Buchman E. *Cosmos Whitepaper*. A Netw Distrib Ledgers. 2019;27.

[48]   Wood G. Polkadot: vision for a heterogeneous multi-chain framework. *White Paper*. 2016;21(2327):4662.

[49]   Polkadot. Polkadot Launch: Nominated Proof of Stake Phase. https://www.polkadot.network/launch-roadmap/npos/ [Accessed: 10/15/2023].

[50]   Gaži P, Kiayias A, and Zindros D. Proof-of-stake sidechains. In: *2019 IEEE Symposium on Security and Privacy (SP)*. IEEE; 2019. p. 139–156.

[51]   The Value Layer of the Internet [homepage on the Internet]. Polygon; 2023 [updated 2023 Oct 19; cited 2023 Oct 19]. Available from: https://polygon.technology/.

Chapter 4
Blockchain-based content caching toward 6G networks

Shaohan Feng[1], Wenbo Wang[2] and Zhengwei Ni[1]

In this chapter, we embark on a journey into the realm of blockchain technology and its ingenious application in the domain of autonomous proactive caching. The notion of proactive caching arises from the ever-mounting challenge of efficiently managing data traffic within the confinements of finite network resources. Prognostications reveal that the velocity of mobile network connections is poised to undergo only a threefold improvement in the forthcoming half-decade. In stark contrast, the panorama of global mobile data traffic has witnessed a staggering 18-fold upsurge over the preceding five years. This meteoric growth can be primarily attributed to the rapid proliferation of on-demand mobile video streaming services, a trend corroborated by the authoritative Cisco VNI report [1]. However, within the labyrinth of this burgeoning data traffic, a substantial proportion comprises frequently requested content. This revelation has ignited a fervent exploration within the research community, as they delve into the realm of proactive content caching as an effective strategy to alleviate the burden on networks. Such proactive caching holds the promise of ensuring reliable content delivery, particularly during periods of peak demand [2]. The significance of this endeavor becomes evident when considering the limitations of network infrastructures. In a world where the explosive growth of data consumption shows no signs of abating, network resources must be harnessed judiciously to deliver a seamless and quality experience to end-users. This pivotal chapter unravels the interplay between blockchain technology and proactive caching, offering insights into how this innovative combination holds the key to overcoming contemporary challenges in the management of data traffic, heralding a new era of efficiency and reliability in content delivery.

In a broader, more holistic perspective, proactive content caching is a multifaceted process that unfolds in two primary stages. The initial stage centers around prefetching, in which various caching nodes, including Wi-Fi Access Points (APs),

[1]School of Information and Electronic Engineering (Sussex Artificial Intelligence Institute), Zhejiang Gongshang University, China
[2]Faculty of Mechanical and Electrical Engineering, Kunming University of Science and Technology (KUST), China

small-cell base stations (SCBSs), and device-to-device (D2D)-enabled nodes, assume the crucial role of caching points. At this stage, they proactively fetch or replicate content from content providers (CPs) before any user-initiated content requests are made. This anticipatory approach is a proactive measure to prepare for and potentially fulfill anticipated content demands. The subsequent stage is dedicated to content delivery. At this stage, the cached content, which has been diligently acquired and stored during prefetching, is efficiently disseminated to mobile users. The content delivery process can employ diverse communication channels, such as fronthaul connections or D2D links. This stage ensures that the cached content is transmitted to mobile users in a swift and responsive manner, enhancing the overall user experience. Recent investigations and studies have solidified the merits of proactive caching, substantiating its potential in addressing critical networking challenges. The advantages are manifold. Proactive caching has been shown to effectively alleviate backhaul congestion, a pressing issue in modern networks [3]. By intelligently prefetching and caching content, it contributes to the reduction of expenses for CPs [4]. Moreover, this proactive strategy significantly elevates the Quality of Experience (QoE) for mobile users, ensuring that they enjoy smoother and more seamless content delivery [2]. Instead of being just a concept, proactive content caching is a pivotal approach that is redefining how networks operate in the face of growing data demands. As the digital landscape continues to evolve, proactive caching emerges as a strategic solution that optimizes network performance, mitigates congestion, reduces costs, and prioritizes the mobile users' experience.

Conventional commercial content delivery networks (CDNs) [5] have been the bedrock of content delivery in the digital landscape, built around centralized accounting mechanisms that orchestrate a myriad of crucial operations. These operations encompass:

- Distributing content: CDNs excel in distributing identical copies of content to end users, ensuring that the desired content is efficiently delivered to the audience, regardless of their geographical location.
- Load balancing: A fundamental task of CDNs is directing client requests to suitable edge servers. This dynamic routing ensures that content is retrieved from the nearest and most efficient source, reducing latency and optimizing content delivery.
- Content replication: CDNs also facilitate the transfer of content from the origin server to CDN edge servers, creating a distributed network of content repositories. This strategic content replication is essential for improving content accessibility and redundancy.
- Cache management: Central to CDNs is the management of content consistency within caches. These systems ensure that cached content remains up to date, eliminating staleness and ensuring users receive the latest content.

The overarching objective of these operations is not merely efficient content delivery but also an intricate process of data collection, monitoring, and analysis. CDNs record client access and closely monitor the utilization of CDN server resources. The data harnessed from this accounting setup serves multifaceted purposes. It is employed for:

- Traffic analysis: The data gathered enables in-depth traffic analysis, shedding light on user behavior, content popularity, and network performance. This analysis empowers CDNs to fine-tune their operations, optimizing content delivery and network management.
- Usage-dependent billing: The data provides the foundation for usage-dependent billing models, ensuring that clients are billed based on their actual resource consumption. This precise billing approach aligns costs with the actual usage of CDN services.
- Resource optimization: Leveraging this wealth of traffic data, CDNs can strategically allocate and optimize their constrained storage resources, computational capabilities, and edge-to-end bandwidth. By doing so, they ensure more effective and efficient content caching, content delivery, and network management.

In summary, conventional CDNs have harnessed centralized accounting mechanisms not only to excel in content delivery but also to inform and fine-tune their operations. The ability to collect and analyze data from these mechanisms is instrumental in ensuring that CDNs continue to meet the ever-evolving demands of content delivery in the digital age.

In the context of a self-organized and decentralized content caching market, caching entities such as APs and SCBSs operate under more stringent resource constraints compared to their counterparts in conventional CDNs. These constraints limit their capacity to cache content from CPs, resulting in a scenario where only a subset of content can be stored locally (see Figure 4.1(a)). However, the decentralized nature of Cache Helpers (CHs) at the network edge, combined with the presence of multiple coexisting CPs, renders the implementation of a centralized accounting server for the maintenance of access logs and resource utilization records impractical. This lack of centralization presents a significant challenge for CHs when it comes to selecting the most appropriate content to cache effectively. Furthermore, the absence of an accounting server in the self-organized content caching market gives rise to a lack of a trusted intermediary for auditing transactions between CHs and CPs. This creates complexities in ensuring precise and transparent payments to the involved parties, namely CPs and CHs.

To address these formidable challenges and to ensure the efficient operation of a self-organized proactive caching system, it becomes imperative to meet several key requirements:

- Decentralized brokerage and accounting: There is a compelling need to facilitate brokerage and accounting procedures between CHs and CPs in a decentralized yet reliable manner. This involves devising mechanisms for tracking content delivery, user access, and resource utilization without relying on a central authority.
- Adaptive CH strategies: Empowering CHs to dynamically adapt to shifts in content demand and supply within the network, even in the absence of a centralized content-delivery accounting server, is vital. CHs must be equipped to make informed decisions regarding what content to cache based on real-time conditions.
- Transparency in allocation: Ensuring transparency in cache selection and content delivery allocation processes for mobile users is essential. Users should have

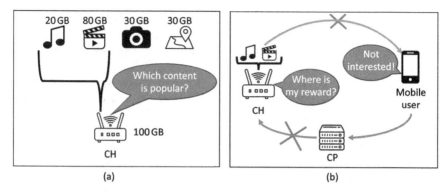

Figure 4.1 (a) Limited caching capacity and (b) issues in self-organized content caching market

insights into the sources and routes of the content they access, even within a decentralized framework.

- Effective incentive mechanisms: To foster content caching among APs and SCBSs, it is crucial to establish effective incentive mechanisms. These mechanisms should motivate caching entities to participate actively in the network's proactive content caching, aligning their interests with the overall performance and efficiency of the network.

Thereby, the self-organized and decentralized nature of proactive content caching markets presents both opportunities and challenges. By addressing the key requirements mentioned earlier, it is possible to create a robust and efficient ecosystem for content caching while retaining decentralization and ensuring equitable participation among all network stakeholders.

To meet these requirements, we have devised a comprehensive solution, implementing a blockchain technology enriched with smart contracts to establish a self-regulating content caching marketplace. This blockchain acts as an immutable public ledger within a decentralized peer-to-peer (P2P) network [6]. All transactions occurring within this blockchain ecosystem undergo collective validation by consensus nodes and are securely recorded in their respective local blockchain replicas. This ensures transparency and immutability in all interactions. Within this context, the processes of content prefetching and delivery are seamlessly orchestrated through smart contracts [7], which automate and enforce the rules of the marketplace. Notably, the blockchain maintains clear and publicly auditable records of content demand and supply within the network, providing all stakeholders with insights into the current state of the market. One of the key innovations in our approach is the integration of CHs' actions in smart contract execution and blockchain consensus maintenance. This cross-layer design leverages the Proof-of-Stake (PoS) consensus mechanism [8], which offers distinct advantages over traditional centralized caching systems like CDN [5].

The followings are the notable advantages of our blockchain-based content caching marketplace:

- Incentivized participation: Our proposed consensus protocol incentivizes CHs for active involvement. By participating in consensus and supporting the network's security and integrity, CHs are rewarded. Importantly, these incentives are designed to require minimal resource consumption, ensuring that participation is accessible and sustainable for all.
- Transparent record keeping: The blockchain maintains a transparent and publicly auditable transaction record. This feature empowers CHs to autonomously monitor the market and adjust their caching strategies based on real-time demand and supply dynamics. This real-time visibility enhances their decision-making capabilities, contributing to the efficient operation of the market.
- Secured interactions: Smart contracts play a crucial role in securing interactions within the trustless content caching market. These contracts provide financial incentives and safeguards that protect the interests of all stakeholders. By automating the execution of agreements, smart contracts ensure that transactions are fair, enforceable, and tamper-proof.

In summary, our blockchain-based content caching marketplace offers a robust and decentralized solution that aligns the interests of all participants, promotes transparency, and enhances market efficiency. It represents a significant step forward in the evolution of content caching systems, particularly in the context of emerging decentralized and self-organized networks.

The organization of the rest of this chapter is as follows. Elaboration on the use of a blockchain powered by smart contracts to establish an autonomous marketplace for content caching is presented in Section 4.1. Section 4.2 models the content caching market based on blockchain principles, likening it to a Chinese restaurant game. Within this context, a case study is conducted in Section 4.2.4 to showcase the advantages of the proposed blockchain-driven content caching marketplace, supported by numerical findings. Finally, Section 4.3 of this chapter offers a summary of key insights.

4.1 Illustration of blockchain-based autonomous content caching market

4.1.1 Network structure

We explore a hierarchical wireless network scenario, exemplified by a densely populated small cell network within an urban area, depicted in Figure 4.2. In this network, there is a group of N CPs that provide a standardized catalog of content items, denoted as $\mathcal{K} \triangleq \{1, \ldots, K\}$, to mobile users. Proactive CHs within the network consist of a total of M edge nodes, including SCBSs and user-deployed Wi-Fi APs. Mobile users do not display preferences when selecting services from a CP, and they randomly subscribe to one of the CPs and pay a flat-rate subscription fee for complete access to $\mathcal{K}$. The frequency of content requests by users remains consistent over an extended period. The content items in $\mathscr{K}$ are organized in a descending order of popularity, determined by the probability of a content item being requested during a specific timeframe. This popularity distribution can be modeled using the Zipf distribution, as outlined in [9]:

$$p_k = \frac{k^{-\beta}}{\sum_{k=1}^{K} k^{-\beta}}, \tag{4.1}$$

where β denotes the skewness of the distribution.

Within a specific timeframe, each CH is limited to caching a solitary content item from a single CP. This constraint is mainly due to the storage and bandwidth limitations of the edge devices. In response, the CP in question not only compensates the CH for content prefetching but also pledges rewards based on the deliveries offloaded by the CH to mobile users. We acknowledge that the delivery cost of content might fluctuate based on the CP. Hence, transactions are restricted to transpire between the mobile users and CPs, as well as between the CPs and CHs, as depicted in Figure 4.2.

4.1.2   Blockchain-based autonomous cache-delivery market

As illustrated in Figure 4.2, a blockchain operates at the core of the decentralized content delivery market, functioning within a virtual P2P network. In this setup, each participant (e.g., CP, CH, and mobile user) within the market is a registered node within the blockchain network. They employ a pair of asymmetric keys: a private key labeled sk_i and a public key denoted as pk_i for node i. The blockchain network associates each node's identity with a unique "transaction address" using the hashcode of its public key, represented as $\mathscr{H}(pk_i)$, utilizing a collision-resistant, irreversible hash function

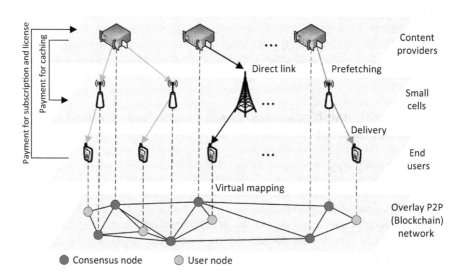

Figure 4.2   Structure of the blockchain network for proactive caching within a hierarchical wireless network with illustration of the payment flow

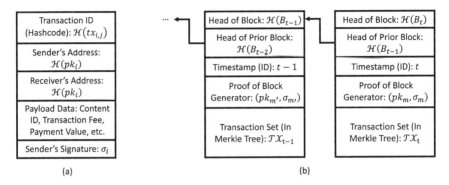

Figure 4.3 Data structures involved in building a blockchain. (a) Fields within an individual transaction. (b) Blockchain represented as a linked list of blocks interconnected through hash functions.

denoted by $\mathcal{H}(\cdot)$. All financial transactions within the caching market are carried out using blockchain tokens, such as Ethers within the Ethereum network [7]. This leads to the two principal transaction types within the marketplace, which can be outlined as follows (also refer to Figure 4.3(a)):

Definition 1 (Transaction). *A transaction, denoted as $tx_{i,j}$, involving blockchain nodes i and j, can be expressed as a 4-tuple: $tx_{i,j} = \langle \mathcal{H}(pk_i), \mathcal{H}(pk_j), d_{i,j}, \sigma_i \rangle$, where*

- *$\mathcal{H}(pk_i)$ and $\mathcal{H}(pk_j)$ denote the virtual on-chain addresses linked to nodes i and j, respectively.*
- *$d_{i,j}$ includes payload data specifying payment value and additional information such as content ID.*
- *The symbol σ_i denotes a verifiable digital signature generated by node i using its secret key sk_i. To be precise, it can be expressed as $\sigma_i = Sign(sk_i, d_{i,j})$.*

A new transaction is initialized by a node through its propagation across the entirety of the blockchain network. This dissemination process is facilitated by employing an open P2P protocol, exemplified by Ethereum's Whisper [7]. The blockchain network is responsible for meticulously maintaining a reliable, accurately sequenced log of these transactions. This chronological record of transactions is achieved by grouping them into sequential data structures called "blocks." Each block is a discrete entity housing a specific set of transactions. To elucidate the technical intricacies and provide clarity on the structural organization of the data, we shall expound upon the arrangement of data within both an individual block and the overarching blockchain itself. A detailed representation of this data structure is meticulously outlined in Figure 4.3(b).

Definition 2 (Block). *A block $B_t = \langle t, \mathcal{TX}_t, (pk_m, \sigma_m), H(B_t), H(B_{t-1}) \rangle$ can be expressed as a 5-tuple, with*

- *t denoting the ID (timestamp) of block B_t within the blockchain.*

- The symbol $\mathscr{TX}_t = \{tx_1, \ldots, tx_l\}$ representing a collection of unique transactions not clashing with previously confirmed transactions in B_0 to B_{t-1}.
- (pk_m, σ_m) containing node m's public key and signature that releases the block. $\sigma_m = Sign (sk_m, \mathscr{TX}_t)$.
- $H(B_t)$ and $H(B_{t-1})$ signifying the headers (hashcodes) of the current block at t and the previous block at $t - 1$. $H(B_t) = \mathscr{H}(t \| \mathscr{TX}_t \| (pk_m, \sigma_m) \| H(B_{t-1}))$.

Definition 3 (Blockchain). *A blockchain $\mathscr{C}(t) = \{B_0, \ldots, B_t\}$ represents a sequence of linked blocks arranged in strictly ascending chronological order. Therein, B_0 serves as the initial block, often termed $\mathscr{C}(t)$'s genesis block, and B_t is specifically denoted as $\mathscr{C}(t)$'s head.*

The utilization of a blockchain, comprising a series of interconnected blocks, each fortified with a unique header containing a hashcode, institutes an unequivocal barrier against any attempt to tamper with transactions in the local copy of the blockchain. Notably, should any entity endeavor to manipulate a transaction within a particular block, the necessity arises to subsequently modify every subsequent block within the chain. This inherent mechanism stands as a pillar of the blockchain's immutability, underscoring its indispensable role as a transparent public ledger meticulously recording a comprehensive array of transactions occurring within the dynamic realm of the content delivery market. In practical terms, this unwavering commitment to transaction integrity bestows CHs with a powerful tool. They possess the capacity to seamlessly and repeatedly query the blockchain for recent transactions initiated by mobile users. This systematic approach equips CHs with a precise and real-time understanding of the frequency of demand for a specific content item $k \in \mathscr{K}$. Through this iterative querying process, CHs gain a competitive edge, allowing them to effectively assess content popularity according to (4.1). In turn, this invaluable data empowers CHs to autonomously make strategic decisions, precisely selecting and caching the most highly sought-after content items.

In the presented context, both CPs and CHs actively participate as consensus nodes in the blockchain network's consensus process. In contrast, mobile devices assume the role of lightweight nodes, primarily dedicated to content delivery requests. Rather than opting for the computationally intensive Proof of Work (PoW) protocol [6,10,11], our endorsement is rooted in a PoS-based consensus mechanism, drawing insights from [8]. The PoS consensus mechanism functions by selecting validators to create new blocks based on the quantity of cryptocurrency they hold and are willing to "stake" or lock up as collateral. Validators with a higher stake enjoy an increased likelihood of being chosen to create a block. This consensus approach fundamentally distinguishes itself by substantially reducing computational power and energy consumption in comparison to the resource-intensive PoW mechanism [12,13]. Additionally, PoS establishes an intrinsic alignment of validators' interests with network security. Validators with a larger stake have more to lose if they engage in malicious activities, thereby providing a built-in incentive for bolstering network security. Conversely, the PoW protocol compels miners to engage in competition to solve intricate mathematical problems, a process that mandates significant computational resources. PoW guarantees network security through its energy-intensive nature, requiring potential attackers to commandeer a majority of the computational power in the network to execute a successful assault. However, the pursuit of computational dominance can usher in centralization risks, as a limited number of entities equipped with substantial computational capabilities may come to dominate the network, thereby undermining the principles of decentralization.

In the context at hand, the envisioned advantages of the PoS consensus mechanism over PoW materialize as follows:

- Energy efficiency: PoW, due to its complex mathematical problem-solving nature, demands substantial computational power and, as a consequence, results in high energy consumption. Conversely, PoS excels in its selection of block creators based on cryptocurrency ownership and stake, manifesting significantly reduced computational power and energy utilization.
- Network security and decentralization: PoW relies on computational resources to secure the network, potentially fostering centralization by entities with extensive computational capabilities. In stark contrast, PoS bolsters network security by harmonizing the interests of network nodes with the overarching goal of system security. Validators with higher stakes are disincentivized from engaging in malicious activities, thus fostering a decentralized and distributed ecosystem.
- Transaction speed and user experience: PoS, owing to its streamlined block creator selection process, typically facilitates faster transaction validation and block creation in comparison to PoW. PoW necessitates miners' competition to solve complex problems, whereas PoS appoints validators based on their cryptocurrency holdings. This distinction in block creation processes frequently translates into accelerated transaction validation, ultimately enhancing content access speed and culminating in an enriched user experience.

In summation, PoS offers a more energy-efficient, secure, and decentralized consensus mechanism than PoW, profoundly resonating with the prerequisites of a decentralized caching market.

To ensure both simplicity and generality, we make certain assumptions in our framework. First, we assume approximate clock synchronization among consensus nodes. This approximation is vital for the consistency of block creation and ensures an orderly progression of the blockchain. Second, the creation of new blocks adheres to a slotted approach, with each slot having a fixed duration in time. This structured approach is necessary for the orderly functioning of the blockchain, ensuring that block creation occurs at regular intervals. Third, the PoS mechanism introduces a secure and random process of leader selection for each time slot. This selection designates a unique consensus node responsible for generating the block within that time slot. This method introduces an element of randomness to the process, enhancing security and decentralization. Fourth, to maintain the sustainability of the proactive content caching ecosystem, we establish several practical assumptions concerning the blockchain's token supply mechanism:

- Initial token allocation: At the genesis block, each CP is endowed with a substantial token allocation, denoted as B_0. This initial allocation forms the foundation of the blockchain's token economy.

- Block reward: Additional tokens are introduced into the blockchain exclusively through a block reward mechanism. For every new block generated, a fixed amount of tokens is rewarded to the consensus node responsible for creating the block. This incentive promotes active participation in the consensus process.
- Token exchange rate: CPs maintain a stable rate for the exchange between tokens and fiat currency. This rate is applicable to both CHs and mobile users, fostering transparency and trust within the ecosystem.
- Minimal transaction fees: Transaction fees, often referred to as *gas* in Ethereum [7], are deliberately set at a minimal level. This minimization of transaction fees ensures that participants in the ecosystem are not burdened by high costs when engaging in transactions. It also encourages the use of the blockchain for various content caching-related activities.

These assumptions collectively contribute to the effective operation of the proactive content caching marketplace, providing the necessary structure and incentives to maintain a sustainable and robust ecosystem.

Based on [8], we provide a formal description of the process for electing a leader responsible for block generation using the PoS mechanism.

Definition 4. *Consider during time slot s_t that the M CHs and N CPs are holding fixed-amount stakes, denoted by $\mathbf{u}(s_t) = [u_1(s_t), \ldots, u_{M+N}(s_t)]^\top$. The process of electing a leader to determine the block issuer involves a deterministic function $F(\cdot)$ and a distribution $\mathcal{D}$. By sampling from $\mathcal{D}$ with a random seed ρ, a unique leader index $m \in (1, M+N)$ will be produced by the function $F(\mathbf{u}, \rho, s_t)$, and the corresponding leader is responsible for following the probability specified by the equation below to generate a block:*

$$p_m^{win}(s_t) = \frac{u_m(s_t)}{\sum_{i=1}^{M+N} u_i(s_t)}, \tag{4.2}$$

where independency exists between s_t and the random variables $m \leftarrow F(\mathcal{S}, \rho, s_t)$.

The PoS-based leader election mechanism employs Follow-the-Satoshi (FtS) [8], a well-established algorithm simulating a biased coin-tossing procedure to randomly select a leader's address. This process entails indexing a subset of tokens controlled by consensus nodes, often referred to as stakeholders. Each token is associated with the owner's address through a randomly chosen token index.* The seeding function, denoted as $\rho \leftarrow \mathcal{D}$, is implemented using the hashcode of the previous block header (i.e., $\sigma \leftarrow \mathcal{H}(B_{s_t-1})$), ensuring randomness in token selection. In this context, $\mathcal{H}(\cdot)$ serves as a trusted uniform random oracle [8], and σ is utilized for random token indexing, employing a straightforward modulo operation. The proposed PoS scheme effectively mitigates the inefficiencies inherent to PoW, which encompass computational resource consumption and the issue of block orphaning, under the

---

*The pre-execution of FtS at $s_t - 1$ can be facilitated via a smart contract, involving a random search within the Merkle tree connected to stake deposits. For a simplified implementation, refer to https://github.com/Realiserad/fts-tree.

assumption of honest behavior from consensus nodes [6]. Here, we define an *epoch* as a predefined time interval comprising a fixed number of time slots, denoted as T. Notably, in contrast to utilizing each stakeholder's balance as their stake in (4.2) (as per [8]), we specify that each CH determines their stake based on the rewards they have received for delivering content during the recent epoch. This unique approach encourages CHs to maintain an active online presence since they gain no profit solely from holding tokens. Conversely, a CP's stake is tied to the number of unverified payments for content deliveries during the preceding epoch. In scenarios where CHs face challenges in completing deliveries or pending transactions accumulate due to malicious actions like Denial of Service (DoS) attacks, orchestrated by malicious CHs, this arrangement ensures that CPs can exert a significant influence on the block generation process. Consequently, the blockchain establishes a robust foundation for a secure and autonomous caching market.

4.1.3 Content caching and delivery via smart contracts

Incorporating smart contracts [7] ensures precise autonomous content delivery. The content delivery process outlined in Section 4.1 encompasses two essential stages: prefetching and delivery, both seamlessly facilitated through smart contracts [14]. In the prefetching stage, CHs and CPs utilize smart contracts to negotiate the allocation of offloaded content, as visually depicted in Figure 4.4. For a given content $k \in \mathcal{K}$, CP n initiates an *order for caching* by deploying a smart contract, defining $o_{n,k}$ as the envisaged delivery price. CH m responds to CP n by utilizing the *offer for caching* function for content k and submits a deposit to the associated smart contract. The smart contract then triggers a *response* event, effectively informing CP n of CH m's response. Importantly, a CP can engage multiple CHs for the delivery task, a concept analogous to Ethereum's "crowdfund contract" [14]. The selection of CH m by CP n is finalized through the smart contract's registration function, following which a copy of content k is transferred to CH m utilizing third-party methods [15,16]. CH m is obligated to provide CP n with an interactive Proof of Retrievability (PoR) [17] for content k, presented as a set of Merkle proofs [17], to secure a refund. Notably, CP n initiates the refund of CH m's deposit only upon successful PoR verification. The conclusion of each epoch prompts CPs to finalize existing contracts, resolving any pending transactions. Subsequently, at the commencement of the next epoch, new contracts in a similar format are deployed.

In the delivery stage, CP n employs a designated smart contract known as the *delivery order* to request the delivery of each content $k \in \mathcal{K}$. This contract functions as an escrow, guaranteeing payment release by CP n only upon successful delivery. CH m initiates the *delivery offer* function, accompanying it with a security deposit submitted to the smart contract to express interest. The impartial allocation of delivery tasks among responsive CHs is managed by CP n, who directs the smart contract to enlist CH m for the designated task. Conversely, the smart contract withholds CP n's delivery payment ($o_{n,k}$) until the intended mobile user provides an interactive Proof of Retrievability (PoR) for content k to CP n. To mitigate collusion attempts and false claims by CHs and mobile users, the smart contract mandates that mobile

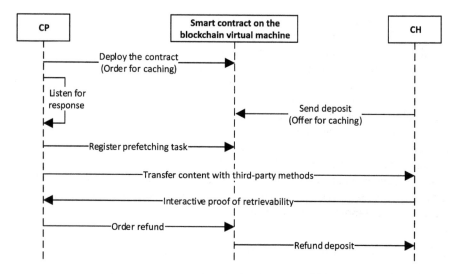

Figure 4.4   Workflow of prefetching content in smart contract

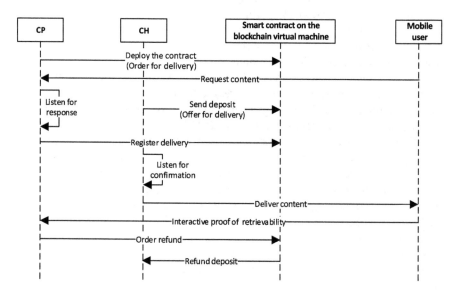

Figure 4.5   Workflow of the content delivery in smart contract

users present the PoR within a stipulated timeframe, thus confirming content receipt. Failure to comply triggers a contract rollback, penalizing CH *m* while ensuring CP *n* receives their security deposit. This design rigorously ensures that a mobile user without a locally stored content copy cannot obtain the PoR from the CH due to potential transmission delays. Additionally, at the commencement of each epoch, the content delivery contract undergoes updates to address any pending transactions.

4.2   Property of blockchain-based content caching market

This section commences with an in-depth exploration of the application of blockchain technology in the context of the content caching market, set within the framework of the Chinese restaurant game [18]. This foundation provides a rich understanding of how blockchain technology can be employed to enhance the dynamics of content caching within the market. Subsequently, a rigorous analysis of the Nash Equilibrium (NE) within the context of this gaming framework is meticulously presented. This analysis delves into the strategic interactions of the various participants, shedding light on the equilibrium points in this complex environment. Building upon this theoretical foundation, a novel decentralized algorithm based on sequential best response strategies is devised to probe and explore the NE. This algorithm offers a practical approach to facilitate the emergence of equilibrium strategies among the participants. To underscore the advantages and practical implications of integrating blockchain technology into the content caching market, a comprehensive case study is meticulously conducted. This case study serves as an exemplar of how blockchain enhances the efficiency, transparency, and autonomy within the content caching ecosystem. Furthermore, the section culminates with the presentation of extensive simulation results. These results offer a quantitative evaluation of the performance of the proposed decentralized NE searching algorithm. The assessments are carried out in terms of both efficiency and reliability, providing empirical evidence of the algorithm's efficacy in a real-world context. This empirical validation adds a practical dimension to the theoretical framework, reinforcing the significance of the findings.

4.2.1   Caching strategies

In each epoch, we consider a network comprising L users who seek content delivery. These users do not display a specific inclination toward subscribing to a particular CP when the content service remains consistent, as elucidated in (4.1). Leveraging this understanding, we can determine the expected content requests for content k in CP n over the epoch using the subsequent formula.

$$L(n, k) = LN^{-1}p_k. \tag{4.3}$$

The subset of CHs that have readily deliverable copies of content k from CP n is denoted as $\mathcal{M}_{n,k}$. Referring to (4.3) and assuming uniform distribution of delivery tasks among responsive CHs by each CP, the anticipated number of delivery tasks assigned to CH $m \in \mathcal{M}_{n,k}$ can be calculated as follows:

$$L_m(n, k) = LN^{-1}M_{n,k}^{-1}p_k, \tag{4.4}$$

where $M_{n,k}$ represents the cardinality of $\mathcal{M}_{n,k}$, and $\sum_{n=1}^{N}\sum_{k=1}^{K} M_{n,k} = M$. Implementing a best-effort delivery strategy, CH m is responsible for offloading all the assigned delivery tasks from CP n. Consequently, within a defined subset of CHs caching content k for CP n (represented as $\mathcal{M}_{n,k}$), we can calculate the expected delivery reward for CH $m \in \mathcal{M}_{n,k}$ using the following expression:

$$r_m^d(n,k) = o_{n,k} L_m(n,k) = o_{n,k} L N^{-1} M_{n,k}^{-1} p_k. \tag{4.5}$$

In instances where CH m assumes the role of the leader for block generation within a specific epoch, it is entitled to a predetermined reward for creating T new blocks. This reward is symbolized by λ, representing the total block generation reward for a given epoch. As expounded in Section 4.1.2, the probability of CH m being chosen as the leader in the subsequent epoch hinges on the ratio between its individual delivery reward and the collective delivery rewards obtained by all CHs within the ongoing epoch. Consequently, leveraging (4.2) and (4.5), if CH m caches content k from CP n, we can derive the anticipated block generation reward for the following epoch using the ensuing expression:

$$r_m^m(n,k) = \lambda \frac{o_{n,k} L_m(n,k)}{\sum_{i=1}^{N} \sum_{j=1}^{K} \sum_{l \in \mathcal{M}(i,j)} o_{i,j} L_l(i,j)}. \tag{4.6}$$

Therein, the symbol $L_l(i,j)$ denotes the expected number of tasks allocated to CH l for delivering content j for CP i.

CH m's activity during an epoch can be precisely characterized as a pair denoting the chosen content and CP, represented as $a_m = (n,k)$. It is essential to underscore that the anticipated compensation from CP n for delivering content k is equitably distributed among the CHs involved (i.e., $\mathcal{M}_{n,k}$). Therefore, for the action $a_m = (n,k)$, the gain for CH m can be computed by integrating (4.5) and (4.6), as articulated below:

$$r_m(a_m) = \frac{o_{n,k} L p_k}{N M_{n,k}} + \lambda \frac{o_{n,k} p_k}{M_{n,k} \sum_{i=1}^{N} \sum_{j=1}^{K} o_{i,j} p_j}. \tag{4.7}$$

Therein, the expression $\sum_{i=1}^{N} \sum_{j=1}^{K} o_{i,j} p_j$ remains unaffected by $M_{i,j}$ since the recalculated stakes are influenced by the unutilized rewards preserved by the CPs. Within the suggested framework for evaluating stakes, the CH's gain in (4.7) relies solely on the collective actions of CHs in the present epoch. In the ensuing subsection, we model the caching market in the framework of non-cooperative game so as to examine CHs' caching strategies.

4.2.2 Chinese restaurant game for modeling content caching market

We define the set of actions, representing CP-content selections for each CH, as $\mathcal{A} \triangleq \{(n,k) | n \in [1,N], k \in [1,K]\}$, and the vector encapsulating the collective actions of the CHs as $\mathbf{a} \triangleq [a_1, \dots, a_M]^\top \in \mathcal{A}^M$. Consequently, the non-cooperative game among the CHs is formally presented as a 3-tuple: $\mathscr{G} = \langle \mathcal{M}, \mathcal{A}, \{r_m(\mathbf{a})\}_{m \in \mathcal{M}, \mathbf{a} \in \mathcal{A}^M} \rangle$. Moreover, we introduce the concept of *action grouping* by defining a vector that delineates the number of CHs selecting a particular action given a collective action $\mathbf{a}$: $\mathbf{g}_{\mathcal{M}}(\mathbf{a}) = [M_{1,1}, \dots, M_a, \dots, M_{N,K}]^\top$. In alignment with (4.7), the *reward potential* for each action is defined as $R_{n,k} = o_{n,k} p_k$. Consequently, for CH m selecting action $a = (n, k)$ and assuming the actions of the other CHs are fixed, (4.7) can be reformulated as follows:

$$r_m(a) = r(R_a, M_a) = \frac{L}{N} \frac{R_a}{M_a} + \frac{\lambda}{\sum_{i=1}^{N} \sum_{j=1}^{K} R_{i,j}} \frac{R_a}{M_a}. \tag{4.8}$$

As $r(R_a, M_a)$ decreases with respect to M_a, M_a illustrates how the adverse network effect influences CH m's payoff upon selecting action a. Upon analyzing the first-order derivative of $r(R_a, M_a)$ concerning R_a, it becomes evident that $r(R_a, M_a)$ increases as R_a rises. Hence, we can analogize game $\mathcal{G}$ to a traditional Chinese restaurant game [18], wherein $\mathcal{A}$ corresponds to the tables in a restaurant, and R_a and M_a mirror the table's size and the number of customers seated at table a, respectively.

We define $\mathbf{a}_{-m} \triangleq [a_1, \ldots, a_{m-1}, \ldots, a_{m+1}, \ldots, a_M]^\top \in \mathcal{A}^{M-1}$ to represent the actions chosen by opponents with respect to CH m in this game. Additionally, the result of action grouping for $\mathbf{a}_{-m}$ is denoted as $\mathbf{g}_\mathcal{M}(\mathbf{a}_{-m}) = [M_{-m,1,1}, \ldots, M_{-m,N,K}]^\top$. Here, $M_{-m,n,k}$ denotes the number of CHs opting for action (n, k). The Best Response (BR) of CH m to $\mathbf{a}_{-m}$ can now be formally defined as follows:

$$BR_m(\mathbf{a}_{-m}) = BR_m(\mathbf{g}_\mathcal{M}(\mathbf{a}_{-m})) = \arg\max_{a \in \mathcal{A}} r(R_a, M_{-m,a} + 1). \tag{4.9}$$

With this, the NE of game $\mathcal{G}$ can be defined as:

Definition 5. *An NE in game $\mathcal{G}$ is characterized by a joint action of the CHs, denoted as $\mathbf{a}^* = [a_1^*, \ldots, a_{m-1}^*, a_m^*, a_{m+1}^*, \ldots, a_M^*]^\top$. Let $\mathbf{g}_\mathcal{M}^*(\mathbf{a}_{-m})$ denote the outcome of action grouping for $\mathbf{a}_{-m}^*$. For all $m \in \mathcal{M}$, the following condition holds:*

$$a_m^* = BR_m(\mathbf{g}_\mathcal{M}^*(\mathbf{a}_{-m})) = \arg\max_{a \in \mathcal{A}} r(R_a, M_{-m,a}^* + 1). \tag{4.10}$$

4.2.3 Nash equilibrium of the game

Note that, as stated in (4.8), when CHs choose the same action, they will all receive an equivalent payoff. This categorizes game $\mathcal{G}$ precisely as an exact potential game.

Theorem 1. *$\mathcal{G}$ is proven to be an exact potential game and possesses at least one pure-strategy NE.*

Proof. We define the following function as the potential function (specifically, Rosenthal's potential function [19]) associated with $\mathbf{a} = [a_1, \ldots, a_M]^\top$ in the analyzed game $\mathcal{G}$:

$$\phi(\mathbf{a}) = \sum_{a \in \mathcal{A}} \sum_{i=1}^{M_a} r(R_a, i), \tag{4.11}$$

where M_a is determined by the action grouping $\mathbf{g}_\mathcal{M}$ of $\mathbf{a}$. When CH m individually changes its action from $a_m = (n, k)$ to $a_m' = (n', k')$, this alteration affects only the CHs selecting actions a_m and a_m'. Hence, with $\mathbf{a}' = [a_1, \ldots, a_{m-1}, a_m', a_{m+1}, \ldots, a_M]$, a new grouping of actions $\mathbf{g}_{\mathcal{M}}(\mathbf{a}') = \left[M'_{1,1}, \ldots, M'_{N,K}\right]^{\top}$ is generated. The only difference from $\mathbf{g}_{\mathcal{M}}(\mathbf{a})$ is that $M_{a_m} = M'_{a_m} + 1$ and $M_{a'_m} = M'_{a'_m} - 1$. Consequently, we obtain

$$\phi(a_m, \mathbf{a}_{-m}) - \phi(a'_m, \mathbf{a}_{-m})$$

$$= \left(\sum_{i=1}^{M_{a_m}} r(R_{a_m}, i) + \sum_{i=1}^{M_{a'_m}} r(R_{a'_m}, i)\right) - \left(\sum_{i=1}^{M_{a_m}-1} r(R_{a_m}, i) + \sum_{i=1}^{M_{a'_m}+1} r(R_{a'_m}, i)\right) (4.12)$$

$$= r(R_{a_m}, M_{a_m}) - r(R_{a'_m}, M_{a'_m} + 1) = r_m(a_m, \mathbf{a}_{-m}) - r_m(a'_m, \mathbf{a}_{-m}).$$

As per Definition 52 outlined in the work [19], it is evident that game $\mathcal{G}$ fulfills the criteria of an exact potential game. Consequently, Theorem 1 can be readily deduced, aligning with the findings stipulated in Theorem 53 in [19].   □

Theorem 2. *In the context of game $\mathcal{G}$, employing sequential best-response dynamics or asynchronous dynamics demonstrates a notable likelihood of converging to a pure NE.*

Proof. With Theorem 1, which rigorously establishes game $\mathcal{G}$ as an exact potential game, the natural extension to Theorem 2 seamlessly aligns with the insights expounded in Theorem 143 in [19].   □

Considering the intrinsic asynchrony prevalent in the selection of caching strategies grounded in the blockchain, we propose an asynchronous best-response algorithm depicted in Algorithm 1. This algorithm is designed to diligently explore the equilibrium strategies within the intricate dynamics of game $\mathcal{G}$. The reliability and efficacy of Algorithm 1 in converging steadfastly towards a pure-strategy NE are underscored by the comprehensive validation elucidated in Theorem 2.

Algorithm 1: Asynchronous best-response algorithm

Data: Randomly Initialize $\mathbf{a}(0) = [a_1(0), \ldots, a_M(0)]^{\top}$;
1 **while** *has not reached convergence* **do**
2   **for** *each CH $m \in \mathcal{M}$* **do**
3        $r_m \leftarrow 0$;
4   **for** $a \in \mathcal{A}$ **do**
5   **if** $r(R_a, M_{-m,a} + 1) > r_m$ **then**
6              $a_m \leftarrow a, r_m \leftarrow r(R_a, M_{-m,a} + 1)$;
7   **end**
8   **end**
9        $a_m(t) \leftarrow a_m$;
10   **end**
11     $t \leftarrow t + 1$;
12 **end**

4.2.4 Case study

In our network model, we consider a scenario involving three CPs, each offering a catalog consisting of six distinct content items. A total of $L = 200$ mobile users are included in this network. To characterize content demand distribution, we set the skewness parameter, as defined in (4.1), to $\beta = 1$. In the initial state, we assume a uniform distribution of rewards associated with content delivery across all possible CP-content pairs. For a comprehensive evaluation of our proposed best-response strategy exploration outlined in Algorithm 1, we present a comparative analysis against two alternative strategies: random content selection and centralized payoff optimization. The results obtained for random content selection are derived through Monte Carlo simulations. Figures 4.6 and 4.7 offer detailed insights into the performance of these strategies. The analysis of our proposed algorithm reveals its superiority over random content selection in terms of both the average payoff for CHs and the overall number of deliveries offloaded. It is important to note, however, that a noticeable performance gap exists between our proposed algorithm and the centralized optimum. This disparity emphasizes the presence of what is commonly referred to as a "pure price of anarchy" within the framework of game $\mathcal{G}$. From a theoretical standpoint,

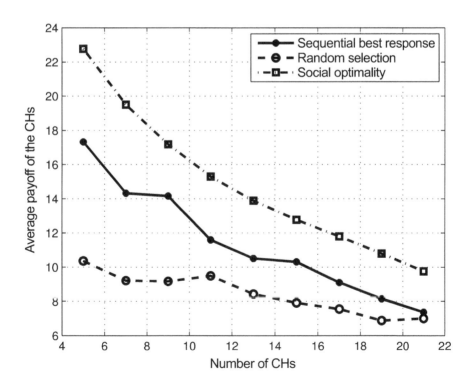

Figure 4.6   Average payoff of the CHs with respect to number of CHs in the network

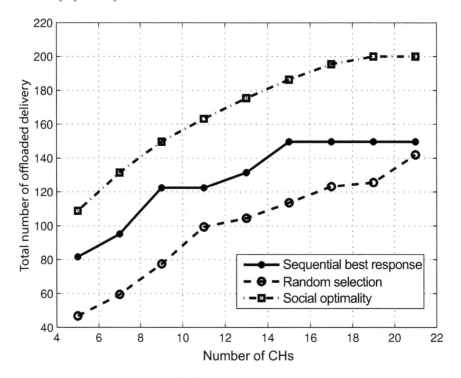

*Figure 4.7   Number of offloaded deliveries to the CHs with respect to number
of CHs*

viewing the caching game $\mathcal{G}$, we can interpret it as a singleton congestion game. This interpretation is based on the individual payoff function expressed in (4.8). Consequently, in the absence of coordination, CHs may exhibit hesitancy in providing caching services to CP-content pairs that offer lower delivery rewards. This hesitancy is observed even though such actions have the potential to enhance the overall social welfare of the CHs. Conversely, when CHs collaborate and share the delivery demands, especially for CP-content pairs with higher rewards, they achieve a superior individual payoff. This observation highlights the intricate dynamics at play within the content caching ecosystem, which are addressed and optimized through our proposed algorithm.

The evaluation of how CPs' reward strategies impact CHs' strategies is depicted in Figures 4.8 and 4.9. To facilitate the analysis, we consider a network configuration that encompasses 200 mobile users, 2 CPs, 24 CHs, and 4 distinct content types. Three distinct reward schemes are investigated within this context:

- Uniform reward scheme: In this scenario, CPs propose a uniform reward for each content type. This uniformity is represented by the condition $o_{n,k} = o_{n',k'}$ for all valid combinations of n, n', k, and k'. The results of this scheme are illustrated by the blue bars in Figures 4.8 and 4.9.

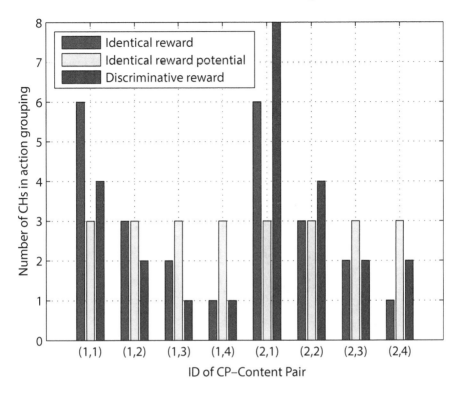

Figure 4.8   Action grouping results with different rewarding schemes

- Equal reward potential: CPs offer varied rewards while maintaining an equal reward potential. This means that the condition $o_{n,k}p_k = o_{n',k'}p_{k'}$ holds for all valid combinations of n, n', k, and k'. The pricing approach for this scheme is depicted by the green bars in Figures 4.8 and 4.9.
- Discriminatory reward scheme: In this scheme, CPs employ a discriminatory reward strategy where $o_{2,k} = 2o_{1,k}$ for all feasible content types k. The results of this pricing strategy are presented by the red bars in Figures 4.8 and 4.9.

Figure 4.8 reveals that the reward scheme with identical reward potential promotes greater fairness among CHs when compared to the other two reward schemes. Moreover, within the reward scheme with identical reward potential, CHs exhibit a greater inclination to handle caching and delivery tasks for less popular content items. In contrast, as observed from the red bars in Figure 4.8, a CP can attract more CHs to manage its traffic offloading by increasing the delivery reward. Furthermore, Figure 4.9 illustrates that at the NE, the payoffs of CHs tend to increase when one CP raises its delivery reward. This observation implies that CPs encounter higher costs when attempting to unilaterally enhance their delivery efficiency, potentially affecting the overall equilibrium of the system. These findings shed light on the complex interplay

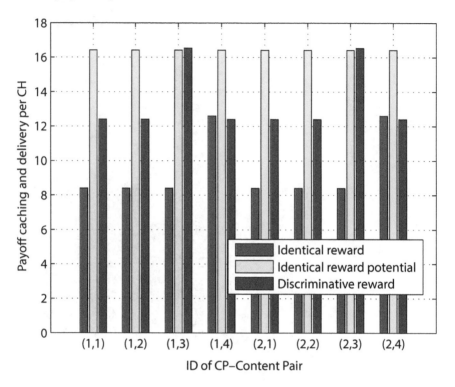

Figure 4.9   Payoff comparison of action groups with different rewarding schemes

between CPs' reward strategies and CHs' actions, providing valuable insights into the
dynamics of the content caching market.

4.3   Conclusion

In this chapter, we have intricately devised an autonomous proactive caching framework within a hierarchical wireless network, seamlessly integrating blockchain
technology. This configuration provides CHs with the autonomy to independently
tailor their strategies, thereby eliminating the need for centralized audit oversight. A
comprehensive suite of distinct smart contracts has been thoughtfully developed to
optimize autonomous task allocations for content caching and delivery, preserving the
integrity of all network components involved. Furthermore, we have architected an
incentive-aligned consensus mechanism for the blockchain, leveraging PoS to motivate CHs for the continuous provision of online services. To deepen our understanding
of the content caching market, we have modeled it as a game reminiscent of a Chinese
restaurant, a structure validated as an exact potential game. To further empower CHs
in determining their NE strategies, we have introduced a decentralized strategy exploration algorithm based on asynchronous best response. This algorithm enables CHs to

adapt to their optimal strategies without necessitating centralized coordination. The contributions made are substantiated through extensive numerical simulations, conclusively demonstrating the efficacy and reliability of our proactive content caching approach. This multifaceted approach marks a significant step towards enhancing the efficiency and autonomy of content caching in wireless networks while fostering the security and transparency of blockchain technology.

References

[1]   Cisco. Cisco Visual Networking Index: Global Mobile Data Traffic Forecast Update, 2016–2021; 2017.

[2]   Dehghan M, Jiang B, Seetharam A, *et al*. On the complexity of optimal request routing and content caching in heterogeneous cache networks. *IEEE/ACM Transactions on Networking*. 2017;25(3):1635–1648.

[3]   Chen B, Yang C, and Molisch AF. Cache-enabled device-to-device communications: offloading Gain and energy cost. *IEEE Transactions on Wireless Communications*. 2017;16(7):4519–4536.

[4]   Tadrous J and Eryilmaz A. On optimal proactive caching for mobile networks with demand uncertainties. *IEEE/ACM Transactions on Networking*. 2016;24(5):2715–2727.

[5]   Pathan AMK and Buyya R. *A Taxonomy and Survey of Content Delivery Networks*. Melbourne, Australia: Grid Computing Distributed System Lab, University of Melbourne; 2007.

[6]   Tschorsch F and Scheuermann B. Bitcoin and beyond: a technical survey on decentralized digital currencies. *IEEE Communications Surveys Tutorials*. 2016;18(3):2084–2123.

[7]   Wood G. Ethereum: a secure decentralised generalised transaction ledger (EIP-150 Revision). Ethereum Project Yellow Paper. 2017, vol. 151.

[8]   Kiayias A, Russell A, David B, *et al*. Ouroboros: a provably secure proof-of-stake blockchain protocol. In: *CRYPTO 2017: 37th Annual International Cryptology Conference, Part I*. Santa Barbara, CA; 2017. pp. 357–388.

[9]   Breslau L, Cao P, Fan L, *et al*. Web caching and Zipf-like distributions: evidence and implications. In: *Eighteenth Annual Joint Conference of the IEEE Computer and Communications Societies*, vol. 1; 1999. pp. 126–134.

[10] Feng S, Xiong Z, Niyato D, *et al*. Cyber risk management with risk aware cyber-insurance in blockchain networks. In: *2018 IEEE Global Communications Conference (GLOBECOM)*; 2018. pp. 1–7.

[11] Feng S, Wang W, Xiong Z, *et al*. On cyber risk management of blockchain networks: a game theoretic approach. *IEEE Transactions on Services Computing*. 2021;14(5):1492–1504.

[12] Xiong Z, Feng S, Wang W, *et al*. Cloud/fog computing resource management and pricing for blockchain networks. *IEEE Internet of Things Journal*. 2019;6(3):4585–4600.

[13] Xiong Z, Feng S, Niyato D, *et al.* Optimal pricing-based edge computing resource management in mobile blockchain. In: *2018 IEEE International Conference on Communications (ICC)*; 2018. pp. 1–6.

[14] Solidity Documentation, Release 0.4.20. Ethereum; 2018. Available from: http://solidity.readthedocs.io/en/latest/.

[15] Feng S, Wang W, Niyato D, *et al.* Dynamic sensor renting in RF-powered crowdsensing service market with blockchain. In: *2019 IEEE Wireless Communications and Networking Conference (WCNC)*; 2019. pp. 1–7.

[16] Feng S, Wang W, Niyato D, *et al.* Competitive data trading in wireless-powered Internet of Things (IoT) crowdsensing systems with blockchain. In: *2018 IEEE International Conference on Communication Systems (ICCS)*; 2018. pp. 289–394.

[17] Kopp H, Mödinger D, Hauck F, *et al.* Design of a privacy-preserving decentralized file storage with financial incentives. In: *2017 IEEE European Symposium on Security and Privacy Workshops (EuroS PW)*, Paris, France; 2017. pp. 14–22.

[18] Wang CY, Chen Y, and Liu KJR. Chinese restaurant game. *IEEE Signal Processing Letters*. 2012;19(12):898–901.

[19] Lasaulce S and Tembine H. *Game Theory and Learning for Wireless Networks: Fundamentals and Applications*. London: Academic Press; 2011.

Chapter 5
PoS-based blockchain-assisted UAV networks

Müge Erel-Özçevik[1]

Nowadays, 5G and 6G applications are irregular and not predictable. Therefore, fixed wireless access cannot meet the requirements of enhanced Mobile Broadband (eMBB), Ultra-Reliable Low Latency (URLLC), and massive Internet of Things (mIOT) content. Due to economic reasons, service providers prefer partial recovery in physical infrastructure instead of full recovery to enhance the capacity of the network. On the other hand, in disaster cases such as earthquakes and floods, fixed wireless components in the physical infrastructure cannot sustain wireless communication until repairment in the disaster area. In sports events and parades, there can be a requirement for extra wireless capacity for a limited time period. For only cases, expenditure for deploying fixed wireless access is not cost-efficient because they are not in use in the out of events. This leads to using unmanned aerial vehicles (UAVs) as a service between multi-providers by hiring them from physical infrastructure. UAVs act as wireless base stations on demand. Thanks to its adaptive altitude in 3D topology, it has been used in several cases such as sports events, natural disasters, and parades.

However, the usage of UAVs as a service should be implemented in a secure manner as an urgent requirement of 5G and 6G. It forwards the control and data packets in a decentralized manner in a topology. Therefore, blockchain which does not need centralized authority is proposed to carry data in a secure manner for UAV networks. The well-known Proof-of-Work (PoW) mechanism cannot be implementable in UAV networks which should respond in a few milliseconds level. Therefore, in this chapter, the consensus mechanisms in blockchain-assisted UAV networks are compared. Here, the three different Proof of Stake (PoS) as List-based, Merkle-Tree-based, and evolutionary algorithms-based mechanisms are detailed. Their superiorities and challenges are argued in terms of UAV applications.

5.1 Introduction to UAV as a service

Fixed wireless access (FWA) provides broadband access for different types of users. The offering speed of FWA is expected to increase three times higher than the cellular network [1]. On the other hand, the forwarding data over FWA is predicted

---

[1]Department of Software Engineering, Manisa Celal Bayar University, Turkey

to reach 19 GB per month, where the FWA equipment will serve over 800 million people by 2028 [2]. There are several 5G and 6G contents such as enhanced Mobile Broadband (eMBB), Ultra-Reliable Low Latency (URLLC), and massive Internet of Things (mIoT). Each traffic type has different requirements. For example, eMBB consumes much more bandwidth than the other types, whereas URLLC needs zero latency. Moreover, more than 70% computing capability is needed for URLLC and mIoT on-edge networks to handle zero-latency requirements. Therefore, 5G and 6G applications are irregular and not predictable [3].

To enhance the increased requirements of 5G and 6G applications, they should have recovery on the access network. However, since the COVID-19 epidemic period, there have been economic restrictions on service providers. Therefore, the service providers avoid extensive expenditure during the recovery of physical equipment. Instead of full recovery on the network devices, the service providers newly prefer the partial recovery on demand of the access network [4].

Unmanned aerial vehicle as a service (UAVaaS) is one of the best examples of partial recovery for service providers [5,6]. UAV-assisted base stations improve the capacity requirement of 5G and 6G applications near FWA. On the other hand, UAVs are usable for unpredictable or temporary deployment needs in such disaster cases, sports/conference events, dense hours in a mall/airport, etc. The service providers can have different policies and strategies. This leads to hiring UAVs from physical infrastructure. Thanks to its adaptive altitude, it can meet the capacity and latency requirements of 5G and 6G applications [7,8].

In the literature, there are many studies about the challenges of UAV-assisted networks. Wireless sensor networks (WSN) are well-known for handling longer network lifetimes with low power. However, UAV-assisted networks carry a higher amount of traffic than WSNs, which results in frequent recharging for flying base stations. Path planning in an energy-efficient way for UAVs is also a current need [9–11].

Nevertheless, these studies do not consider the security of the data and control channels. Security is an urgent requirement of 5G and 6G applications, and, therefore, it is the main challenge for UAV-assisted networks. Due to forwarding extensive data, the data integrity and the trustworthiness of UAVs as a service mechanism for service providers bring about vital security problems. The protection of privacy for end-user and service providers has become a more challenging issue in UAV networks [12].

Due to being deployed in an ad-hoc manner, UAV-assisted base stations do not execute under centralized authority. Therefore, blockchain can be implemented in UAV networks with distributed security without any need for centralized authority [13]. With blockchain, the number of transactions is increased when compared the conventional databases. Therefore, this decreases the cost of a blockchain-based system. In general, each transaction has ID, nonce value, the hash value of the previous block, and the signatures of pairs who sign the smart contract. In UAV-assisted networks, the hiring information of UAV as a service, the physical and service provider details are stored in blockchain.

There are many consensus mechanisms to validate the blockchain. They are listed as PoW and PoS mechanisms. While considering UAV-assisted networks, PoW is not implementable in the validation of blockchain. The transaction blocks may be built faster than the processing and validation of a transaction in PoW. The high number of transaction arrival negatively affects the delay and throughput requirements of 5G and 6G applications [14]. Therefore, the PoS mechanism is more implementable for UAV networks [15,16]. However, there is a trade-off between security level and processing time on PoS consensus mechanisms in UAV-assisted networks. This chapter introduces three PoS mechanisms listed as List-based, Merkle-Tree-based, and Evaluation-based proof of blockchains.

In the remaining chapter, Section 5.2 gives a general structure of blockchain-assisted UAV network architecture. Section 5.3 details the three consensus mechanisms for UAVs as a service. Section 5.4 compares these mechanisms in terms of their pros and cons according to the implementation in UAV networks. Finally, the chapter is concluded in Section 5.5.

5.2 Blockchain-assisted UAV network architecture

The blockchain-assisted UAV network architecture is separated into three parts: UAV network, FWA, and core network. In the UAV network, there are several UAVs that act as base stations to serve end-users located out of the fixed wireless area. Here, UAVs are used as a service on the demand of service providers, for which the centralized controllers are deployed in the core network. The FWA service acts as a relay node in order to can serve the traffic flows of end-users in a guaranteed service. The core network is accounted for the control centers of infrastructure providers and different service providers that provide several contents to end-users such as YouTube, Netflix, Spotify, Amazon web services, and Microsoft 365.

In Figure 5.1, the blockchain-assisted UAV network architecture is exemplified by deployed three different providers: service providers 1 and 2, and the infrastructure

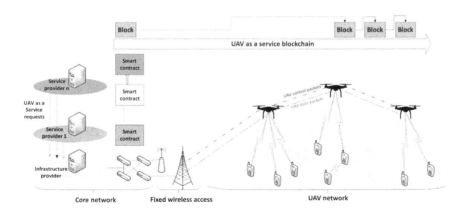

Figure 5.1   Blockchain-assisted UAV network architecture.

provider. Here, the former is the requester of UAV as a service, whereas the latter is the physical provider of UAV on demand. Once there is a demand from an end-user located out of the coverage area of FWA, the service provider requests a UAV from the infrastructure provider to serve its subscriber. The core network orchestrates the transaction data, which will later be called a smart contract. The transaction is built up between service and infrastructure providers. It consists of such following items: unique identification numbers of transaction, service, and infrastructure providers; a nonce value which is either generated randomly or taken as a return value from an evolution-based algorithm, start and finish time to use UAV as a service, and the charging value which will later be called as UAV-coin. Both sides of the smart contract should agree on the transaction data and each of them should sign it. Afterward, the signed transaction data is stored in the blockchain by running a consensus mechanism to validate the blocks in a secure manner.

The consensus mechanism, i.e. also called the validation procedure, can be executed as PoW or PoS. In both of them, service providers can be a miner to validate a transaction and store data as a block into the blockchain. They can exchange their computing power for UAV-coin. Then, it can hire a UAV and use it as a service so far as these coins meet the service fee. Each service provider acts as a miner to find a unique hash value. Either the first one that finds a nonce value that decrypts the hashed data and returns the first four-digits as zero or the best one who randomly offers a UAV-coin fee is selected as a winner who earns total UAV-coin offerings and this winner generates a block by using its nonce value. The communication details and block generation processes are figured out in the following section.

5.3   PoS mechanisms in UAV networks

Figure 5.2 gives the communication details of blockchain-assisted UAV networks. It figures out a general flow of blockchain-assisted UAV networks. The control signaling may be differentiated in other studies of the literature, which can stem from the varied physical dependencies of UAV networks. In general, the flow of using UAV as a service and constructing blockchain by the smart contracts made up between providers can be described into three processes: initializing UAV as a service, executing a PoS mechanism, and controlling UAV signaling to perform the smart contract that has been already stored in a blockchain.

First, the system is triggered if there is an end-user located out of the FWA. Because of being out of coverage of FWA, this request is not being relied on a real control packet but it is based on the location of the end-user which is predicted by the core network. In that case, the service provider prefers to use UAV as a service to meet its subscriber demand. Instead of physical deployment and a huge amount of expenditure, it can hire UAVs to act as base stations of the provider in return for UAV-coin. Therefore, it sends UAV as a service request to the infrastructure provider so as to can check whether or not there is an available UAV on the topology. This message is delivered to available UAVs to prepare for resource allocation. After taking

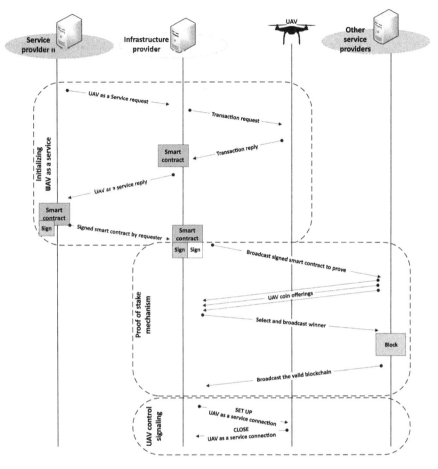

Figure 5.2 Communication diagram for blockchain-assisted UAV networks

a positive reply from UAV, a smart contract is built by the infrastructure and service provider. Each side should sign the smart contract before sending it to the validation procedure. This securely protects the transaction data by using an asymmetric encryption algorithm. The transaction is hashed/encrypted by SHA-256, which can only be decrypted by private and public keys of the sides [17]. Therefore, a malicious node cannot decrypt and change the transaction before the block is generated. It can only use an illegal copy of the transaction data, but a copy of the transaction would not be a part of the valid block made out in the second process of Figure 5.2 [6].

Second, an encrypted smart contract that is rather secure due to being signed between the service and the infrastructure provider is broadcasted to the network to start the validation procedure between miners. In this part, some blockchains use a PoW mechanism [18]. For example, bitcoin uses PoW to generate a unique block.

The winner is selected according to the first miner who finds a unique nonce value of a block that outputs the first four digits as zero in hashed data. Being first is of immense importance to be selected as a winner who can transfer its computing power to coins. However, it takes up too much time to generate a block by PoW, and this cannot be acceptable for UAV networks. On the other hand, the UAV network is closed architecture. Namely, there is no need for any exchange of UAV-coin for other current cryptocurrencies. Therefore, PoS mechanisms is preferred to validate a block in a low processing delay [15,16]. Ethereum currently uses PoS that builds a block by either randomly selected as a miner between many validators or selected validator according to offering the best coin between all that are determined independently. Thanks to overcoming competing challenges as in the PoW, PoS highly reduces the producing delay of a valid block. After the winner is selected by using PoS, the transaction is generated as a valid block, and it is broadcasted to the UAV network to add distributed blockchains in different nodes.

Third, physical controlling is performed for UAVs as a service. The radio bearers between UAVs and end-users, and also between UAVs and any equipment of FWA, are set up [19]. Therefore, the cellular connections for dedicated bearers, which would serve end-user IP traffic, are performed. The policy and charging strategy of infrastructure providers according to UAV-coin determined in the smart contract is periodically checked, and FWA tracks the quality of service parameters of the end-user, accordingly.

While generating a hash value of the block, different consensus mechanisms can be used for UAV networks. In this chapter, we detail the immensely important ones. They can be differentiated as List-based and Merkle-tree-based blockchain constructions, and these are novel data structures to store data in a blockchain. On the other hand, Proof of Evolution (PoE) is another novel approach to provide rather a secure mechanism to determine a nonce value in PoS. These three proof of blockchain mechanisms for UAV networks are detailed in the following subsections.

5.3.1   List-based proof of blockchain in UAV networks

The List-based blockchain in UAV networks is exemplified in Figure 5.3. Once a request is taken from any of the service providers who would like to serve UAV as a

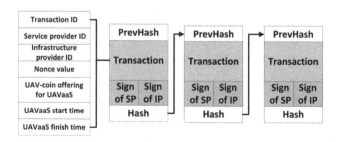

Figure 5.3   List-based blockchain in UAV networks

service, a transaction is built by the infrastructure provider. A transaction may have the following fields:

- Transaction ID which is unique for the distributed UAV database.
- Service and infrastructure providers IDs which are also unique and interpreted as sender and receiver of smart transaction, respectively.
- Nonce value determined as randomly by a given fixed interval.
- UAV-coin fee in exchange for UAV as a service.
- Start time to use UAV as a service.
- Finish time to use UAV as a service.

Afterward, each party of the transaction signs this transaction by encrypting it using via asymmetric encryption key [17]. The signature of the service provider is shown in the figure as the "Sign of SP," whereas it is illustrated with the "Sign of IP" for the infrastructure provider. This protects the data from decrypting by a malicious user. Then, the encrypted transaction, i.e. namely signed smart contract, is sent to the network in order to be validated and stored in a blockchain. The validation procedure is performed via any PoS mechanism so as to can keep 5G and beyond end-to-end delay requirement [2]. Each miner in a UAV-assisted blockchain which is the controller of service providers gives their offerings in the currency of UAV-coin. At this point, each offering is determined randomly per miner without any tip from the others. The infrastructure provider takes all offerings from the miner and selects the one who gives the largest UAV-coin to be a miner as a winner. The winner miner builds a block by creating a random nonce value. By taking the hash value of the previous block in a list-based blockchain stored distributedly, encrypted transaction, and adding a new nonce value determined by itself, it calculates the hash value of whole data. Then, it broadcasts the newly generated block into the blockchain. The copies of this list-based blockchain are also stored in various providers.

5.3.2 Merkle-tree-based proof of blockchain in UAV networks

The Merkle-tree-based blockchain in UAV networks is illustrated in Figure 5.4. Until a new block is generated by the winner miner, all steps are the same as the processes of a List-based blockchain. Afterward, the selected winner takes an encrypted transaction and adds a randomly selected nonce value in a block. The main difference in the Merkle-tree-based blockchain is the inimitable way of calculating the hash value of a Merkle root. First, the winner calculates all hash values of the transactions. Second, each block in two pairs of leaves is taken as an argument of a new hashing function in a tree. Until this process reaches the Merkle root, the recursive hash calculation is repeated. As a result, the Merkle root keeps the whole hash value of the blocks in the Merkle tree.

According to the literature, it has several advantages to aggregating the data that would have been stored in a blockchain. It reduces the number of blocks stored in a blockchain with a highly sized transaction. This results in less computational work for

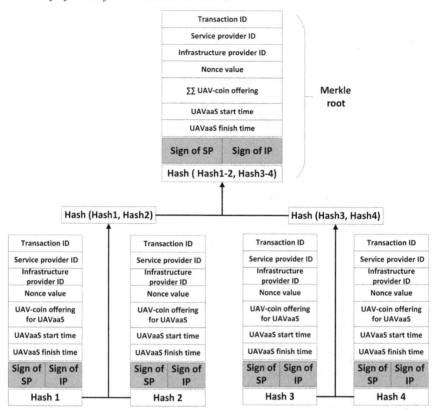

Figure 5.4   Merkle-tree-based blockchain in UAV networks

the validation procedure in a blockchain [6]. However, this construction can be built in a unidirectional. Data stored in a leaf cannot be readable in detail after a Merkle root is created. It can be used in cases where the transaction data of leaves are not considered in the future and the data are available to aggregate. This is exemplified in Table 5.2 by a given comparative example for List-based and Merkle-tree-based blockchains in UAV networks.

In Table 5.1, four smart contracts are taken by the infrastructure provider as the transaction requests from service provider 1. Their incoming arrivals are different. The important point is that their start and finish times can be combined. According to serving times, they are listed, respectively, and they can schedule the service without any gap in the time interval. This makes the transactions combinable. Although the details of each transaction cannot be readable after a Merkle root is generated, the combined data is valid and enough for the exchange in the UAV-coin currency.

Table 5.1 A comparative example for list-based and Merkle-tree-based blockchain in UAV networks

List-based blockchain in UAV networks		Merkle-tree-based blockchain in UAV networks	
Transaction 1	Service Provider 1 takes UAV as a Service from 10.00 to 10.30 in exchange for 30 UAV-Coins	Block 1	Service Provider 1
Transaction 2	Service Provider 1 takes UAV as a Service from 10.30 to 11.00 in exchange for 10 UAV-Coins		Takes UAV as a Service
Transaction 3	Service Provider 1 takes UAV as a Service from 11.00 to 11.20 in exchange for 40 UAV-Coins		From 10.00 to 12.00
Transaction 4	Service Provider 1 takes UAV as a Service from 11.20 to 12.00 in exchange for 100 UAV-Coins		In exchange for 180 UAV-Coins

5.3.3 Evolution algorithm-based proof of blockchain in UAV networks

The evolution algorithm-based proof of blockchain in UAV networks is illustrated in Figure 5.5. Determining the winner miner is different from the processes of List-based and Merkle-tree-based blockchains. Here, each miner executes an evolutionary-based algorithm separately. These algorithms can be a genetic algorithm, ant colony optimization, artificial-bee colony, particle swarm optimization, etc. [20,21]. The main thing is sharing a best between miners for each iteration. The shared bests are taken into account and the next iteration is performed by adding the shared best to the solution pool.

In Figure 5.5, the genetic algorithm-based proof of evolution is exemplified. Each miner has its own chromosome pool and each chromosome is a feasible solution for any optimization problem such as warehouse location problem, travel salesman problem, shortest path problem, and assignment problem [22,23]. First, each miner initializes its pool by a random generator and considers the feasibility of the candidate solutions. Second, the miners calculate the fitness value for each solution which

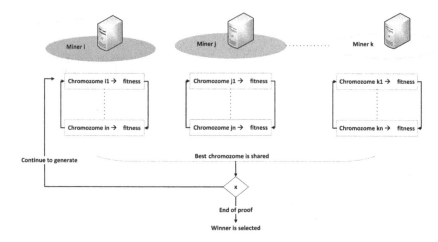

Figure 5.5 Proof of evolution-based blockchain in UAV networks

outputs the result for the objective function of the executed problem. Then, miners perform specific steps on its' solution pool in each iteration. These steps are parent selection, recombination, mutation, and survivor selection for the genetic algorithm-based proof of evolution mechanism:

- *Parent selection*: In this step, each miner selects parents to find a new generation, randomly. This selection can be performed from the sorted list of chromosomes according to fitness value. However, this way is not to guarantee reaching global optimum value for different search spaces of the problems. This directly affects the result of the problem, which does not damage the security level of the blockchain.
- *Recombination*: After the parents are selected, the chromosome pairs to be recombined are selected randomly or, respectively, from a sorted list. Recombination can be performed in different ways. According to the complexity level, the crossing-over points are determined such as one, two, and three points. By selecting these points fixed or randomly, a new generation is built by taking from either the mother's or the father's remaining chromosomes. At the end of this step, a new generation pool is ready to be performed on the remained processes.
- *Mutation*: After a new generation pool is created, some chromosomes can be mutated. The mutation is also executed over one, two, three genes, etc., where the genes are determined fixed or randomly. After this step, each generation can be used plainly, or it is checked whether it is feasible or not according to the constraints of its optimization problem. If the whole pool is preferred to be feasible, each new generation is moved into a feasible search space by gene manipulation.
- *Survivor selection*: Between the new generation pool, the best generation is selected to survive in the next iteration. By also considering the previous and new generation pools, the best chromosomes survived into the pool according to their fitness values, and the remained ones disappear.

Table 5.2   Block items in proof of evolution-based algorithm for UAV networks

ID of winner miner	Best chromosome	Fitness	Iteration number
3	2 2 2 2 2 2 2 2 2 2 2 2 2 2 2 2 2 2 2 2 2 1 2 1 2 1 1 1 0 2 1 1 1 1 1 1 1 1 1 1 2 1 1 1 0 1 1 1 1 1	0.129 Watt	1000

After these steps, the best chromosomes of the miners are shared with the others over the network. The best of bests is determined in each miner and the best chromosome is taken into the generation pool for the next iteration.

Here, there is a trade-off between the security level and the processing time of generation. The iteration number directly defines the security level of the blockchain. If the iteration number is increased, the miner gets in close to the global optimum which means finding a unique nonce value for a block. Nevertheless, increasing the number of iterations also rises the processing time of the blockchain. Executing this mechanism until the unique value that decodes the first four digit-zero by using the SHA-256 algorithm generates a block in nearly the same processing time with PoW. Therefore, determining the number of iterations is also another research challenge for proof of evolution-based blockchain.

After a predetermined iteration is executed, a miner that finds the best chromosome while comparing other shared bests is selected as a winner who generates a block. In Table 5.2, the items of each block being taken to be the input parameters of the hashing algorithm are shown. These are the ID of Winner Miner, Best Chromosome, Fitness value, and the Iteration Number as the security level of blockchain. In this table, the result of an assignment problem is shown. There are three UAVs where the ids are 0, 1, and 2. The chromosome of the best solution defines the assignments of each user in the UAV networks. According to this case, the average energy consumption of UAVs is calculated as 0.129 W/s [24,25]. This data is hashed by the SHA-256 algorithm and taken as the Nonce value of a block. The winner generates the block and shared it with the blockchain network.

5.4   Comparison of PoS mechanisms in UAV networks

5.4.1   Performance evaluation

In the performance evaluation, the blockchains are implemented by using Java-based hashing algorithms. Taken real results are simulated by using MATLAB® 2021b to handle delay analysis of UAV networks. The test-bed is run over 2.3 GHz Dual-Core

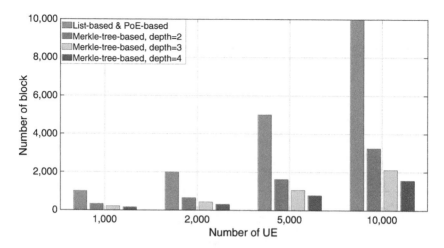

*Figure 5.6   Total number of blocks in the whole topology for different blockchain
             data structures in UAV networks*

Intel Core i5-based controller with 8 GB RAM. The topology includes 10,000 User
Equipment (UEs) for 10 UAVs, where each UAV base stations can serve at most
1,000 UEs. The total number of block that would be processed in a blockchain, the
processing time, the security level of different structures, etc., are analyzed by the
increased UEs with different parameters.

In Figure 5.6, the total number of blocks that are required to validate in a
blockchain is given for different blockchain structure in UAV networks. As the number of UEs is increased from 1,000 to 10,000, the total blocks are also the same for
the List-based blockchain. Because there is an assumption that each UE creates only
one smart contract (block) to use UAV as a service per evaluation time. However,
the number of blocks that are required to validate in a blockchain decreases as the
depth of Merkle-tree increases from 2 to 4. For example, the number of blocks in a
tree varies as 925, 912, and 906 when the depth is 2, 3, and 4, respectively. The gap
between List-based and Merkle-tree-based blockchains rises when the total number
of UE is 10,000. Here, the total number of blocks is nearly reduced by 67%, 78%,
and 84% when the depth is 2, 3, and 4, respectively. This would directly decrease the
processing time of a blockchain in UAV networks.

In Figure 5.7, the block validation time is compared for different blockchains
when the number of UEs and the depth parameter of the Merkle tree are increased.
The validation time to check the security of the blockchain should be acceptable for
different structures. As the number of UE is increased from 4 to 64 in a List-based
blockchain per UAV, the blockchain validation time is under 4.5 ms level. After this
level, List-based blockchain is not suitable due to exceeding the 5G delay requirement
per UAV. Therefore, the Merkle-tree depth is increased from 2 to 6 to decrease total
number of blocks that are required to validate in a blockchain. However, the depth
can be increased up to 5. When it is 6, the validation time in Merkle-tree exceeds

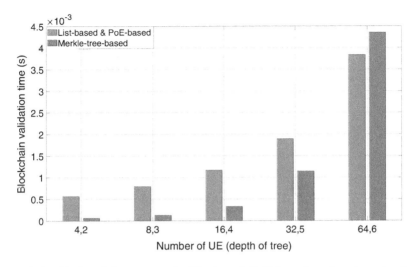

Figure 5.7　Block validation time for List-based, PoE-based, and various depths of Merkle-Tree in UAV networks

Table 5.3　Processing time and security level comparison for PoW-based, PoE-based, and List-based blockchains for UAV networks

Block processing type	PoW-based	PoE-based	List-based
Processing time for a block	14,347 s	0.377 s	0.0008106 s
Security level of blockchain	94%	87%	75%

the List-based blockchain. This is caused by the more recursive calls in Merkle-tree to validate the whole blockchain. As a result, the depth can be at most 5 for the Merkle-tree-based blockchain.

In Table 5.3, the total processing time for a block generation and their security levels are compared for PoW-based, PoE-based, and List-based blockchains. In PoW-based blockchain, mining a block takes too much time which is analyzed as 14,347 s whereas it handles the best security level while comparing the other. When the mining block is harder, the decrypting also takes too much time which makes decomposed data invalid in a time process. In PoE-based blockchain, the security level is defined as the optimality result of the genetic algorithm approach for a specific UE admission problem in UAV networks. On average, it generates a block in 0.377 s by 87% security level. In a List-based blockchain, the nonce value is taken randomly when the block is generated; therefore, the block can be processed at a microsecond level. Nevertheless, the security level becomes lower than the others by 75%.

In Figure 5.8, the processing time and the security level of PoE-based blockchain are analyzed by different parameters of the genetic algorithm. As the number of chromosomes and iterations is increased from 10 to 50, the algorithm reaches optimality

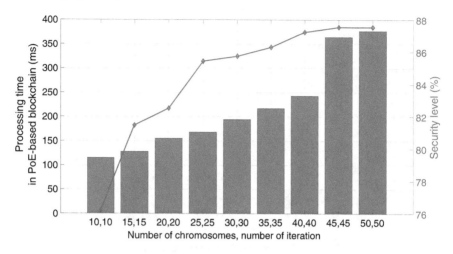

Figure 5.8   Processing time and security level analysis for PoE-based blockchain in UAV networks

and this is seen as the rise in security level from 76% to 87%. The increases in the parameters make it harder to decrypt a block, and therefore, the processing time for a block takes more time than List-based blockchain. When the number of chromosomes and iterations are 50 and 50, respectively, a block can be generated at 400 ms level. After this threshold, PoE-based blockchain is not suitable per UAV because the block processing time exceeds the delay requirement of 5G and beyond [19].

5.4.2   Interpretation of the results

As a result, UAV networks need secured data without any centralized authority. The blockchain is a well-known decentralized security mechanism to protect data integrity. However, the execution of blockchain in UAV networks needs different conservation. The PoW consensus mechanism for blockchain takes overtime than required in 5G and beyond UAV networks as shown in Table 5.3. The block processing should be under a few milliseconds level for UAV networks as analyzed in Figure 5.8. Therefore, PoS mechanisms are preferred to build a blockchain-based UAV as a service.

In this chapter, three PoS mechanisms were compared according to their pros and cons as follows:

- *List-based proof of blockchain*: It keeps the linearity of blockchain by taking the hash value of previous block and this is taken an input argument while generating a new hash of the next block. Each data of transaction can be stored into blockchain separately. Nevertheless, this increases the number of blocks to be executed, and, therefore, the load of miner rises considerably as analyzed in Figure 5.6. On the other hand, the nonce value of block is generated randomly according to an interval. If this interval is selected too narrow, the security level would be low. Namely, the decoding of the block becomes easy for malicious miners. It can be said that this mechanism outputs block in a fastest way as compared with the studies in the literature while it is providing less security than Merkle-tree and Evolutionary-based proof of blockchains as given in Table 5.3.

- *Merkle-tree-based proof of blockchain*: It does not directly represents each data with one block in blockchain. Merkle-tree structure decreases the number of block that would be validated by proof mechanism, and this indirectly reduces the blockchain processing time while comparing the linear-based proof of blockchain as analyzed in Figures 5.6 and 5.7. Thanks to complex structure of Merkle-tree, the security level of blockchain is also higher than List-based blockchain. The decoding of a block is almost impossible from the root to leaves. However, once the transactions are combined from leaves to the root of Merkle-tree, there is no down way to decompose the transaction as in leaves. This structure can be used in specific data that can be aggregated in UAV networks.

- *Evolutionary algorithm-based proof of blockchain*: This mechanism builds a blockchain in a list-based structure, however, the nonce value of a block is generated by evolutionary-based algorithms. It can also solve an optimization problem while executing a block without the need for another processing in miners. The security level is determined by the number of iterations of the evolutionary algorithm. If it is taken high, the processing time for a block would be nearly the same as the PoW mechanism, which is not implementable in UAV networks as analyzed in Figure 5.8. Proof of evolution makes the security level high by increasing processing time more than list-based immensely less than PoW as exemplified in Table 5.3. Therefore, there is a trade-off between the security level of blockchain and the processing time.

5.5   Conclusion

Recently, FWA has not met the requirements of 5G and 6G applications. On the other hand, the service providers have preferred partial recovery instead of full recovery to enhance the capacity of infrastructure because of economic restrictions since the COVID-19 pandemic. This leads UAV-assisted base stations to enhance the capacity for unpredictable contents such as eMBB, URLLC, and mIoT. Thanks to UAVs' adaptive altitude in 3D topology, they have been used in several cases such as sports events, natural disasters, and parades. There are many studies in the literature which consider the energy-efficient path planning of UAV-assisted base stations in order to increase network lifetime. However, they do not consider the urgent security demand of 5G and 6G applications while using UAVs as a service.

Therefore, the blockchain-assisted UAV networks are detailed in this chapter. First, the network architecture for UAV as a service is handled where the smart contracts between service and infrastructure providers are stored in blockchain by the offering of UAV-coin. Second, the communication parts from requesting a UAV to partially use it until the generated smart contract is saved into the blockchain are detailed. Third, the consensus mechanisms for UAV applications are studied in terms of their pros and cons. These proof of blockchain mechanisms are listed into three such as List-based, Merkle-tree-based, and Evolutionary-based proof of blockchains. Finally, the usage of these three proofs of blockchains in UAV-assisted networks is summarized in a separated comparison section by performance evaluation. In the future, proof of evaluation-based blockchain would be more suitable for UAV networks by considering the processing time of a block by handling 5G and beyond delay requirements and also keeping the security level high.

References

[1]   Cisco. Cisco Annual Internet Report (2018–2023), White Paper, C11-741490, Technical Report. Cisco Public. 03-2020.

[2]   Ericsson Mobility Report, Technical Report. EAB-22:010742 uen rev d. Ericsson. Nov 2022.

[3]   Elayoubi SE, Jemaa SB, Altman Z, *et al*. 5G RAN slicing for verticals: enablers and challenges. *IEEE Communications Magazine*. 2019;57(1):28–34.

[4]   Li X, Casellas R, Landi G, *et al*. 5G-Crosshaul network slicing: enabling multi-tenancy in mobile transport networks. *IEEE Communications Magazine*. 2017;55(8):128–137.

[5]   Erel-Özçevik M. UAV-coin: blockchain assisted UAV as a service. In: *2022 Innovations in Intelligent Systems and Applications Conference (ASYU)*; 2022. p. 1–6.

[6]   Erel-Özçevik M. Two-layered blockchain-based admission control for secure UAV networks. *Turkish Journal of Electrical Engineering and Computer Sciences*. 2022;38(6):2165–2178.

[7]   Aloqaily M, Bouachir O, Boukerche A, *et al*. Design guidelines for blockchain-assisted 5G-UAV networks. *IEEE Network*. 2021;35(1):64–71.

[8]   Yapp J, Seker R, and Babiceanu R. UAV as a service: enabling on-demand access and on-the-fly re-tasking of multi-tenant UAVs using cloud services. In: *2016 IEEE/AIAA 35th Digital Avionics Systems Conference (DASC)*; 2016. p. 1–8.

[9]   Shen T and Ochiai H. A UAV-enabled wireless powered sensor network based on NOMA and cooperative relaying with altitude optimization. *IEEE Open Journal of the Communications Society*. 2021;2:21–34.

[10]   Zhang Y, Mou Z, Gao F, *et al*. Hierarchical deep reinforcement learning for backscattering data collection with multiple UAVs. *IEEE Internet of Things Journal*. 2021;8(5):3786–3800.

[11]   Bozkaya E, Foerster KT, Schmid S, *et al*. AirNet: energy-aware deployment and scheduling of aerial networks. *IEEE Transactions on Vehicular Technology*. 2020;69(10):12252–12263.

[12]   Li X, Russell P, Mladin C, *et al*. Blockchain-enabled applications in next-generation wireless systems: challenges and opportunities. *IEEE Wireless Communications*. 2021;28(2):86–95.

[13]   Gorla P, Chamola V, Hassija V, *et al*. Blockchain based framework for modeling and evaluating 5G spectrum sharing. *IEEE Network*. 2021;35(2):229–235.

[14] Zaghloul E, Li T, Mutka MW, *et al*. Bitcoin and blockchain: security and privacy. *IEEE Internet of Things Journal*. 2020;7(10):10288–10313.

[15] Nguyen CT, Hoang DT, Nguyen DN, *et al*. Proof-of-stake consensus mechanisms for future blockchain networks: fundamentals, applications and opportunities. *IEEE Access*. 2019;7:85727–85745.

[16] Li X, Xu J, Fan X, *et al*. Puncturable signatures and applications in proof-of-stake blockchain protocols. *IEEE Transactions on Information Forensics and Security*. 2020;15:3872–3885.

[17] Martino R and Cilardo A. SHA-2 acceleration meeting the needs of emerging applications: a comparative survey. *IEEE Access*. 2020;8:28415–28436.

[18] Tran TH, Pham HL, Phan TD, *et al*. BCA: a 530-mW multicore blockchain accelerator for power-constrained devices in securing decentralized networks. *IEEE Transactions on Circuits and Systems I: Regular Papers*. 2021;68(10):4245–4258.

[19] 5G-NR; Medium Access Control (MAC) Protocol Specification (Version 15.6.0 Release 15). 3GPP TS 38321; 2019.

[20] Sun G, Dai M, Zhang F, *et al*. Blockchain-enhanced high-confidence energy sharing in Internet of Electric Vehicles. *IEEE Internet of Things Journal*. 2020;7(9):7868–7882.

[21] Bhoware A, Jajulwar K, Ghodmare S, *et al*. Performance analysis of network management system using bioinspired-blockchain technique for IP networks. In: *2023 3rd International Conference on Smart Data Intelligence (ICSMDI)*; 2023. p. 201–205.

[22] Han Y, Guan X, and Shi L. Optimization based method for supply location selection and routing in large-scale emergency material delivery. *IEEE Transactions on Automation Science and Engineering*. 2011;8(4):683–693.

[23] Daoqing Z and Mingyan J. Parallel discrete lion swarm optimization algorithm for solving traveling salesman problem. *Journal of Systems Engineering and Electronics*. 2020;31(4):751–760.

[24] Ghazzai H, Ben Ghorbel M, Kadri A, *et al*. Energy-efficient management of unmanned aerial vehicles for underlay cognitive radio systems. *IEEE Transactions on Green Communications and Networking*. 2017;1(4):434–443.

[25] Bozkaya E, Erel-Özçevik M, Bilen T, *et al*. Proof of evaluation-based energy and delay aware computation offloading for digital twin edge network. *Ad Hoc Networks*. 2023;149:103254. Available from: https://www.sciencedirect.com/science/article/pii/S1570870523001749.

Chapter 6

Leveraging Proof-of-Stake to mitigate frauds in mobile roaming management

Hoang-Anh Pham[1] and Nguyen Huynh-Tuong[2]

The global revenue generated from mobile services in 2022 was $5.2 trillion, with a subscriber base of over 5.4 billion individuals, owing to the widespread use of IT technology and smart gadgets [1]. Mobile service providers (MSPs) are encountering several challenges, particularly in the realm of roaming services, despite the ongoing growth in subscriber numbers and profits. One of the significant issues faced by MSPs is fraud control, which results in an annual loss of about $32.7 billion globally [2]. Roaming fraud is a deceptive practice that capitalizes on the inadequacies in the management of data exchanges between two MSPs with the intention of illicitly accessing and utilizing free-riding services. Specifically, when a user transitions from their primary mobile network to a secondary one and remotely utilizes services provided by the primary network through the facilities of the secondary network, the primary network is obligated to compensate the secondary network for the expenses associated with the user's service usage, as outlined in the roaming agreement.

Nevertheless, the Home Public Mobile Network (HPMN) may have difficulties in accurately billing the subscriber as a result of the latency in data transmission between the HPMN and the Visitor Public Mobile Network (VPMN). This latency refers to the time gap between the subscriber's service usage completion and the HPMN's receipt of the service report from the VPMN [3]. An instance of fraudulent activity can occur when a subscriber illicitly acquires a subscription from the HPMN, employing methods such as SIM cloning or utilizing false identities. Subsequently, this subscriber proceeds to use roaming services within the VPMN. The detection and response to roaming fraud incidents are typically reliant on receiving service reports by the HPMN, a process that can exceed 4 h. The primary factor contributing to the difficulty in detecting and preventing roaming frauds within contemporary roaming systems is the extended duration of delays, combined with challenges related to interoperability among various mobile networks. These factors have resulted in substantial financial losses, reaching up to €40,000 in extreme occurrences [4].

[1] Faculty of Computer Science and Engineering, Ho Chi Minh City University of Technology (HCMUT), VNU-HCM, Vietnam
[2] Faculty of Information Technology, Industrial University of Ho Chi Minh City (IUH), Vietnam

In recent times, there has been a notable acceleration in the advancement of blockchain technology, which has facilitated the emergence of applications based on blockchain in diverse domains such as Internet-of-Things [5,6], cloud computing [7], education [8], healthcare [9], and service providers. The Proof-of-Stake (PoS) consensus mechanism has gained prominence as a viable solution for data management in networks comprising devices with limited processing capability, primarily due to its notable benefits of low latency and minimal computational requirements [10]. Blockchain technology has the potential to mitigate data exchange delays in conventional roaming systems effectively. This capability can enable mobile operators to promptly identify and address fraudulent activities, resulting in a reduction of financial losses. Furthermore, the privacy of mobile roamers can be augmented by using blockchain's sophisticated cryptographic methods, including digital signatures and asymmetric keys. This measure can effectively safeguard the privacy of individuals by ensuring the protection of their sensitive data, including details pertaining to their trip destinations and past travel experiences.

It should be noted that the act of deanonymization, such as the endeavor to establish a connection between a blockchain account and an IP address [11,12], or the attempt to deduce transaction patterns [12], has the potential to undermine the privacy of users. Nevertheless, the efficacy of such assaults is limited when directed toward mobile users who are roaming, as the IP addresses assigned to these users are typically dynamic. In addition, contemporary systems frequently depend on Data Clearing Houses (DCHs) for processing and transmitting roaming service records. Furthermore, aside from the intermediary cost that mobile operators are obligated to pay to the DCH, the dependence on this centralized body results in a situation where data interchange within the current system becomes unfeasible in the event of DCH downtime. This chapter introduces BlockRoam, a PoS-based blockchain approach aimed at mitigating the issue of significant latency observed in current roaming systems [21].

For the readers' convenience, Table 6.1 summarizes some acronyms with corresponding explanations that are frequently used in this chapter.

Table 6.1   Acronyms with the corresponding explanations

Acronym	Explanation	Acronym	Explanation
MSP	Mobile Service Provider	PoW	Proof-of-Work
HPMN	Home Public Mobile Network	PoS	Proof-of-Stake
VPMN	Visited Public Mobile Network	PoA	Proof-of-Activity
DCH	Data Clearing House	CoA	Chain-of-Activity
CDR	Call Detail Record	DPoS	Delegated Proof-of-Stake
TAP	Transfer Account Procedure	SC	Smart Contract
HLR	Home Location Register	VLR	Visitor Location Register

The remainder of this chapter is organized as follows. Section 6.1 describes the problem statement. Then, Section 6.2 provides an overview of blockchain technology and existing mobile roaming systems. The BlockRoam solution, including its security and performance analysis, is presented in Section 6.3. Subsequently, Section 6.4 presents a concise overview of an economic model that relies on the Stackelberg game framework. This model's objective is to optimize the profits of both network users and the stake pool, hence fostering increased user engagement. Finally, conclusions are summarized in Section 6.5.

6.1 Problem statement

A typical roaming fraud prevention system is composed of both preventive and reactive levels, as depicted in Figure 6.1. The implementation of a preventative layer serves to deter instances of fraud by verifying the identification of subscribers, conducting audits of subscribers' credit, imposing limitations on the duration of services, and employing other relevant measures. While these techniques can effectively address roaming fraud, they can also have adverse effects on the quality of service (QoS) experienced by subscribers. For instance, the frequent validation and service limitations associated with these procedures can lead to a decrease in customer satisfaction. The reactive layer generally encompasses four primary steps for identifying and responding to instances of roaming fraud assaults. The data pertaining to roaming, such as service records, that is shared between Mobile Service Providers (MSPs) undergoes two key stages: data collection and fraud detection. At the data collection stage, this information is initially gathered. Subsequently, during the fraud detection stage, the obtained data is processed with the aim of identifying potential instances of fraudulent activity [3]. Thereafter, every instance is manually supervised during the supervision stage. In the event that a fraudulent attack is verified during the response phase, the utilization of the service is discontinued. Within the various stages of the roaming fraud protection system, it is commonly seen that data collecting presents a significant bottleneck. The techniques utilized in this phase are capable of facilitating data gathering in near real-time but with a restricted number of subscribers. For instance, the Fraud Information Gathering System (FIGS) [13] enables data collecting in near real-time, while the Near Real Time Roaming Data Exchange (NRTRDE) [14] reduces the latency in data exchange to a mere 4 h. The activation of subsequent stages within the system is contingent upon the prior collection of data, as the system operates sequentially. Therefore, it is essential to note that while fraud attacks like SIM cloning can occur within the HPMN, their impact is significantly amplified in the context of roaming. This is primarily attributed to the time lag in data exchange, resulting in a delay of approximately 18 h, on average, before a fraud attack can be effectively halted using the existing system [4].

Blockchain has gained prominence as a reliable and efficient data management solution in numerous decentralized networks because of its exceptional performance in maintaining data integrity, decentralization, and safeguarding privacy. Recently, certain organizations such as IBM, Deutsche Telekom, SK Telecom, and Enterprise

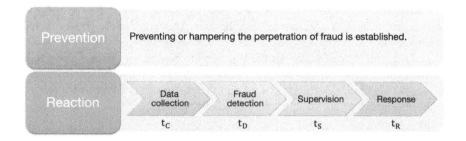

Figure 6.1   An existing fraud protection system [21]

Ethereum Alliance have introduced blockchain-based solutions for mobile roaming. These solutions primarily aim to address issues related to identity management, automating billing processes, and preventing fraud [15–17]. These proposed solutions primarily center around the enhancement of blockchain technology's asymmetric keys and digital signatures for effectively managing subscriber identities. Additionally, the implementation of smart contracts is suggested to facilitate the establishment of roaming agreements and automate billing procedures. By using advanced identity management systems and automated billing processes, the occurrence of fraudulent attacks can be substantially mitigated. Nevertheless, most of these proposed solutions are currently in the nascent phase of their development and encountering various technical obstacles.

Many existing data management systems that utilize blockchain technology commonly adopt the Proof-of-Work (PoW) consensus, such as the well-known example of Bitcoin [18]. Nevertheless, it is worth noting that the PoW process entails a substantial energy expenditure. For instance, the energy consumption of Bitcoin network surpasses that of numerous nations, as reported in a study [19]. Furthermore, networks that rely on PoW often experience significant delays in achieving consensus, with an average time frame of approximately 1 h [10]. Therefore, a novel consensus process known as Proof-of-Stake (PoS) has been devised, exhibiting notable advantages compared to the PoW. These advantages encompass diminished energy usage and latency [10]. Recently, a blockchain network called Bubbletone has been created as a solution for MSPs to combat the issue of roaming fraud. The Bubbletone system utilizes a consensus mechanism based on the PoS algorithm and employs smart contracts to facilitate interactions between MSPs and subscribers inside the roaming environment. This Blockchain-based platform offers a comprehensive solution for a wide range of MSP-to-MSP and MSP-to-subscriber interactions. However, a comprehensive discussion of the consensus mechanism design is lacking in the study conducted by [20].

Furthermore, the increased involvement of users, particularly mobile subscribers, in a PoS-based Blockchain network leads to enhanced network performance and security. Therefore, it is crucial to provide incentives that encourage a greater number of people to engage in the network. In contemporary PoS Blockchain systems, some stakes, such as network tokens, are allocated to users as a form of compensation for their involvement in consensus formation. Nevertheless, a user possessing a limited number of stakes exhibits a decreased probability of obtaining the reward. Furthermore, as exemplified by the work of [20], many blockchain networks enforce a substantial stake prerequisite for engaging in consensus. As a result, the individuals or groups with a vested interest, commonly referred to as stakeholders, are motivated to participate in a stake pool established by MSPs to maximize their potential profits. In addition, a stake pool has the potential to generate revenue by the collection of a percentage from the rewards allocated to stakeholders based on their investments.

Consequently, the establishment of a stake pool can yield advantages by effectively motivating a greater number of customers and MSPs to participate in the network. Hence, the configuration of stake pool and network parameters has a substantial influence on the efficiency of a blockchain network; yet, scholarly investigations pertaining to this subject remain constrained. Our previous study in [10] examined the process of stake pool building in PoS-based blockchain networks. However, this study focuses solely on the investment methods of users without taking into account any changes in the pricing policy of the stake pool. In practical application, the pool must strategically develop its pricing policy in order to optimize revenues and incentivize increased investment from stakeholders.

6.2 Background

6.2.1 Current roaming systems

The current roaming process is illustrated in Figure 6.2. Within the current framework, an initial establishment of a roaming agreement occurs between two MSPs. Afterward, when a subscriber wishes to access services offered by their HPMN while being physically located inside the coverage area of the VPMN, the subscriber begins a request to the VPMN. Following this, the VPMN initiates inquiries to the HPMN about the services for which the user has been enrolled. The data indicated above is stored in the Home Location Register (HLR) database owned by the HPMN. Assuming the accuracy of the subscription details, the VPMN will authorize the subscriber with the requisite permissions to access the corresponding services, such as voice or data service, through the Mobile Switching Center/Visitor Location Register (MSC/VLR). The Call Detail Records (CDRs) are thereafter forwarded to both networks, where they undergo processing for the purpose of subscription billings and the preparation of bills. Subsequently, the VPMN proceeds to transmit a Transfer Account Procedure (TAP) file containing the CDR data to the HPMN. In general, a DCH entity fulfills the function of an intermediary responsible for validating and transmitting TAP files related to the VPMN. After receiving the TAP files, the HPMN will proceed to compensate the VPMN based on the predetermined roaming agreement [3].

Instances of fraud attacks in roaming arise when a subscriber successfully accesses roaming Instances of fraud attacks in roaming arise when a subscriber successfully accesses roaming services, although the HPMN encounters difficulties in billing the user for the rendered services. In this scenario, the HPMN is obligated to compensate the VPNM for the utilization of its facilities during the roaming procedure,

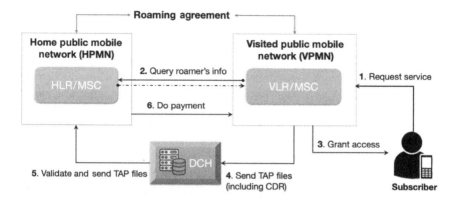

Figure 6.2   Illustration of a typical roaming system [21]

potentially leading to substantial financial detriment. As an illustration, a deceitful Subscriber Identity Module (SIM) has been seen to consume an average of 18 h of service. In certain cases, the associated financial loss has been reported to reach as high as €40,000 per hour [4]. The susceptibility of the present roaming system to roaming fraud attacks mostly stems from the latency in data exchange between the HPMN and the VPMN. Despite the implementation of the Near Real Time Roaming Data Exchange scheme (NRTRDE) as described in the referenced work [14], it is important to note that there exists a potential delay of up to 4 h in the data exchange process. Consequently, this delay may significantly impede the timely detection and accurate determination of fraudulent activities. Despite the identification of fraudulent activities, the HPMN encounters challenges in responding effectively due to its limited authority over the VPMN's infrastructure [3].

6.2.2   Blockchain fundamentals

A blockchain is a linear arrangement of blocks whereby each block contains data in the form of transactions distributed among the network participants. When a user generates a transaction, it undergoes first verification by miners, which are nodes actively participating in the consensus process, in order to authenticate the transaction. Once the transaction verification process is completed and it is successfully incorporated into a newly created block, the block will be disseminated to all other nodes within the network. According to the distributed consensus procedure, a block is chosen from the set of blocks offered by miners for inclusion in the chain [23]. In addition to the inclusion of transactions, a block in a blockchain also incorporates a hash pointer that is generated by hash functions. These hash functions are responsible for mapping all the contents of the block, as well as the pointer from the previous block, to the pointer of the current block. Consequently, each alteration made to preceding blocks will provide a distinct hash value in the subsequent block, and this modification can be traced back to the initial block of the blockchain. Consequently, the entire blockchain possesses tamper-evident properties, whereby any endeavor to modify preceding blocks may be promptly identified. One of the most significant advantages of blockchain technology in comparison to alternative security systems is its critical nature. One further benefit of a blockchain network is its decentralized nature, which eliminates the presence of a singular point of failure. Consequently, the network's functionality remains intact even in the event of node failures. In contrast, in the present roaming system, the failure of the DCH results in the inability to send CDRs and TAP files, hence, causing a complete halt in system functionality.

A smart contract refers to a computer program kept within the blockchain network and comprises a collection of rules established by users. The contract enforcement will be facilitated by utilizing a consensus mechanism contingent upon fulfilling the stipulated rules. The visibility of a smart contract's content extends to all participants inside the network, hence, guaranteeing transparency [22]. For instance, an HPMN and a VPMN have the capability to engage in negotiations and establish a smart contract on the blockchain. This contract is activated when a transaction containing CDR data is transmitted to the designated address of the smart contract. Subsequently, upon verification and inclusion of the transaction in the blockchain, all participants in consensus proceed to execute the contractual code and initiate the corresponding events in accordance with the stipulations outlined in the agreement. For instance, the HPMN immediately fulfills its payment obligations to the VPMN per the agreed-upon terms.

The distributed consensus mechanism serves as the fundamental framework of a blockchain network, overseeing and regulating the majority of its operations. Its primary function is to establish a robust safeguard, wherein any attempts to modify data stored within a block are rendered exceedingly arduous without the collective agreement of a significant number of nodes within the network. Presently, a majority of blockchain networks have used the Proof of Work (PoW) consensus procedures. Within the PoW system, participants engage in a competitive process of seeking solutions. This technique entails that individuals with greater computational capabilities possess increased prospects of becoming the block winner, responsible for appending a new block to the chain and receiving the associated reward. The implementation of this competition results in the inefficient utilization of energy within PoW-based blockchain networks. Furthermore, blockchain networks that rely on PoW can have significant delays in achieving agreement as a result of security considerations. The utilization of PoW consensus algorithms may not be suitable for implementing mobile roaming systems that necessitate minimal latency for preventing fraudulent activities.

In contrast to the PoW, the PoS consensus mechanism assigns each block in PoS-based blockchain networks to a pre-selected authorized participant, known as the leader, for the purpose of mining. This selection is determined by the stakes held by the various stakeholders within the network. The mechanism described exhibits numerous advantages in comparison to the PoW system. These advantages encompass reduced energy usage and latency. Consequently, PoS-based blockchain applications can be efficiently utilized in networks comprising a large number of users [10]. Currently, multiple iterations of the PoS algorithm exist, each possessing some favorable attributes that make them suited for managing roaming, as well as certain shortcomings that impede their effectiveness in this particular context. The following will thoroughly examine the pros and disadvantages associated with each technique.

- Proof-of-Activity (PoA) [29] is considered to be among the initial proposals for PoS techniques. The mechanism employed in this system utilizes the block header of preceding blocks to ascertain the leader for the present block. This approach guarantees impartial randomization and mitigates the risk of grinding attacks, as demonstrated in the study conducted by PoA [29]. Nevertheless, it is essential to note that the method in question operates as a hybrid PoW and PoS system, hence, inheriting certain disadvantages associated with the PoW mechanism, such as substantial energy consumption and prolonged delays.
- Casper [26] represents an additional example of a PoW and PoS hybrid system. Despite the demonstrated efficacy of this mechanism in ensuring security and countering several threats, its performance is constrained due to the presence of the PoW mechanism.
- Chain-of-Activity (CoA) [28] is classified as a pure PoS system, which enables it to achieve a comparatively low delay in transaction confirmation time, specifically 6 min. Additionally, it demands minimal energy usage. However, the study lacks thorough proof of the security of this method, and the real-world application network associated with it has a relatively low transaction throughput of 60 transactions per second.
- Tendermint [27], built upon the principles of Byzantine Fault Tolerance (BFT) protocol, demonstrates the capability to achieve significantly reduced latency and increased transaction processing capacity. Nevertheless, the article does not include a comprehensive discussion on the selection process of validators, which is crucial for Tendermint's reliance on their voting for consensus. Furthermore, it is worth noting that this particular technique exhibits a significant communication cost, namely on the order of $O(n^3)$. Additionally, it is important to highlight that the security analysis presented in the work lacks comprehensiveness as it fails to address many potential attacks.
- Ouroboros [25] is a PoS mechanism that possesses a robust theoretical foundation and has undergone a thorough security examination. The mechanism's efficacy has been demonstrated to be robust, as it successfully fulfills the persistence and liveness properties with a high degree of certainty, as stated in [32]. Furthermore, it possesses the capability to mitigate numerous types of attacks effectively. Nevertheless, when faced with a formidable opponent, the duration of the delay experiences a substantial augmentation.
- Algorand [30] has been empirically demonstrated to possess robust security measures and is capable of achieving exceptional performance levels. Nevertheless, it should be noted that the mechanism has a limited capacity to withstand adversarial behavior, with a maximum tolerable ratio of 1/3. Additionally, it is worth mentioning that it lacks an incentive mechanism and a comprehensive examination of potential attacks
- Delegated Proof-of-Stake (DPoS) [31] is a variant of the PoS consensus mechanism that utilizes a committee-based approach for block creation. However, this process necessitates a greater degree of communication, has a higher susceptibility to centralization, and has a worse capacity to withstand a smaller ratio of adversarial actors compared to alternative PoS mechanisms.

Table 6.2   Overview of several PoS consensus mechanisms [21]

Consensus algorithm	Delay	Communication complexity	Energy consumption	Transaction throughput	Attack mitigation	Security analysis
Proof-of-Activity [29]	Long	Low	High	–	Be able	Not extensive
Chain-of-Activity [28]	Low	Low	–	Low	Be able	Not extensive
Casper [26]	Long	–	High	–	Be able	Secure
Tendermint [27]	Low	High	–	–	–	Not extensive
Ouroboros [25]	Long	Low	–	–	Be able	Secure
Algorand [30]	Low	Low	–	High	–	Secure
DPoS [31]	Low	High	–	–	–	Secure

Table 6.2 provides a concise overview of the primary benefits and drawbacks associated with the consensus algorithms under several aspects. Upon examination of the table, it becomes evident that each consensus technique possesses inherent security vulnerabilities or performance constraints that render them ill-suited for the roaming management application. These concerns will be resolved by a proposed consensus mechanism in BlockRoam [21].

6.3   BlockRoam

The proposed BlockRoam system is composed of two primary elements: the roaming management platform and the consensus method. The roaming management platform facilitates intricate user interactions, automates diverse roaming procedures, and employs blockchain network tokens as a global currency for financial transactions. In addition to facilitating roaming procedures, the network also engages in the consensus mechanism to uphold the operational efficiency and security of the network. Furthermore, it serves as a repository for various data, including roaming agreements, subscriber information, and transaction history. Additionally, the network is responsible for executing roaming processes, such as payment transactions and processing CDRs.

6.3.1   Roaming management procedure

Two MSPs establish a roaming agreement that encompasses the provision of tariff plans for services rendered to their respective customers, as well as the terms and conditions for payment between the two MSPs. As depicted in Figure 6.3, the roaming agreement is established as a smart contract and kept within the blockchain. The

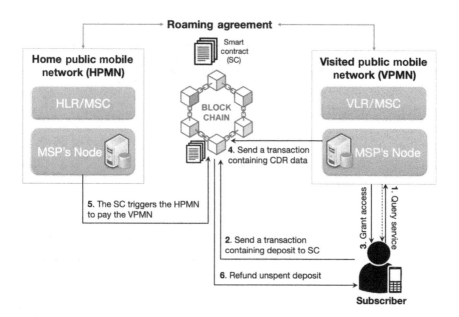

Figure 6.3   The roaming management procedure in BlockRoam system [21]

roaming process, which serves as the primary procedure of the roaming management platform, encompasses a series of fundamental steps as follows:

- **Step 1:** When a subscriber, commonly referred to as a roamer, desires to utilize services provided by their HPMN, they initiate a query to the VPMN. In response, the VPMN provides the roamer with a list of tariff plans that are accessible based on the established roaming agreement between the VPMN and the HPMN.
- **Step 2:** Once the subscriber has given consent to utilize the service, they proceed to transmit a transaction comprising an adequate quantity of digital tokens to the designated address of the smart contract.
- **Step 3:** Upon successful verification and transmission of the transaction, the VPMN will authorize the subscriber to utilize roaming services.
- **Step 4:** Upon the termination of the subscriber's roaming service, the VPMN transmits a transaction to the address of the smart contract. This transaction encompasses the CDR data pertaining to the rendered service.
- **Step 5:** The service fee is automatically computed by SC and thereafter transmitted to the HPMN. The SC additionally initiates a transaction from the HPMN to the VPMN to facilitate payment for the provided service.
- **Step 6:** Finally, the smart contract transfers unspent tokens back to the subscriber.

Compare with traditional roaming system, the proposed roaming procedure has the following advantages:

- *Roaming fraud prevention*: The primary impediment to the prevention and response to fraudulent attacks is the substantial latency in data exchange, i.e., a delay of up to 4 h. The proposed method utilizes the PoS mechanism to enhance the efficiency of data exchange, resulting in a significantly reduced average processing time of roughly 3 min. Consequently, this enables the timely detection of fraudulent assaults. Furthermore, the utilization of smart contracts facilitates the immediate execution of the invoicing procedure upon the completion of service usage. Consequently, the occurrence of roaming fraud can be significantly reduced.

- *Cost saving*: The proposed BlockRoam involves the storage of CDRs in a blockchain framework, where these records are subsequently processed through smart contracts. Consequently, the necessity of the DCHs is rendered obsolete, resulting in the elimination of intermediary charges. Additionally, the proposed system can automate a range of activities, including billing for subscribers and handling HPMN payments. This functionality has the potential to yield further reductions in operational expenses. In addition, it is worth noting that the proposed system's energy consumption is far lower compared to PoW-based systems, resulting in a substantially reduced energy cost.

- *Security and privacy*: By employing cryptographically robust procedures, the enhancement of privacy and security for subscribers can be notably achieved. In the network, every subscriber employs a pair of public and private keys to facilitate their identification as well as verification processes. The network solely requires the subscriber's digital signature, which can be readily authenticated and exceedingly challenging to counterfeit. Furthermore, this measure ensures the preservation of subscribers' anonymity, as their actual identity in real life is entirely disconnected from their network identity.

6.3.2   BlockRoam's consensus mechanism

As previously stated, the existing PoS solutions are unsuitable for the roaming management application due to either inherent security risks or insufficient performance capabilities. Therefore, a novel consensus mechanism is introduced in the context of this specific domain. Furthermore, we conduct assessments to showcase the capability of this consensus mechanism in meeting rigorous security standards and achieving higher performance in comparison to current methodologies.

6.3.2.1   Epochs and time slots

As proposed in [21], the consensus mechanism divides time into discrete epochs, whereby each epoch consists of a predetermined number of time slots denoted as N_e. At the first time slot of epoch e_k, a committee, including multiple users who are stakeholders, carries out an election process to select a leader for each time slot within epoch e_k. The election protocol is responsible for selecting committee members for the era e_{k+1}. In the event that a leader neglects to transmit its block inside its allocated time slot, resulting in its offline status during its designated time slot, an empty block will be appended to the blockchain. The leader is further directed to refrain from modifying its broadcast segments at any subsequent point.

6.3.2.2 Leader and committee election protocol

The committee members associated with epoch e_k employ the Publicly Verifiable Secret Sharing (PVSS) protocol [24] to create seeds for the Follow-the-Satoshi (FTS) algorithm [10], which facilitates the selection of leaders and committee members. The PVSS protocol facilitates the generation of unbiased random strings by protocol participants while also enabling any network user to check the authenticity of these strings. Furthermore, it should be noted that the PVSS protocol can withstand an adversarial ratio of up to 1/2. Additionally, this protocol has high efficiency in terms of communication complexity, specifically denoted as $O(m)$ where m represents the total count of committee members, as stated in the reference [24]. After generating random strings, they are employed as the initial values for the FTS algorithm. The FTS algorithm, which functions as a hash function capable of accepting any text as input, produces token indices as its output (PoS, citation). The individuals who currently own these tokens are subsequently selected as the leaders of epoch e_k and as committee members for epoch e_{k+1}.

6.3.2.3 Incentive mechanism

Besides the election protocol for leaders and committees, the incentive mechanism is pivotal in ensuring stakeholders appropriately adhere to the consensus mechanism. To reach this goal, the incentive mechanism needs to effectively encourage people to participate in the consensus process by putting in place a system of rewards while also discouraging bad behavior by putting in place a system of penalties. Within the framework of the incentive system, a leader is entitled to a predetermined quantity of tokens upon successfully appending a new block to the blockchain. The probability P_n of selecting user n using the FTS method in a network of N stakeholders is calculated by (6.1):

$$P_i = \frac{s_n}{\sum_{n=1}^{N} s_n} \tag{6.1}$$

where s_n is the number of stakes (so-called tokens) held by stakeholder n. As seen by (6.1), stakeholders with more stakes are more likely to be chosen as the leader and thereby acquire the associated reward. Regarding the penalty scheme, it is necessary for the leader to provide a deposit that will be securely held throughout its designated epoch to prevent bride, nothing-at-stake [10], and transaction denial attacks [25]. Committee members' stakes are also securely locked during their tenure on the committee in order to mitigate the risk of potential long-term attacks [10].

6.3.2.4 Security analysis

To maintain the blockchain's operations and security, it is imperative that the consensus mechanism must adhere to the following properties [32]:

- **Persistence**: Once a transaction has been verified and confirmed by a trustworthy user, it will subsequently be confirmed by all other trustworthy users, and its status will remain consistent across all honest users.
- **Liveness**: A valid transaction will be confirmed by all trusted users after a sufficient period of time.

In BlockRoam, the persistence guarantees that it becomes irrevocable once a transaction has been validated. Without persistence, an individual engaging in fraudulent activities can exploit roaming services without incurring any charges. An instance of fraudulent activity can be observed when an individual with malicious intent executes a double-spending attack. This attack involves the initial step of transmitting a transaction denoted as Tx_1 to the smart contract. Subsequently, following the authorization of the VPMN, the perpetrator proceeds to disseminate a transaction denoted as Tx_2, wherein the tokens originating from Tx_1 are transferred to an alternative address, such as the fraudster's secondary account. If the confirmation of Tx_1 has not occurred, it is essential to note that Tx_2 remains valid and has the potential to be confirmed by trustworthy users.

The persistence feature ensures data immutability, while the liveness property ensures that all valid transactions will ultimately be incorporated into the chain. Without liveness, an attacker could effectively obstruct all transactions originating from the MSP, hence, impeding the initiation of the roaming process. In [32], it was proven that the assurance of persistence and liveness properties is contingent upon the consensus mechanism's satisfaction of the following properties, such as Common prefix (CP), Chain growth (CG), and Chain quality (CQ). The consensus mechanism in Blockchain was proved to be able to satisfy these three properties with exceedingly high probabilities via Theorem 1 in [21].

Additionally, to evaluate the effectiveness of the proposed system's roaming fraud protection capabilities, the analysis focuses on the average resolution time, represented as t_{total}. This metric denotes the mean time interval between the incidence of a roaming fraud assault and the implementation of the corresponding countermeasures. As seen in Figure 6.1, the variable t_{total} represents the cumulative time of each step at the reactive layer, denoted as t_C, t_D, t_S, and t_R, respectively. Given the much reduced t_C of the proposed system in comparison to the conventional roaming system, specifically around 3 min versus 4 h, the total duration t_{total} of our system is around 4 h less than that of the traditional roaming system.

As Theorem 2 in [21], BlockRoam was also proved to be able effectively mitigate and prevent emerging attacks on blockchain systems, including grinding, bribe, double spending, nothing-at-stakes, and long-range attacks. According to the Ouroboros protocol [25], if the adversary gains control over more than 50% of the overall network stakes, the guarantees of both persistence and liveness are compromised. As a result, it is no longer possible to effectively resist attacks such as nothing-at-stakes, double-spending, and transaction denial attacks.

6.3.2.5 Performance analysis

Table 6.3 shows an examination of the transaction confirmation times across various adversarial ratios in three distinct blockchain networks: a PoW network (Bitcoin), an existing PoS network (Cardano), and the proposed BlockRoam network. The transaction confirmation time refers to the duration required for the occurrence of a common prefix violation probability $Pr_{CP} \leq 0.1\%$. According to [19], the value of κ can be ascertained, and, afterward, κ is multiplied by the slot time in order to get the transaction confirmation time. The designated time interval for our slot is established to be

Table 6.3   Transaction confirmation times in minutes

Adversarial ratio	0.10	0.15	0.20	0.25	0.30	0.35	0.40	0.45
Bitcoin	50	80	110	150	240	410	890	3400
Cardano	5	8	12	18	31	60	148	663
BlockRoam	1	1.3	1.6	1.6	2	2.3	2.6	3

20 s, aligning with the duration specified in the Cardano protocol [34]. The Bitcoin and Cardano's transaction confirmation times are collected from [25].

As observed in Table 6.3, the duration of transaction confirmation time increases proportionally with the number of stakes controlled by the adversary. Moreover, 51% attack has the potential to compromise the integrity and security of the majority of PoW-based and PoS-based blockchain networks [25]. Specifically, it is noteworthy that an adversary who possesses a computational power exceeding 51% of the total computational power in a PoW network or holds more than 51% of the total stakes in a PoS network has the capability to execute various assaults. These attacks encompass but are not limited to nothing-at-stakes, double-spending, and transaction denial attacks. Hence, it is imperative to enhance the participation rate in our PoS blockchain system to augment the overall stake of the network. This would subsequently enhance the possibility of common prefix violation and expedite transaction confirmation time. The subsequent section will introduce a proficient economic model that has the capability to maximize profits for the participants concurrently. This model serves as an incentive for their active involvement in the network, thereby enhancing both the performance and security of the network.

6.4   Economic model

In a PoS-based blockchain network, the likelihood of an individual user, also known as a stakeholder, with a limited number of stakes being chosen as the leader, is rather low. In addition, when a stakeholder becomes the leader, it is required to be present online during its designated time slot in order to carry out the following duties: (1) collect transactions from other users, (2) verify the authenticity of these transactions, (3) construct a block comprising of legitimate transactions, and (4) disseminate the block to the entire network. Hence, in the event of a deficient stakeholder connection, the ability to generate a valid block is compromised, resulting in the forfeiture of the block reward. Therefore, it is imperative for stakeholders engaging in the consensus process to uphold a robust network connection, resulting in an operational expense ranging from $40 to $300 per month [35]. It is common for minor stakeholders to consolidate their stakes in order to enhance their chances of assuming leadership roles and distributing operational costs. This practice leads to the establishment of stake pools, as exemplified by previous studies [36–38]. The establishment of a stake pool also confers advantages to the blockchain since it prevents the processing of transactions in instances when the leader fails to generate a valid block. This, in turn, results in a reduction in transaction throughput. In BlockRoam, it is likely that stakeholders, such as subscribers, would demonstrate a greater inclination towards participating in stake pools, which are organized by MSPs. This inclination can be attributed to their desire to minimize operating expenses and achieve more consistent revenue streams. A stake pool typically imposes a fee on the profits earned by stakeholders upon joining the pool. For instance, the Stakecube pool levies a fee of 3% on every reward received by a shareholder [37]. This section presents an economic model using the Stackelberg game theory to optimize the combined profitability of the stake pool and stakeholders. This approach offers advantages for both MSPs and BlockRoam's operation and security.

This study considers a blockchain network of one stake pool and N stakeholders with corresponding stake budgets $\mathbf{B} = (B_1, \ldots, B_N)$ and operational costs $\mathbf{C} = (C_1, \ldots, C_N)$. The stake pool possesses its own stake denoted as σ, and it establishes predetermined values for a cost c and a charge α for those who express interest in becoming pool members. The pool's fee encompasses both the initial joining fee and the ongoing expenses required for the pool's management and maintenance. The cost charged by the pool represents the pool owner's profit margin, typically varying between 1% and 9% in real-world stake pools [36–38]. The stakeholders can invest p_i stakes to the pool and m_i stakes for self-mining, subject to the constraint that the sum of their investments does not exceed their budget, denoted as B_i (i.e., $p_i + m_i \leq B_i$). Let $\mathcal{N}_p$ be the set of stakeholders who make investments in the pool. We define P^w as the probability that the pool is chosen as the leader and receives a block reward, denoted as R. The variable R exhibits a direct relationship with the pool's stakes in relation to the overall stakes throughout the network. The P^w is determined as (6.2):

$$P^w = \frac{\sigma + \sum_{n \in \mathcal{N}_p} p_n}{\sigma + \sum_{n \in \mathcal{N}_p} p_n + \sum_{j=1}^{N} m_j} \tag{6.2}$$

Upon receiving the reward denoted as R, the pool proceeds to calculate the individual reward for each stakeholder r_i^p as (6.3). This calculation is based on the percentage, denoted as P_i^p, which represents the stakeholder i's stakes in relation to the total stakes held by the pool:

$$P_i^p = \frac{p_i}{\sigma + \sum_{n \in \mathcal{N}_p} p_n} \tag{6.3}$$

The pool imposes a fee of α percent on each stakeholder's reward and incurs a cost of ce^{-p_i} prior to distributing the reward to the stakeholders. Due to the exponential decrease in cost as the stakes increase, stakeholders are incentivized to invest more stakes in the pool. Therefore, when a stakeholder i invests a number of stakes p_i into the pool, the expected reward for that stakeholder, denoted as r_i^p, can be determined by (6.4):

$$r_i^p = P^w P_i^p (1 - \alpha)R - ce^{-p_i} = \frac{p_i}{\sigma + \sum_{n \in \mathcal{N}_p} p_n + \sum_{j=1}^{N} m_j}(1 - \alpha)R - ce^{-p_i}$$

$$(6.4)$$

If stakeholder i utilizes m_i stakes for self-mining, the anticipated reward can be calculated as (6.5):

$$r_i^m = \left(\frac{m_i}{\sigma + \sum_{n \in \mathcal{N}_p} p_n + \sum_{j=1}^{N} m_j} \right) R - C_i,$$

$$(6.5)$$

where $\dfrac{m_i}{\sigma + \sum_{n \in \mathcal{N}_p} p_n + \sum_{j=1}^{N} m_j}$ is the proportion of stakeholder i's stakes. Then, the total profit of the pool is comprised of two components: the profits generated from its own stakes, which corresponds to the first item in (6.6), and the costs and fees imposed on the stakeholders, represented by the second term in (6.6):

$$U_p = \frac{\sigma}{\sigma + \sum_{n \in \mathcal{N}_p} p_n + \sum_{j=1}^{N} m_j} R + \sum_{i \in \mathcal{N}_p} \left(\frac{p_i \alpha}{\sigma + \sum_{n \in \mathcal{N}_p} p_n + \sum_{j=1}^{N} m_j} R + ce^{-p_i} \right)$$

$$(6.6)$$

6.4.1   Stackelberg game formulation

In practice, a pool initially discloses its cost and fee. For instance, the Stakecube pool provides information regarding its membership fee on its official website (Pool2). Based on the provided facts, the stakeholders will make a determination regarding the appropriate investment. Consequently, the interaction between stakeholders and the stake pool can be conceptualized as a Stackelberg game with a single-leader-multiple-followers Stackelberg game [39]. In this game, the stake pool assumes the role of the leader by initially disclosing its plan, which encompasses the charges and fees associated with joining the pool. Subsequently, the stakeholders, acting as followers, will deliberate their decisions, such as whether or not to invest in the pool.

The leader and follower's strategies i are denoted as s_p and s_i, respectively. In addition, we represent $\mathcal{S}_i$ as the collection of all potential strategies for follower i. The optimal response s_i^* of a follower i can be defined as the collection of strategies that yield the follower the highest payout, given a fixed strategy $s_p = (\alpha, c)$ of the leader, as represented in (6.7):

$$U_i(s_i^*, s_p) \geq U_i(s_i', s_p), \forall s_i' \in \mathcal{S}_i$$

$$(6.7)$$

The Stackelberg strategy for the leader can be defined as a strategy denoted by s_p^*, which satisfies the following conditions as (6.8) based on the follower's best response:

$$s_p^* = \underset{s_p}{\text{argmax }} U_p(s_p, s_i^*)$$

$$(6.8)$$

The Stackelberg solution can be formally represented as the tuple (s_p^*, s_i^*), where s_p^* and s_i^* denote the optimal strategies of the leader and the follower, respectively. Furthermore, the associated utility tuple (U_p^*, U_i^*) represents the Stackelberg equilibrium, which signifies the game's outcome. In order to determine the Stackelberg equilibrium, it is necessary to partition the game into two stages. In the initial phase, the leader announces its strategy. Subsequently, during the second phase, the followers ascertain their tactics by drawing upon the leader's strategy as a guiding principle. The subsequent analysis employs a backward-induction approach to investigate the Stackelberg equilibrium of the game.

6.4.1.1 Follower strategy

According to the proof of Theorem 3 in [21], it can be stated that the optimal strategy for a follower is to invest all of its stakes towards either investing in the pool or engaging in self-mining activities. Given that a stakeholder's optimal strategy is investing all of its stakes, the optimal response can be determined based on p_i^* or m_i^*. Henceforth, we represent the optimal response of follower i as the number of stakes it invests in the pool p_i^*. The optimal response p_i^* of follower i can be formulated as a function of the cost and charge associated with the pool by (6.9):

$$p_i^*(\alpha, c) = \begin{cases} 0 & \text{if } C_i < \dfrac{B_i \alpha R}{\sigma + \sum_{j=1}^{N} B_j} + ce^{-B_i}, \\[4mm] B_i & \text{if } C_i \geq \dfrac{B_i \alpha R}{\sigma + \sum_{j=1}^{N} B_j} + ce^{-B_i}. \end{cases} \qquad (6.9)$$

Based on (6.9), it can be inferred that upon considering a fixed leader's strategy, there exists a unique best strategy for each follower. This finding was also stated by Theorem 4 in [21].

6.4.1.2 Leader strategy

The utilization of the backward induction mechanism [39] enables the determination of the optimal strategy for the leader. This approach is identified as the one that results in the highest payoff as (6.10), considering the optimal response of all followers:

$$s_p^* = \underset{s_p = (c, \alpha)}{\operatorname{argmax}} U_p(s_p, p_i^*) = \frac{\sigma}{\sigma + \sum_{j=1}^{N} B_j} R + \sum_{i \in \mathcal{N}_p} \left(\frac{p_i^* \alpha}{\sigma + \sum_{j=1}^{N} B_j} R + ce^{-B_i} \right) \qquad (6.10)$$

Given that the total network stakes may be regarded as a constant value, it follows that the profit derived from the pool owner's stake remains constant (the first term in (6.10)) and does not necessitate optimization.

Moreover, $p_i^*(\alpha, c)$ can be represented by a corresponding binary decision variable x_i because it only takes two different values (i.e., 0 or B_i), such that when $x_i = 1$,

$p_i^* = B_i$, and when $x_i = 0$, $p_i^* = 0$. This facilitates the conversion of the optimization problem (6.10) into a MIP optimization as (6.11):

$$
\begin{aligned}
\max_{\alpha,c,\mathbf{x}} \quad & \sum_{i=1}^{N} x_i \left(\frac{B_i R \alpha}{\sigma + \sum_{j=1}^{N} B_j} + ce^{-B_i} \right), \\
\text{s.t.} \quad & \frac{B_i R \alpha}{\sigma + \sum_{j=1}^{N} B_j} + ce^{-B_i} \leq L(1 - x_i) + C_i \quad \forall i \in \mathcal{N}, \\
& x_i \in \{0, 1\} \quad\quad\quad\quad\quad\quad\quad\quad\quad \forall i \in \mathcal{N},
\end{aligned}
\tag{6.11}
$$

where L is a sufficiently large number. The objective of (6.11) is to determine the optimal values of the variables $(\alpha, c, \mathbf{x})$ in order to obtain the best profit of the pool. The first set of constraints guarantees that only when the pool charges follower i an amount less than C_i, the variable x_i can be assigned a value of 1, hence, enabling the inclusion of the corresponding profit in the overall profit of the pool. The second set of constraints guarantees the binary nature of every x_i. However, it should be noted that the objective function exhibits nonlinearity due to a multiplication operation involving two decision variables, namely x_i and α, making it much more complex to solve [41]. Therefore, we convert (6.11) into an equivalent MILP model as (6.12):

$$
\begin{aligned}
\max_{\alpha,c,\mathbf{x},\mathbf{y}} \quad & \sum_{i=1}^{N} y_i, \\
\text{s.t.} \quad & \frac{B_i R \alpha}{\sum_{j=1}^{N} B_j} + ce^{-B_i} \leq L(1 - x_i) + C_i \quad \forall i \in \mathcal{N}, \\
& y_i - Lx_i \leq 0 \quad\quad\quad\quad\quad\quad\quad\quad \forall i \in \mathcal{N}, \\
& y_i - L(1 - x_i) \leq \frac{B_i R \alpha}{\sum_{j=1}^{N} B_j} + ce^{-B_i} \quad \forall i \in \mathcal{N}, \\
& x_i \in \{0, 1\} \quad\quad\quad\quad\quad\quad\quad\quad\quad \forall i \in \mathcal{N}, \\
& y_i \in \mathbb{R}^+ \quad\quad\quad\quad\quad\quad\quad\quad\quad\quad \forall i \in \mathcal{N}.
\end{aligned}
\tag{6.12}
$$

The conversion from the MIP model (6.11) to the MILP model (6.12) is accomplished using a standard transformation technique that guarantees the equivalence of the two models [40]. In particular, a novel collection of continuous variables denoted as $\mathbf{y} = \{y_1, \ldots, y_N\}$ was introduced to represent the potential profit that might be generated by follower i in the pool. Two more sets of auxiliary constraints, specifically the second and third ones, are included to establish an upper limit for the variable y_i.

6.4.1.3   Existence of the Stackelberg equilibrium

The proof of the existence of the Stackelberg equilibrium is established by demonstrating the existence of the optimal solutions of (6.12), stated by Theorem 5 in [21].

6.4.1.4   Uniqueness of the Stackelberg equilibrium

Although there is always at least one Stackelberg equilibrium in this particular game, it is important to note that the uniqueness of this equilibrium cannot be assured due to the continuous nature of both α and c variables. Consequently, it is feasible to identify numerous combinations of α and c that produce equivalent optimal utility.

The leader's primary objective in the traditional Stackelberg game model is to maximize the profit, while the secondary objective involves minimizing the parameter α. This dual objective serves two functions: to attract followers with high stakes (since the fee charged by the pool is directly proportional to the investments) and to ascertain the singular optimal strategy for the game. The proposed methodology demonstrates the ability to consistently attain a distinct Stackelberg equilibrium, as substantiated by Theorem 6 in [21].

Based on the distinctive Stackelberg equilibrium observed, the stake pool can strategically determine optimal parameters such as cost and fee. This enables the pool to maximize its profits and effectively attract more stakeholders to invest in the pool. Simultaneously, stakeholders are empowered to ascertain their most advantageous investment strategies, thereby maximizing their profits.

6.4.2   Performance evaluation

6.4.2.1   Leader and follower's utilities

To provide a thorough understanding of the relationship between the leader and the followers in different circumstances, three small game instances, denoted as $\mathcal{G}_1$ to $\mathcal{G}_3$, are examined. In these cases, we analyze the utility functions of both the stake pool and the stakeholders. In this study, we focus on investigating their utilities associated with various fees and charges, thereby illustrating the influence of the stake pool strategy on the profitability of both stakeholders and the stake pool. In $\mathcal{G}_1$, we examine a compact game that involves a stakeholder and a single stake pool. The game parameters are set as follows: $C_1 = 0.1$, $b_1 = 5$, $R = 10$, and $\sigma = 10$. Then, we process to expand the game to $\mathcal{G}_2$ by incorporating five additional followers with the same configurations as the follower in $\mathcal{G}_1$, while keeping all other parameters unchanged. Subsequently, in $\mathcal{G}_3$, the parameters are kept the same as those of $\mathcal{G}_2$, with the exception that the followers possess different budgets $\mathbf{B} = (5, 10, 13, 6, 8)$, operational costs $\mathbf{C} = (0.1, 0.3, 0.2, 0.6, 0.5)$, and $R = 50$.

The optimal response function of follower 1 in $\mathcal{G}_1$ is depicted in Figure 6.4(a). The profit of follower 1 can be ascertained based on its optimal response. The profit of the follower diminishes when the fees and costs associated with the pool increase, as depicted in Figure 6.4(b); nonetheless, it remains superior to the profits obtained by self-mining. The profit generated by the pool is depicted in Figure 6.4(c). Given that there exists a sole follower in $\mathcal{G}_1$, the pool's profit solely originates from follower 1, hence, establishing an upper limit defined by C_1. The game considers pairs of (c, α) that fulfill the conditions $\dfrac{\alpha R B_i}{\sigma + C_i} + ce^{-B_i} = C_i = \dfrac{50}{15}\alpha + 0.007c = 0.1$. These pairs are referred to as Stackelberg solutions, and they result in the existence of numerous Stackelberg equilibria. However, according to the proposed method, it is

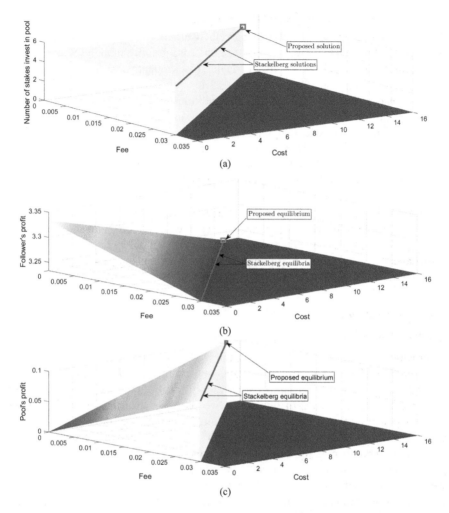

Figure 6.4   Profit and best response of the leader and follower in $\mathcal{G}_1$ [21]. (a) Best response function of follower 1. (b) Profit of follower 1. (c) Pool's profit

possible to determine the unique Stackelberg equilibrium for this particular game at the coordinates $(c^*, \alpha^*) = (14.8, 0)$.

In $\mathcal{G}_2$, the followers' optimal response and profit functions are equivalent, as illustrated in Figure 6.5(a) and 6.5(b), respectively, because they have same budgets and incur same operational costs. The functions exhibit similarities to those in $\mathcal{G}_1$, with the exception that the fee threshold is elevated to 7% due to more followers in $\mathcal{G}_2$. In this game, pool's profit is upper-bounded by $5C_i$ and the unique proposed equilibrium is characterized by the solution $(c^*, \alpha^*) = (14.8, 0)$, as indicated in Figure 6.5(c).

Figure 6.6(a) shows the optimal strategy for each follower in $\mathcal{G}_3$. In general, there exists a positive relationship between a follower's budget and their willingness

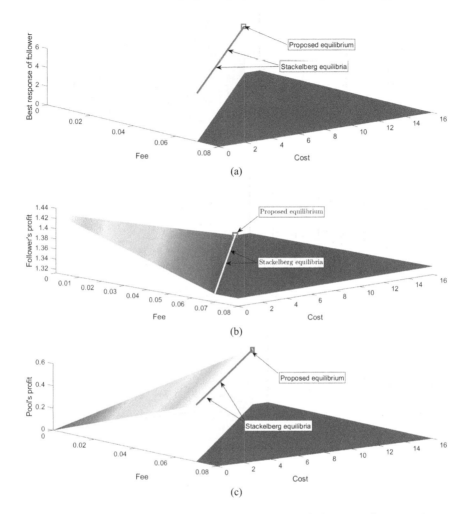

Figure 6.5   Profit and best response of the leader and follower in $\mathscr{G}_2$ [21]. (a) Best response function of follower 1. (b) Profit of follower 1. (c) Pool's profit.

to accept a lower fee, while simultaneously exhibiting a negative relationship with the associated cost. For instance, follower 3, with the highest budget, entertains a remuneration not exceeding 1.6%. Conversely, follower 1, with the lowest budget, accommodates costs that do not exceed a threshold of 15. This phenomenon can be attributed to the proportional correlation between the budget and the fee imposed by the pool, along with the exponential decline in costs as the budget expands.

Figure 6.6(b) shows the pool's profit in $\mathscr{G}_3$ with the leader's optimal strategy $(c^*, \alpha^*) = (171.3, 3.0\%)$ and optimal profit $U_p^* = 1.19$. Meanwhile, the profit the pool receives from each follower is illustrated in Figure 6.6(c). It is noteworthy that in the achieved Stackelberg equilibrium of $\mathscr{G}_3$, follower 3 refrains from making any

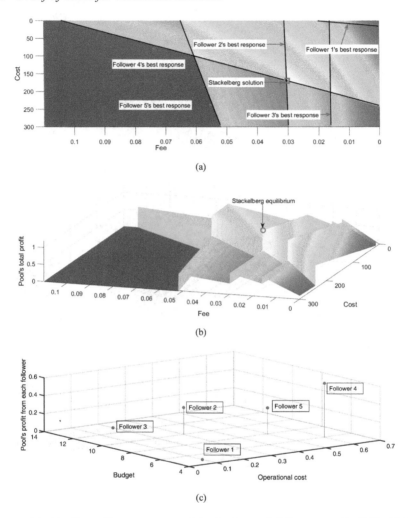

Figure 6.6   Profit and best response of the leader and followers in $\mathscr{G}_3$ [21]. (a) Best responses of followers. (b) Pool's total profit. (c) Pool's profit from each follower.

investment in the pool despite possessing the highest stakes. One possible explanation is that follower 3 has a comparatively reduced operational cost, which consequently increases its likelihood of engaging in mining activities when the cost and fee associated with the pool are excessively high. When the pool attempts to encourage all followers to invest by decreasing the values of α and c, its profit is just $U_p = 0.68$.

Additional series of comprehensive simulations for more general cases have been conducted to evaluate the efficacy of the proposed game theoretic model. Simulation results have demonstrated that the model can yield supplementary advantages for both the stake pool and its stakeholders. The detail analysis and discussion are presented in [21].

6.4.2.2 Network security and performance

We also conducted numerous simulations of adversarial attack scenarios to evaluate the impact of the economic model on the network's security and performance. Under such adversarial attacks with three levels (weak, medium, and strong), we compute the common prefix violation probability and transaction confirmation time both with and without the presence of a stake pool.

As observed from Figure 6.7, it can be noticed that instances involving a stake pool exhibit a decreased risk of common prefix violation in comparison to instances without a stake pool. For example, the network has a violation probability of 1.28% for the medium adversary setting. Conversely, without a stake pool, the probability increases to 2.20%. In the absence of a stake pool, it may have negative utility for participants with small stakes if they engage in the consensus process. This is due to the fact that their operational costs exceed the possible profits they may obtain. As a result, stakeholders that possess small stakes may face exclusion from the consensus process, leading to a reduction in the collective network stakes. Consequently, the adversarial ratio has the potential to be augmented, thereby increasing the adversary's likelihood of effectively compromising the network.

From Figure 6.8, the transaction confirmation time for instances with a stake pool is observed to be reduced compared to instances without a stake pool, similar to the chance of a common prefix violation. The stakeholders must wait for a larger number of blocks (higher κ) to confirm a transaction when the probability of a common prefix violation exceeds 0.1%. Given the aforementioned discussion on instances without

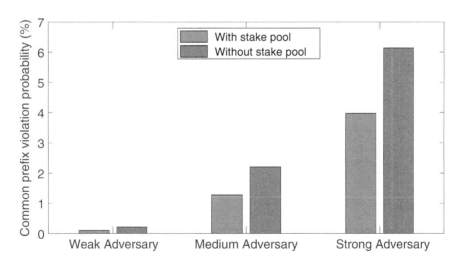

Figure 6.7   Common prefix violation probability under different adversarial power [21]

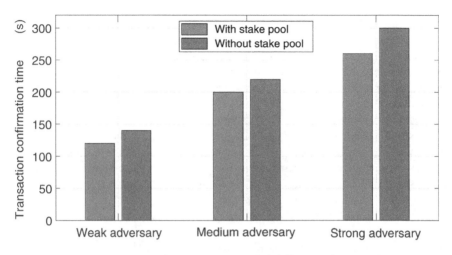

Figure 6.8   Transaction confirmation time under different adversarial power [21]

stake pools, it may be inferred that the duration for confirming transactions is also extended in such circumstances.

6.4.2.3   Summary of findings

Some key findings are summarized as follows:

- Based on the analytical results, it has been demonstrated that the best strategy for a stakeholder is to invest all its stakes to the blockchain network, as this strategy yields optimal outcomes.
- It has also been demonstrated that the optimal approach for each stakeholder is to allocate their investments entirely toward either the collective pool or individual self-mining endeavors.
- In the context of a decision-making framework for a leader, it may be asserted that there always exists an optimal and unique set of tactics that are deemed beneficial for both the stakeholders and the owner of the stake pool. This strategy also attracts stakeholders who possess significant investments in the stake pool.
- The proposed economic model has the potential to improve both security and performance of the network.

6.5   Conclusion

Roaming fraud poses a significant vulnerability to mobile service providers (MSPs), particularly those who exploit the significant latency in the data exchange process of modern roaming management systems, leading to yearly losses in the billions of dollars. This chapter introduced a methodology named BlockRoam [21] that utilizes a revised PoS consensus algorithm and smart contracts within a blockchain framework to ensure the secure data flow between MSPs and mobile customers to manage roaming services. The proposed methodology can potentially decrease the duration needed for the exchange of information significantly, thus effectively addressing concerns related to roaming fraud. The comprehensive research illustrates that enhancing the security and efficiency of a PoS-based blockchain network may be achieved by providing incentives to encourage greater participation of users, such as subscribers, inside the network. Moreover, individuals utilizing these networks often participate in stake pools, such as those established by MSPs, to augment their financial gains. Consequently, a theoretical framework rooted in Stackelberg game theory is developed to optimize the economic profits of network users and the stake pool, thereby fostering increased user engagement. Additionally, a technique is proposed to guarantee the distinctiveness of the equilibrium in this particular game. The performance evaluation findings demonstrate that the economic model developed in the BlockRoam facilitates the generation of supplementary profits for MSPs while concurrently fostering more investment in the blockchain network.

References

[1]   GSMA Intelligence, "The Mobile Economy 2023," GSM Association, 2023. Available: https://data.gsmaintelligence.com/research/research/research-2023/the-mobile-economy-2023 [Accessed: 12-Sep-2023].

[2]   L. Papachristou, "Report: US$32.7 Billion Lost in Telecom Fraud Annually," *Organized Crime and Corruption Reporting Project*. Available: https://www-.occrp.org/en/27-ccwatch/cc-watch-briefs/9436-report-us-32-7-billion-lost-in-telecom-fraud-annually [Accessed: 12-Sep-2023].

[3]   G. Macia-Fernandez, P. Garcia-Teodoro, and J. Diaz-Verdejo, "Fraud in roaming scenarios: an overview," in *IEEE Wireless Communications*, vol. 16, no. 6, pp. 88–94, 2009. doi: 10.1109/MWC.2009.5361183.

[4]   Starhome Mach, "Starhome Mach: Operator's Roaming Fraud Losses Can Reach €40,000 Per Hour," *PR Newswire: Press Release Distribution, Targeting, Monitoring and Marketing*, 29-Jun-2018. Available: https://www.prnewswire.com/news-releases/starhome-mach-operators-roaming-fraud-losses-can-reach-40000-per-hour-598836021.html [Accessed: 12-Sep-2023].

[5]   K. Christidis and M. Devetsikiotis, "Blockchains and Smart Contracts for the Internet of Things," in *IEEE Access*, vol. 4, pp. 2292–2303, 2016, doi: 10.1109/ACCESS.2016.2566339.

[6]   O. Novo, "Blockchain meets IoT: an architecture for scalable access management in IoT," in *IEEE Internet of Things Journal*, vol. 5, no. 2, pp. 1184–1195, 2018, doi: 10.1109/JIOT.2018.2812239.

[7]   K. Gai, J. Guo, L. Zhu, and S. Yu, "Blockchain meets cloud computing: a survey," in *IEEE Communications Surveys & Tutorials*, vol. 22, no. 3, pp. 2009–2030, 2020, doi: 10.1109/COMST.2020.2989392.

[8] M. Turkanović, M. Hólbl, K. košič, M. Heričko and A. Kamišalić, "EduCTX: a blockchain-based higher education credit platform," in *IEEE Access*, vol. 6, pp. 5112–5127, 2018, doi: 10.1109/ACCESS.2018.2789929.

[9] A. Shahnaz, U. Qamar, and A. Khalid, "Using blockchain for electronic health records," in *IEEE Access*, vol. 7, pp. 147782–147795, 2019, doi: 10.1109/ ACCESS.2019.2946373.

[10] C. T. Nguyen, D. T. Hoang, D. N. Nguyen, D. Niyato, H. T. Nguyen, and E. Dutkiewicz, "Proof-of-Stake consensus mechanisms for future blockchain networks: fundamentals, applications and opportunities," in *IEEE Access*, vol. 7, pp. 85727–85745, 2019. doi: 10.1109/ACCESS.2019.2925010

[11] R. Henry, A. Herzberg, and A. Kate, "Blockchain access privacy: challenges and directions," *IEEE Security & Privacy*, vol. 16, no. 4, pp. 38–45, 2018. doi: 10.1109/MSP.2018.3111245.

[12] Q. Feng, D. He, S. Zeadally, M. K. Khan, and N. Kumar, "A survey on privacy protection in blockchain system," *Journal of Network and Computer Applications*, vol. 126, pp. 45–58, 2019. doi: 10.1016/j.jnca.2018. 10.020.

[13] 3GPP, "3GPP TS 22.031 V15.0.0," Technical Specification 22.031, June 2018.

[14] GSMA, "GSMA Speeds Up The Transfer Of Roaming Call Records," *Newsroom*, 21-Mar-2012. Available: https://www.gsma.com/newsroom/press-release/gsma-speeds-up-the-transfer-of-roaming-call-records/ [Accessed: 13-Nov- 2019].

[15] IBM, *Reimagining Telecommunications with Blockchains*, IBM Institute for Business Value. Available: https://www.ibm.com/thought-leadership/ institute-business-value/report/blockchaintelco [Accessed: 16-Aug-2019].

[16] Deutsche Telekom AG, "Deutsche Telekom and SK Telecom pave the way for the future," *Deutsche Telekom*, 26-Feb-2019. Available: https://www. telekom.com/en/media/media-information/archive/deutsche-telekom-and-sk-telecom-pave-the-way-for-the-future-564180 [Accessed: 16-Aug-2019].

[17] M. Boddy, "EEA publishes blockchain uses for T-mobile and other major telecoms," *Cointelegraph*, 30-Aug-2019. Available: https://cointelegraph.com/ news/enterprise-ethereum-alliance-publishes-on-blockchain-uses-in-telecoms [Accessed: 20-Sep-2019].

[18] S. Nakamoto (May 2008). *Bitcoin: A Peer-to-Peer Electronic Cash System*. Available: https://bitcoin.org/bitcoin.pdf.

[19] "Bitcoin Energy Consumption Index," *Digiconomist*. Available: https:// digiconomist.net/bitcoin-energy-consumption [Accessed: 13-Nov- 2019].

[20] A. Kulichevskiy (03-Oct-2017). *Bubbletone Blockchain White Paper*. Available: https://icos.icobox.io/uploads/whitepaper/2017/10/59e8dcfa89537.pdf [Accessed: 16-Aug-2019].

[21] C. T. Nguyen, D. N. Nguyen, D. T. Hoang, *et al.*, "BlockRoam: blockchain-based roaming management system for future mobile networks," in *IEEE Transactions on Mobile Computing*, vol. 21, no. 11, pp. 3880–3894, 2022, doi: 10.1109/TMC.2021.3065672.

[22] L. Luu, D. Chu, H. Olickel, P. Saxena, and A. Hobor, "Making smart contracts smarter," in *Proceedings of the 2016 ACM SIGSAC Conference on Computer and Communications Security – CCS16*, Vienna, Austria, Oct. 2016, pp. 254–269. doi: 10.1145/2976749.2978309.

[23] W. Wang, D. T. Hoang, P. Hu, *et al.*, "A survey on consensus mechanisms and mining strategy management in blockchain networks," in *IEEE Access*, vol. 7, pp. 22328–22370, Jan. 2019. doi: 10.1109/ACCESS.2019.2896108.

[24] B. Schoenmakers, "A simple publicly verifiable secret sharing scheme and its application to electronic voting," *Annual International Cryptology Conference*, Santa Barbara, CA, USA, Aug. 15–19, 1999, pp. 148–164. doi: 10.1007/3-540-48405-1_10.

[25] A. Kiayias, A. Russell, B. David, and R. Oliynykov, "Ouroboros: a provably secure proof-of-stake blockchain protocol," in *Proceedings of the 37th Annual International Cryptology Conference (CRYPTO)*, Santa Barbara, CA, USA, Aug. 2017, pp. 357–388. Available: https://eprint.iacr.org/2016/889.pdf.

[26] V. Buterin and V. Griffith, "Casper the friendly finality gadget," 2017, *arXiv preprint arXiv:1710.09437*. Available: https://arxiv.org/abs/1710.09437.

[27] E. Buchman, J. Kwon, and Z. Milosevic (Sep 2018), *The Latest Gossip on BFT Consensus*. Available: https://tendermint.com/static/docs/tendermint.pdf.

[28] I. Bentov, A. Gabizon, and A. Mizrahi, "Cryptocurrencies without proof of work," in *International Conference on Financial Cryptography and Data Security*. Barbados, Feb. 2016, pp. 142–157. doi:10.1007/978-3-662-53357-4_10.

[29] I. Bentov, C. Lee, A. Mizrahi, and M. Rosenfeld, "Proof of activity: extending Bitcoin's proof of work via proof of stake (extended abstract)," *ACM SIGMETRICS Performance Evaluation Review*, vol. 42, no. 3, pp. 34–37, Dec. 2014. doi: 10.1145/2695533.2695545.

[30] Y. Gilad, R. Hemo, S. Micali, G. Vlachos, and N. Zeldovich, "Algorand: scaling Byzantine agreements for cryptocurrencies," in *Proceedings of the 26th Symposium on Operating Systems Principles*, Oct. 2017, pp. 51–68. doi: 10.1145/3132747.3132757.

[31] Y. Xiao, N. Zhang, W. Lou, and Y. T. Hou, "A survey of distributed consensus protocols for blockchain networks," 2020, *arXiv preprint arXiv:1904.04098*. Available: https://arxiv.org/abs/1904.04098.

[32] J. Garay, A. Kiayias, and N. Leonardos, "The Bitcoin backbone protocol: analysis and applications," in E. Oswald, M. Fischlin, Eds., *Advances in Cryptology - EUROCRYPT 2015 Lecture Notes in Computer Science*, vol. 9057. Berlin: Springer, 2015, pp. 281–310. doi: 10.1007/978-3-662-46803-6_10.

[33] M. Mitzenmacher and E. Upfal, *Probability and Computing: Randomization and Probabilistic Techniques in Algorithms and Data Analysis*. Cambridge: Cambridge University Press, 2017.

[34] "Cardano Blockchain Explorer," *Cardano Blockchain Explorer*. Available: https://cardanoexplorer.com/ [Accessed: 05-Dec-2019].

[35]   Jotunn, "How Many Stake Pools?," *Cardano Forum*, 21-Sep-2018. Available: https://forum.cardano.org/t/how-many-stake-pools/16132/12 [Accessed: 25-Sep-2019].

[36]   "Ultrapool," *Decred Voting Service – Welcome*. Available: https://ultrapool.eu/ [Accessed: 16-Aug-2019].

[37]   "Stakecube," *Crypto Shib*. Available: https://cryptoshib.com/stakecube/ [Accessed: 16-Aug-2019].

[38]   "Earn Profits by Holdings Cryptoassets," *MyCointainer*. Available: https://www.mycointainer.com/ [Accessed: 16-Aug-2019].

[39]   Z. Han, D. Niyato, W. Saad, T. Başar, and A. Hjørungnes, *Game Theory in Wireless and Communication Networks: Theory, Models, and Applications*. Cambridge: Cambridge University Press, 2012.

[40]   F. Glover, "Improved linear integer programming formulations of nonlinear integer problems," in *Management Science*, vol. 22, no. 4, pp. 455–460, 1975. doi: 10.1287/mnsc.22.4.455.

[41]   M. X. Goemans, *Advanced Algorithms*. Massachusetts Institute of Technology. Laboratory for Computer Science, 1994.

[42]   StakingRewards, "Cardano," *Digital Asset Research Platform for Staking & Dividends*. Available: https://stakingrewards.com/asset/ada [Accessed: 16-Aug-2019].

[43]   StakingRewards, "Algorand," *Digital Asset Research Platform for Staking & Dividends*. Available: https://stakingrewards.com/asset/algo [Accessed: 16-Aug-2019].

[44]   StakingRewards, "Cosmos," *Digital Asset Research Platform for Staking & Dividends*. Available: https://stakingrewards.com/asset/atom [Accessed: 16-Aug-2019].

[45]   StakingRewards, "Tezos," *Digital Asset Research Platform for Staking & Dividends*. Available: https://stakingrewards.com/asset/xtz [Accessed: 16-Aug-2019].

[46]   StakingRewards, "NEM," *Digital Asset Research Platform for Staking & Dividends*. Available: https://stakingrewards.com/asset/xem [Accessed: 16-Aug-2019].

Chapter 7

Trading and wealth evolution in the Proof of Stake protocol

Wenpin Tang[1]

A blockchain is a digit ledger allowing the secure transfer of assets in a distributed network without an intermediary, hence, achieving decentralisation. As the Internet is a technology to facilitate the digit flow of information, the blockchain is a technology to facilitate the digit exchange of value. Blockchain technology has shown great potential, with a wide range of applications including cryptocurrency [1,2], healthcare [3,4], supply chain [5,6], and non-fungible tokens [7,8]. See Part 2 of this book for other applications of the blockchain. Recently, a large number of financial institutions seek to launch crypto exchanges in the stock market [9].

The core of a blockchain is the consensus protocol, which specifies a set of rules for the participants (miners or validators) to agree on an ever-growing log of transactions so as to form a distributed ledger. There are two major blockchain protocols, *Proof of Work* (PoW [1]) and *Proof of Stake* (PoS [2,10]):

- In the PoW protocol, miners compete with each other by solving a hashing puzzle. The miner who solves the puzzle first receives a reward (a number of coins) and whose work validates a new block's addition to the blockchain. Hence, while the competition is open to everyone, the chance of winning is proportional to a miner's computing power. The PoW coins include Bitcoin and Dogecoin.
- In the PoS protocol, there is a bidding mechanism to select a miner to do the work of validating a new block. Participants who choose to join the bidding are required to commit some stakes (coins they own), and the winning probability is proportional to the number of stakes committed. The PoS coins include Ethereum and BNB.

As of July 15, 2023, `Cryptoslate` lists 326 PoW coins with a total $628B (51%) market capitalisation, and 248 PoS coins with a total $321B (26%) market capitalisation. One major pitfall of the PoW protocol is that competition among the miners has led to exploding levels of energy consumption, and hence raised the issue of sustainability [11,12]. Refs. [13–15] also discussed the drawbacks of the PoW

[1]Department of Industrial Engineering and Operations Research, Columbia University, USA

blockchain from economic perspectives. These concerns have created a strong incentive among blockchain practitioners to switch from the PoW to the PoS ecosystem, as was pioneered by Ethereum 2.0 in September 2022 [16].

In this chapter, we present recent research on the PoS protocol, with a focus on its wealth evolution. There are three major components in the PoS ecosystem:

(a) *User–miner interface*: The users seek to get their transactions settled and published on the blockchain by the miners. Since each block has a maximum capacity, most blockchains adopt a 'pay your bid' auction, in which the users bid to have the miners include their transactions in the blockchain. (In general, the more a user bids, the more likely her transaction will be settled shortly.) The activity of the user–miner interface relies on the blockchain adoption, and the problem is to design a good transaction fee mechanism, e.g., satisfying some incentive-compatible conditions.

(b) *Built-in PoS protocol*: Each miner selects a set of transactions from the mempool (according to the bids mentioned in (a)) and includes them into a block. As explained earlier, the miners then commit their stakes in a PoS election, and the elected miner gains the right to add the new block to the blockchain. In return, the elected miner will receive transaction fees from the users, and block rewards from the blockchain. The PoS protocol may have additional hard-coded rules, e.g., the longest chain. The key issue is the security level facing to various attacks.

(c) *Speculation and trading*: As the blockchain is a digit exchange vehicle, there is a cryptocurrency (crypto) attached to it. Along with the increasing blockchain adoption, crypto has become a new financial instrument. This leads to the crypto trading. The trading parties are the miners and the investors (i.e., the crypto market). The investors may be the blockchain users who trade the crypto for use, or the speculators who seek profit from crypto holdings. The problem is to understand the trading strategy and wealth evolution of the participants in the crypto market.

See Figure 7.1 for an illustration of the aforementioned components in the PoS ecosystem. Here we concentrate on part (c). Refer to [17–19] for discussions related to part (a), and [20–23] for developments in part (b).

As the readers may have observed, the miners play a particularly important role in the blockchain ecosystem: they manage the user–miner interface (in part (a)); they maintain the blockchain (in part (b)); they provide liquidity in the crypto trading (in part (c)). For the miners, they can commit their stakes to participate in the PoS mining process, trade their stakes on the crypto market for instantaneous profit, or a combination of the two. The most obvious questions are how the miner allocates her stakes between PoS mining and trading (called a *strategy*), and what is her wealth evolution. The former question is concerned with the miner's optimal strategy, while the latter studies the level of decentralisation in the PoS economy. Being more specific, we ask:

1. Does the PoS protocol lead to centralisation or the rich-get-richer phenomenon (assuming no trading)? This question is related to the PoS protocol design.

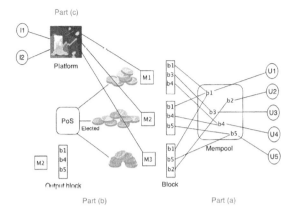

Figure 7.1   Miner–user–investor activities in the PoS protocol

2. For each individual miner, what is her best strategy? This question asks for a miner's trading incentive in the PoS protocol.
3. What is the wealth evolution of the whole (miner) population if each miner follows the best response to the others? This question is concerned with the miner's collective behaviour in a PoS trading environment.

We will answer these questions in the following sections. The remainder of the paper is organized as follows. In Section 7.1, we study the question (1), which hinges on a Pólya urn representation of the PoS election/protocol. Our main finding is that a large miner's shares are stable over the time, while those of a small miner can be much more fluctuated. As a consequence, the PoS protocol alone will lead to neither centralisation, nor decentralisation. In Section 7.2, we allow for trading in the PoS protocol, and provide a sufficient condition under which the miners have no incentive to trade. To address the question (2), we formulate and solve an optimal control problem in Section 7.3. The optimal control framework also allows us to analyse the question (3) via a mean field model in Section 7.4. Numerical experiments show that allowing trading in the PoS protocol does lead to decentralisation, which manifests the market power. In Section 7.5, we conclude with a few open problems and future directions. We emphasise that each PoS blockchain may have specific rules (e.g., block validity, the longest chain rule, etc.), and we will not take these blockchain-specific rules into account. Our analysis applies to the generic PoS protocol which will be defined accordingly.

7.1   Stability of the PoS protocol

We consider the question (1) in this section. Recall that the miners who choose to join the PoS election are required to commit their coins, and the winning probability is proportional to the number of coins committed. To study the PoS protocol itself, we assume in this section that no trading is allowed, and all the miners will participate in the PoS mining process. Hence, the number of coins committed by each miner is equal to that she owns. At first glance, the miner who owns the largest number of coins is more likely to win the PoS election, which will in turn generate more and more coins for her. This is called the rich-get-richer phenomenon, which fundamentally violates the decentralised nature of any blockchain. We will show that the wealth evolution of a PoS miner depends on the reward type and her coin possession level.

Now we describe formally the PoS protocol without trading. Time is discrete, indexed by $t \in \{0, 1, \ldots\}$. Let K be the number of miners, and $N \in \mathbb{R}_+$ be the number of initial coins in the PoS blockchain. The miners are indexed by $[K] := \{1, \ldots, K\}$, and miner k's initial coins are $n_{k,0}$ with $\sum_{k=1}^{K} n_{k,0} = N$. We define the *share* as the fraction of coins each miner owns. So the initial shares ($\pi_{k,0}$, $k \in [K]$) are given by

$$\pi_{k,0} := \frac{n_{k,0}}{N}, \quad k \in [K]. \tag{7.1}$$

Similarly, denote by $n_{k,t}$ the number of coins owned by miner k at time t, and the corresponding share is

$$\pi_{k,t} := \frac{n_{k,t}}{N_t}, \quad k \in [K], \quad \text{with} \quad N_t := \sum_{k=1}^{K} n_{k,t}. \tag{7.2}$$

Here N_t is the total number of coins at time t, with $N_0 = N$. We shall often refer to N_t as the 'volume of coins', or simply 'volume'.

At time t, miner k is selected at random with probability $\pi_{k,t-1}$. Once selected, the miner receives a deterministic reward of $R_t \in \mathbb{R}_+$ coins (which may include transaction fees and block rewards). Denote by $S_{k,t}$ the random event that miner k is selected at time t. So the number of coins owned by each miner evolves as

$$n_{k,t} = n_{k,t-1} + R_t 1_{S_{k,t}}, \quad k \in [K]. \tag{7.3}$$

Note that the volume satisfies $N_t = N_{t-1} + R_t$. Combining (7.2) and (7.3) yields a recursion of the shares:

$$\pi_{k,t} = \frac{N_{t-1}}{N_t} \pi_{k,t-1} + \frac{R_t}{N_t} 1_{S_{k,t}}, \quad k \in [K]. \tag{7.4}$$

which is a (time-dependent) Pólya urn model [24].

We consider the long-time evolution of the shares ($\pi_{k,t}$, $k \in [K]$). Let $\mathscr{F}_t$ be the filtration generated by the random events ($S_{k,r} : k \in [K], r \leq t$). Observe that for each $k \in [K]$, the process ($\pi_{k,t}$, $t \geq 0$) is an $\mathscr{F}_t$-martingale. By the martingale convergence theorem (see [25, Theorem 4.2.11]),

$$(\pi_{1,t}, \ldots, \pi_{K,t}) \longrightarrow (\pi_{1,\infty}, \ldots, \pi_{K,\infty}) \quad \text{as } t \to \infty \text{ with probability 1}, \tag{7.5}$$

where ($\pi_{1,\infty}, \ldots, \pi_{K,\infty}$) is some random probability distribution on $[K]$.

To quantify the wealth evolution of miner k, there are two obvious metrics:

$$|\pi_{k,t} - \pi_{k,0}| \text{ (difference)} \quad \text{and} \quad \frac{\pi_{k,t}}{\pi_{k,0}} \text{ (ratio).} \tag{7.6}$$

If $|\pi_{k,t} - \pi_{k,0}|$ is close to 0, or $\frac{\pi_{k,t}}{\pi_{k,0}}$ is close to 1 (as t is large), we say that the share $\pi_{k,t}$ is *stable* or *concentrated*. This is the desired case as it implies that the PoS protocol will not lead to centralisation. Note that if $\pi_{k,t}$ is of constant order, there is no difference in considering $|\pi_{k,t} - \pi_{k,0}|$ or $\pi_{k,t}/\pi_{k,0}$. However, when $\pi_{k,t}$ is small, the two metrics may exhibit different results: $|\pi_{k,t} - \pi_{k,0}|$ is (trivially) close to 0 $(0 - 0)$, while $\pi_{k,t}/\pi_{k,0}$ is indeterminate $(0/0)$.

First, assume that $R_t \equiv R$ (constant reward), where the limiting $(\pi_{1,\infty}, \ldots, \pi_{K,\infty})$ can be identified. Let $\Gamma(z) := \int_0^\infty x^{z-1} e^{-x} dx$ be the Gamma function. Recall that the Dirichlet distribution with parameters $(a_1, \ldots, a_K)$, which we denote by $\mathrm{Dir}(a_1, \ldots, a_K)$, has support on the standard simplex $\{(x_1, \ldots, x_K) \in \mathbb{R}_+^K : \sum_{k=1}^K x_k = 1\}$ and has density:

$$f(x_1, \ldots, x_K) = \frac{\Gamma\left(\sum_{k=1}^K a_k\right)}{\prod_{k=1}^K \Gamma(a_k)} \prod_{k=1}^K x_k^{a_k - 1}. \tag{7.7}$$

The following theorem elucidates the wealth evolution of a PoS miner with a constant reward.

Theorem 1. *[26,27] Assume that the coin reward is $R_t \equiv R > 0$. Then the miner shares have a limiting distribution*

$$(\pi_{1,\infty}, \ldots, \pi_{K,\infty}) \stackrel{d}{=} \mathrm{Dir}\left(\frac{n_{1,0}}{R}, \ldots, \frac{n_{K,0}}{R}\right). \tag{7.8}$$

Moreover,

(i) *For $n_{k,0} = f(N)$ such that $f(N) \to \infty$ as $N \to \infty$, we have for each $\varepsilon > 0$ and for each $t \geq 1$ or $t = \infty$:*

$$\mathbb{P}(|\pi_{k,t} - \pi_{k,0}| > \varepsilon) \to 0 \quad and \quad \mathbb{P}\left(\left|\frac{\pi_{k,t}}{\pi_{k,0}} - 1\right| > \varepsilon\right) \to 0, \quad as\ N \to \infty. \tag{7.9}$$

(ii) *For $n_{k,0} = \Theta(1)$, we have for each $\varepsilon > 0$, $\mathbb{P}(|\pi_{k,\infty} - \pi_{k,0}| > \varepsilon) \to 0$ as $N \to \infty$, and the convergence in distribution:*

$$\frac{\pi_{k,\infty}}{\pi_{k,0}} \stackrel{d}{\longrightarrow} \frac{R}{n_{k,0}} \gamma\left(\frac{n_{k,0}}{R}\right), \quad as\ N \to \infty, \tag{7.10}$$

where $\gamma\left(\frac{n_{k,0}}{R}\right)$ is a Gamma random variable with density $x^{\frac{n_{k,0}}{R}-1} e^{-x} 1_{x>0} / \Gamma\left(\frac{n_{k,0}}{R}\right)$.

Let us make a few comments. The theorem reveals a *phase transition* of shares in the long run between large and small miners. Part (i) shows that for large miners, their shares are stable (which holds not only for extremely large miners with initial coins $n_{k,0} = \Theta(N)$ but for less rich large miners with $n_{k,0} \gg 1$, $n_{k,0} = o(N)$). Consequently, the PoS protocol with constant reward will lead to neither centralisation, nor decentralisation. On the other hand, the evolution of shares for small miners has a different limiting behaviour. Part (ii) shows that a small miner's share is volatile in

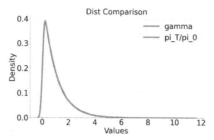

Figure 7.2   Constant reward: instability of $\pi_{k,t}/\pi_{k,0}$ for small miners. Blue curve: histogram of $\pi_{k,50,000}/\pi_{k,0}$ with $n_{k,0} = R = 1$ and $N = 100$. Orange curve: Gamma distribution.

such a way that the ratio $\pi_{k,\infty}/\pi_{k,0}$ is close to a gamma distribution independent of the initial coin offerings, and hence $\mathrm{Var}(\pi_{k,\infty}/\pi_{k,0}) \approx \frac{1}{n_{k,0}}$. For instance, if $n_{k,0} = R = 1$ the limiting distribution of the ratio $\pi_{k,\infty}/\pi_{k,0}$ reduces to the exponential distribution with parameter 1. (See Figure 7.2 for an illustration of this approximation.) In this case, we have

$$\mathbb{P}\left(\frac{\pi_{k,\infty}}{\pi_{k,0}} > \theta\right) \approx e^{-\theta} \quad \text{as } N \to \infty.$$

Thus, with probability $e^{-2} \approx 0.135$ a small miner's share will double, and with probability $1 - e^{-0.5} \approx 0.393$, this miner's share will be halved.

Next we consider the wealth evolution of a PoS miner with a decreasing reward. Though the limiting $(\pi_{1,\infty}, \ldots, \pi_{K,\infty})$ is not explicit, we can still characterise a miner's share stability in terms of her coin possession level.

Theorem 2. *[27] Assume that the coin reward is R_t with $R_t \geq R_{t+1}$ for each $t \geq 0$.*

1. *If R_t is bounded away from 0, i.e., $\lim_{t\geq 0} R_t = \underline{R} > 0$, then*
   (i) *For $n_{k,0} = f(N)$ such that $f(N) \to \infty$ as $N \to \infty$, we have for each $\varepsilon > 0$ and each $t \geq 1$ or $t = \infty$:*

$$\mathbb{P}\left(\left|\frac{\pi_{k,t}}{\pi_{k,0}} - 1\right| > \varepsilon\right) \to 0, \quad \text{as } N \to \infty. \tag{7.11}$$

   (ii) *For $n_{k,0} = \Theta(1)$, we have $\mathrm{Var}\left(\frac{\pi_{k,\infty}}{\pi_{k,0}}\right) = \Theta(1)$. Moreover, there is $c > 0$ independent of N such that for $\varepsilon > 0$ sufficiently small:*

$$\mathbb{P}\left(\left|\frac{\pi_{k,\infty}}{\pi_{k,0}} - 1\right| > \varepsilon\right) \geq c. \tag{7.12}$$

2. *If $R_t = \Theta(t^{-\alpha})$ for $\alpha > 0$, then for each $\varepsilon > 0$ and each $t \geq 1$ or $t = \infty$:*

$$\mathbb{P}\left(\left|\frac{\pi_{k,t}}{\pi_{k,0}} - 1\right| > \varepsilon\right) \to 0, \quad \text{as } N \to \infty. \tag{7.13}$$

The theorem distinguishes two ways that the reward function decreases, leading to different phase transition results. Part (1) assumes that the reward function decreases to a nonzero value. In this case, the threshold to identify large and small miners is $n_{k,0} = \Theta(1)$, which is the same as that of the PoS protocol with a constant reward. This may not be surprising, since the underlying dynamics is not much different from the one with a constant reward. For large miners, the ratio $\pi_{k,\infty}/\pi_{k,0}$ is close to 1; while for small miners there is the *anti-concentration* bound (7.12), indicating that the evolution of a small miner's share is no longer stable, and may be volatile. Part (2) considers a fast decreasing reward $R_t = \Theta(t^{-\alpha})$ for $\alpha > 0$. In this case, there is no phase transition, and the ratio $\pi_{k,\infty}/\pi_{k,0}$ concentrates at 1 for every miner.

To conclude this section, we present the results of the wealth evolution of a PoS miner with an increasing reward.

Theorem 3. *[27] Assume that the coin reward $R_t = \rho N_{t-1}^\gamma$ for some $\rho > 0$ and $\gamma > 0$.*

1. *If $\gamma > 1$, then $\pi_{k,\infty} \in \{0, 1\}$ almost surely with*

$$\mathbb{P}(\pi_{k,\infty} = 1) = \pi_{k,0}, \quad \mathbb{P}(\pi_{k,\infty} = 0) = 1 - \pi_{k,0} \tag{7.14}$$

2. *If $\gamma < 1$, then*
   (i) *For $n_{k,0} = f(N)$ such that $f(N)/N^\gamma \to \infty$ as $N \to \infty$, we have for each $\varepsilon > 0$ and each $t \geq 1$ or $t = \infty$:*

$$\mathbb{P}\left(\left|\frac{\pi_{k,t}}{\pi_{k,0}} - 1\right| > \varepsilon\right) \to 0 \quad as \ N \to \infty. \tag{7.15}$$

   (ii) *For $n_{k,0} = \Theta(N^\gamma)$, we have $Var\left(\frac{\pi_{k,\infty}}{\pi_{k,0}}\right) = \Theta(1)$. Moreover, there exists $c > 0$ independent of N such that for $\varepsilon > 0$ sufficiently small:*

$$\mathbb{P}\left(\left|\frac{\pi_{k,\infty}}{\pi_{k,0}} - 1\right| > \varepsilon\right) \geq c. \tag{7.16}$$

   For $n_{k,0} = o(N^\gamma)$, we have $Var\left(\frac{\pi_{k,\infty}}{\pi_{k,0}}\right) \to \infty$ as $N \to \infty$.

The theorem considers two increasing reward schemes: a geometric reward and a sub-geometric one. Part (1) assumes a geometric reward and shows that with probability one, all the shares will eventually go to one miner in such a way that

$$\mathbb{P}(\pi_k = 1 \text{ and } \pi_j = 0 \text{ for all } j \neq k) = \pi_{k,0}, \quad k \in [K].$$

We call this *chaotic centralisation* because the underlying dynamics will lead to the dictatorship, with the dictator being selected in a random manner. (See Figure 7.3 for an illustration of chaotic centralisation.) Part (2) considers a polynomial reward $R_t = \Theta(t^{\frac{1}{1-\gamma}})$ for $\gamma < 1$. In this case, there is a phase transition in the stability of $\pi_{k,t}/\pi_{k,0}$, with the threshold $n_{k,0} = \Theta(N^\gamma)$.

We also mention that it is possible to study the wealth evolution in the PoS protocol with infinite population ($K = \infty$), see [27, Section 3].

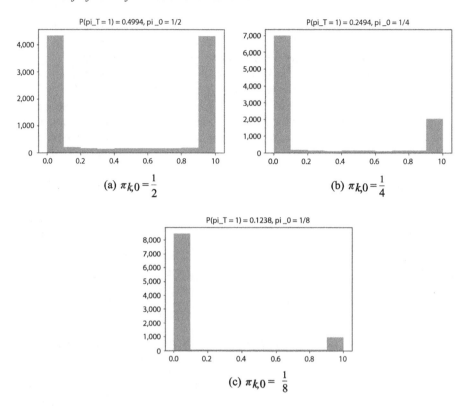

Figure 7.3 Increasing reward: chaotic centralisation. Histogram of $\pi_{k,5000}$ with $\rho = 0.001, \gamma = 1.1, N = 1,000$ and $\pi_{k,0} \in \{1/2, 1/4, 1/8\}$.

7.2 Participation and PoS trading

We consider the question (2) in this section and provide conditions under which no miner will have incentive to trade (so Theorems 1– 3 continue to hold). So far, we have not considered the possibility of allowing the miners to trade coins (among themselves). In the new setting of allowing trading, we need to modify the problem formulation presented in Section 7.1. First, for each $k \in [K]$, let $v_{k,t}$ be the number of coins that miner k will trade at time t. Then, instead of (7.3), the number of coins $n_{k,t}$ evolves as

$$n_{k,t} = \underbrace{n_{k,t-1} + R_t 1_{S_{k,t}}}_{n'_{k,t}} + v_{k,t}, \tag{7.17}$$

i.e., $n'_{k,t}$ denotes the number of coins miner k owns in between time $t - 1$ and t, excluding those traded in period t. Note that $v_{k,t}$ will be up to miner k to decide, as opposed to the random event $S_{k,t}$ which is exogenous; in particular, $v_{k,t}$ can be negative (as well as positive or zero). We will elaborate more on this below, but note that $v_{k,t}$ will be constrained such that after the updating in (7.17) $n_{k,t}$ will remain nonnegative.

Let $\{P_t, t \geq 0\}$ be the price process of each (unit of) coin, which is a stochastic process assumed to be independent of the randomness induced by the PoS selection (specifically, the process $\{S_{k,t}\}$). Hence, we augment the filtration $\{\mathscr{F}_t\}_{t\geq 0}$ with that of the exogenous price process $\{P_t, t \geq 0\}$ to a new filtration denoted $\{\mathscr{G}_t\}_{t\geq 0}$. This assumption need not be so far off, as the crypto's price tends to be affected by market shocks (such as macroeconomics, geopolitics, and breaking news) much more than by trading activities.

Let $b_{k,t}$ denote (units of) the risk-free asset that miner k holds at time t, and $r_{\text{free}} > 0$ the risk-free (interest) rate. As we are mainly concerned with the effect of exchanging coins to each individual, we allow miners to trade coins only internally among themselves, but not risk-free assets between them. Hence, each miner has to trade risk-free asset with a third-party instead of trading that with another bidder.

The decision for each miner k at t is a tuple, $(v_{k,t}, b_{k,t})$. Moreover, there is a terminal time, denoted $T_k \geq 1$, by which time miner k has to sell all assets, including both any risk-free asset and any coins owned at that time. T_k can either be deterministic or random. In the latter case, assume it has a finite expectation and is either adapted to $\{\mathscr{G}_t\}_{t\geq 0}$, or independent of all other randomness (in which case augment $\{\mathscr{G}_t\}$ accordingly). We also allow miner k to liquidate prior to T_k at a stopping time τ_k relative to $\{\mathscr{G}_t\}_{t\geq 0}$. Thus, miner k will also decide at which time τ_k to stop and exit. Abuse τ_k for the minimum of τ_k and T_k.

Let $c_{k,t}$ denote the (free) cash flow (or, 'consumption') of miner k at time t, i.e.,

$$c_{k,t} = (1 + r_{\text{free}})b_{k,t-1} - b_{k,t} - v_{k,t}P_t, \quad \forall 1 \leq t < \tau_k; \tag{C1}$$

with

$$b_{k,0} = 0, \ b_{k,t} \geq 0, \quad 0 \leq n_{k,t} = n'_{k,t} + v_{k,t} \leq N_t, \quad \forall 1 \leq t < \tau_k; \tag{C2}$$

and

$$c_{k,\tau_k} = (1 + r_{\text{free}})b_{k,\tau_k - 1} + n'_{k,\tau_k}P_{\tau_k}, \quad \text{and } v_{k,\tau_k} = b_{k,\tau_k} = 0. \tag{C3}$$

The equation in (C1) is a budget constraint, which defines what's available for 'consumption' in period t. The requirements in (C2) are all in the spirit of disallowing shorting, on both the free asset $b_{k,t}$ and the traded coins $v_{k,t}$. In particular, the latter is constrained such that $v_{k,t} \geq -n'_{k,t}$, i.e., miner k cannot sell more than what's in possession at t; it also ensures that no miner can own a number of coins beyond the total volume ($n_{k,t} \leq N_t$). (C3) specifies how the assets are liquidated at the exit time τ_k: both v_{k,τ_k} and b_{k,τ_k} will be set at zero, and all remaining coins n'_{k,τ_k} liquidated (cashed out at P_{τ_k} per unit).

Denote by τ_k and $(v, b) := \{(v_{k,t}, b_{k,t}), \ 1 \leq t \leq \tau_k\}$ miner k's decision (process) or 'strategy'. The objective of miner k is to solve the consumption–investment problem:

$$U_k^* := \max_{\tau_k,(v,b)} U_k := \max_{\tau_k,(v,b)} \mathbb{E}\left(\sum_{t=1}^{\tau_k} \delta_k^t c_{k,t}\right), \quad \text{subject to (C1), (C2), and (C3);}$$

(7.18)

where $\delta_k \in (0, 1]$ is a discount factor, a given parameter measuring the risk sensitivity of miner k.

We need to introduce two more processes that are related and central to understanding the PoS protocol in the presence of trading. The first one is $\{M_t, t \geq 1\}$, where $M_t := N_t P_t$ denotes the market value of the coins at time t. The second one is $\{\Pi_{k,t}, t \geq 0\}$, for each bidder k, defined as follows:

$$\Pi_{k,0} := n_{k,0} P_0, \quad \text{and} \quad \Pi_{k,t} := \delta_k^t n_{k,t}' P_t - \sum_{j=1}^{t-1} \delta_k^j v_{k,j} P_j, \quad t \geq 1;$$

(7.19)

where $n_{k,t+1}'$ follows (7.17). The process $\{\Pi_{k,t}\}$ connects to the utility U_k in (7.18). To see this, summing up both sides of (C1) and (C3) over t (along with $b_{k,0} = 0$ in (C2)), we get

$$\sum_{t \leq \tau_k} \delta_k^t c_{k,t} = \sum_{t \leq \tau_k} \delta_k^t c_{k,t} = \delta_k^{\tau_k} n_{\tau_k}' P_{\tau_k} - \sum_{t=1}^{\tau_k-1} \delta_k^t v_{k,t} P_t + \sum_{t=1}^{\tau_k-1} \delta_k^t \left[(1 + r_{\text{free}})\delta_k - 1\right] b_{k,t}.$$

(7.20)

Observe that the first two terms on the right-hand side are equal to Π_{k,τ_k}, so we can rewrite the above as follows, emphasizing the exit time τ_k and the strategy (v, b),

$$U_k(\tau_k, v, b) = \mathbb{E}\left[\Pi_{k,\tau_k}(v)\right] + \mathbb{E}\left(\sum_{t=1}^{\tau_k-1} \delta_k^t \left[(1 + r_{\text{free}})\delta_k - 1\right] b_{k,t}\right);$$

(7.21)

hence, the right-hand side above is *separable*: the first term depends on (v) only while the second term, the summation, on (b) only. Moreover, the second term is ≤ 0 provided $(1 + r_{\text{free}})\delta_k \leq 1$, along with b being non-negative, part of the feasibility in (C2). In this case, we will have $U_k \leq \mathbb{E}(\Pi_{k,\tau_k}(v))$, which implies $U_k^* \leq \max_{\tau_k,v} \mathbb{E}(\Pi_{k,\tau_k}(v))$, with equality holding when $b_{k,t} = 0$ for all $t = 1, \ldots, \tau_k$.

We are ready to present the result of the utility maximisation problem in (7.18). Two strategies are singled out: the '*buy-out*' strategy, in which miner k buys up all coins available at time 1, and then participate in the PoS mining process until the end; and the '*non-participation*' strategy, in which miner k turns all $n_{k,0}$ coins into cash, and then never participates in either PoS mining or trading for all $t \geq 1$. Note that the non-participation strategy is executed at $\tau_k = 0$; as such, it complements the feasible class, which is for $\tau_k \geq 1$ and presumes participation. The buy-out strategy clearly belongs to the feasible class.

Theorem 4 (Buy-out strategy versus non-participation). *[26,28] Assume the following two conditions:*

$$\text{(a)} \quad \delta_k(1 + r_{free}) \leq 1 \quad \text{and} \quad \text{(b)} \quad \mathbb{E}(M_{t+1} \mid \mathcal{G}_t) = (1 + r_{cryp})M_t. \tag{7.22}$$

Then with condition (a), the maximal utility U_k^* is achieved by setting $b_{k,t} = 0$ for all $t = 1, \ldots, T_k$; i.e., $U_k^* = \max_v \mathbb{E}(\Pi_{k,T_k})$. In addition, all three parts of the following will hold.

(i) *If $\delta_k(1 + r_{cryp}) \leq 1$, then any feasible strategy will provide no greater utility for miner k than the non-participation strategy, i.e., $U_k^* \leq n_{k,0}P_0$.*

(ii) *If $\delta_k(1 + r_{cryp}) \geq 1$, then any feasible strategy will provide no greater utility for miner k than the buy-out strategy. In this case, miner k will buy all available coins at time 1, and participate in the PoS mining process until the terminal time T_k.*

(iii) *If $\delta_k(1 + r_{cryp}) = 1$, then miner k is indifferent between the non-participation and the buy-out strategy with any exit time, both of which will provide no less utility than any feasible strategy. All strategies achieve the same utility (which is $\Pi_{k,0} = n_0 P_{k,0}$).*

Moreover, when $\delta_k = \delta := (1 + r_{cryp})^{-1}$ for all k, no miner will have any incentive to trade. Consequently, the long-term behaviour of $\pi_{k,t}$ characterised in Theorems 1–3 will hold.

In what remains of this section, we make a few remarks on Theorem 4, in particular, to motivate and explain its required conditions. First, the rate r_{cryp}, which is determined by condition (b), is the (expected) rate of return of each coin, i.e., it is the counterpart of r_{free}, the rate for the risk-free asset. For all practical purpose, we can assume $r_{crpt} \geq r_{free}$, even though this is not assumed in the theorem. When this relation holds, condition (a) will become superfluous in cases (i) and (iii).

Second, the factor δ_k in the utility objective in (7.18) plays a key role in characterizing phase transitions in terms of $\delta_k(1 + r_{cryp})$. In case (i), the inequality $\delta_k \leq 1/(1 + r_{cryp})$ implies miner k is seriously risk-averse; and this is reflected in k's non-participation strategy. In case (ii), the inequality holds in the opposite direction, implying miner k is lightly risk-averse or even a risk taker. Accordingly, k's strategy is to aggressively sweep up all the available coins to reach monopoly and participate (but not trade) until the terminal time. In case (iii), the inequality becomes an equality $\delta_k = 1/(1 + r_{cryp})$, and $(\Pi_{k,t})$ becomes a martingale. Thus, miner k is indifferent between non-participation and participation, and, in the latter case, indifferent to all (feasible) strategies, including the buy-out (and the no-trading) strategy. Indeed, the equality $\delta_k = 1/(1 + r_{cryp})$ is both necessary and sufficient for the no-trading strategy.

Next, we emphasise that the two conditions in (7.22) play very different roles. Condition (b) makes $(\Pi_{k,t})$ a super- or sub-martingale or a martingale, according to miner k's risk sensitivity as specified by the inequalities and equality applied to δ_k in the three cases. Yet, to solve the maximisation problem in (7.18), $(\Pi_{k,t})$ needs to be connected to the utility; and this is the role played by condition (a), under which, it is necessary (for optimality) to set $b_{k,t} = 0$ for all $t \geq 1$, and applicable to all three cases. In this sense, condition (a) alone solves half of the maximisation problem, the $b_{k,t}$ half of the strategy. In fact, it is more than half, as the optimal v strategy is only needed in the sub-martingale case; and, even there, condition (a) pins down the fact that to participate (even without trading) is better than non-participation.

Theorem 4 is easily extended to the case where the rates $r_{\mathrm{cryp}}(t)$ and $r_{\mathrm{free}}(t)$ may vary over the time. In this case, it suffices to modify the conditions in case (i) to $\left(1 + \sup_{t < T_k} r_{\mathrm{cryp}}(t)\right) \delta_k \leq 1$ and $\left(1 + \sup_{t < T_k} r_{\mathrm{free}}(t)\right) \delta_k \leq 1$; the conditions in case (ii) to $\left(1 + \inf_{t < T_k} r_{\mathrm{cryp}}(t)\right) \delta_k \geq 1$ and $\left(1 + \sup_{t < T_k} r_{\mathrm{free}}(t)\right) \delta_k \leq 1$; and the conditions in case (iii) to $\delta_k = (1 + r_{\mathrm{cryp}})^{-1}$ and $\sup_{t < T_k} r_{\mathrm{free}}(t) \leq r_{\mathrm{cryp}}$, with r_{cryp} being constant. Then, Theorem 4 will continue to hold.

Finally, the last part of the theorem considers the wealth evolution of a homogenous miner population. It is also worth considering the wealth evolution of a heterogeneous miner population (e.g., with different risk sensitivity, holding periods, etc.) See [29] for a study on the reward effect on the wealth distribution of the miners with different coin holding horizons.

7.3 PoS trading with volume constraint – a continuous-time control setup

We continue to consider the question (2) in this section. As shown in Theorem 4, the miner's strategy is either not to participate (in both PoS mining and trading) or to sweep up all available coins immediately. The latter, being a market manipulation, rarely occurs in practice due to regulation. One way to prohibit the 'buy-out' strategy is to limit the number of coins that can be traded at a time. This motivates the study of the PoS trading with volume constraint.

To simplify the analysis, we adopt a continuous-time control approach. Time is continuous, indexed by $t \in [0, T]$, for a fixed $T > 0$ representing the length of a finite horizon. Let $\{N(t), 0 \leq t \leq T\}$ (with $N(0) := N$) denote the process of the volume of coins, which is increasing in time and sufficiently smooth. So the derivative $N'(t)$ represents the instantaneous rate of 'reward' by the PoS protocol. For instance, we will consider below, as a special case, the process $N(t)$ of a polynomial form:

$$N_\alpha(t) = (N^{\frac{1}{\alpha}} + t)^\alpha, \quad t \geq 0. \tag{7.23}$$

The parametric family (7.23) covers different rewarding schemes according to the values of α: for $0 < \alpha < 1$, the process $N_\alpha(t)$ corresponds to a decreasing reward; for $\alpha = 1$, the process $N_1(t) = N + t$ gives a rate one constant reward; for $\alpha > 1$, the process $N_\alpha(t)$ amounts to an increasing reward.

Let $K \geq 2$ be the number of miners, who are indexed by $k \in [K] := \{1, \ldots, K\}$. For each miner k, let $\{X_k(t), 0 \leq t \leq T\}$ (with $X_k(0) = x_k$) denote the process of the number of coins that miner k holds, with $X_k(t) \geq 0$ and $\sum_{k=1}^{K} X_k(t) = N(t)$ for all $t \in [0, T]$. For our continuous-time PoS model here, in which the time required for each round of voting is 'infinitesimal', imagine there are M rounds of election during any given time interval $[t, t + \Delta t]$. (Each round in Ethereum takes about 10 s, corresponding to the block-generation time [30].) In each round miner k gets either some coin(s) or nothing, so the average total number of coins k will get over the M rounds is (by law of large numbers when M is large),

$$\underbrace{\frac{X_k(t)}{N(t)} \frac{N'(t) \Delta t}{M}}_{\text{average number of coins in each round}} \times \underbrace{M}_{\text{number of rounds}} = \frac{X_k(t)}{N(t)} N'(t) \Delta t.$$

Hence, replacing Δt by the infinitesimal dt, we know miner k will receive (on average) $\frac{X_k(t)}{N(t)} N'(t) dt$ coins, where $\frac{X_k(t)}{N(t)}$ is k's winning probability, and $N'(t) dt$ is the reward issued by the blockchain in $[t, t + dt]$.

The miners are allowed to trade (buy or sell) their coins. Miner k will buy $v_k(t) dt$ coins in $[t, t + dt]$ if $v_k(t) > 0$, and sell $-v_k(t) dt$ coins if $v_k(t) < 0$. This leads to the following dynamics of miner k's coins under trading:

$$X'_k(t) = v_k(t) + \frac{N'(t)}{N(t)} X_k(t) \quad \text{for } 0 \leq t \leq \tau_k \wedge T := \mathscr{T}_k, \tag{7.24}$$

where $\tau_k := \inf\{t > 0 : X_k(t) = 0\}$ is the first time at which the process $X_k(t)$ reaches zero. It is reasonable to stop the trading process if a miner runs out of coins or gets all available coins: if $\mathscr{T}_k = \tau_k$, then miner k liquidates all his coins by time τ_k, and $X_k(\mathscr{T}_k) = 0$; if $\mathscr{T}_k = \max_{j \neq k} \tau_j$, then miner k gets all issued coins by time $\max_{j \neq k} \tau_j$, and, hence, $X_k(\mathscr{T}_k) = N(\mathscr{T}_k)$. We set $X_k(t) = X_k(\mathscr{T}_k)$ for $t > \mathscr{T}_k$.

The problem is for each miner k to decide how to trade coins with others under the PoS protocol. Similar to Section 7.2, let $\{P(t), 0 \leq t \leq T\}$ be the price process of each (unit of) coin, which is a stochastic process assumed to be independent of the dynamics in (7.24). Let $b_k(t)$ denote the (units of) risk-free asset that miner k holds at time t, and let $r > 0$ denote the risk-free (interest) rate. Recall that all K miners are allowed to trade coins only internally among themselves, whereas each miner can only exchange cash with an external source (say, a bank).

Let $\{c_k(t), 0 \leq t \leq T\}$ be the process of consumption, or cash flow of miner k, which follows the dynamics below:

$$dc_k(t) = rb_k(t) dt - db_k(t) - P(t) v_k(t) dt, \quad 0 \leq t \leq \mathscr{T}_k; \tag{C1}$$

with

$$b_k(0) = 0, \quad b_k(t) \geq 0 \text{ for } 0 \leq t \leq \mathscr{T}_k, \quad 0 \leq X_k(t) \leq N(t) \text{ for } 0 \leq t \leq \mathscr{T}_k. \tag{C2}$$

Set $b_k(t) = b_k(\mathscr{T}_k)$ and $v_k(t) = 0$ for $t > \mathscr{T}_k$. The conditions (C1)–(C2) are the continuous analogue to those in Section 7.2. We also require that the trading strategy be bounded: there is $\bar{v}_k > 0$ such that

$$|v_k(t)| \leq \bar{v}_k. \tag{C3}$$

The objective of miner k is:

$$\sup_{\{(v_k(t),b_k(t))\}} J(v_k, b_k) := \mathbb{E}\left\{ \int_0^{\mathcal{T}_k} e^{-\beta_k t} \left[dc_k(t) + \ell_k(X_k(t))dt \right] \right.$$

$$\left. + e^{-\beta_k \mathcal{T}_k} \left[b_k(\mathcal{T}_k) + h_k(X_k(\mathcal{T}_k)) \right] \right\} \tag{7.25}$$

$$\text{subject to } (7.24), (C1), (C2), \textit{and } (C3),$$

where $\beta_k > 0$ is a discount factor; $\ell_k(\cdot)$ and $h_k(\cdot)$ are two utility functions representing, respectively, the running profit and the terminal profit.

While generally following Merton's consumption–investment framework, our formulation takes into account some distinct features of the PoS blockchain. One notable point is the utilities ℓ and h are expressed as functions of the number of coins $X_k(t)$, as opposed to their value $P(t)X_k(t)$. To the extent that $P(t)$ is treated as exogenous, this difference may seem to be trivial. Yet, it is a reflection of the more substantial fact that crypto-participants tend to mentally decouple the utility of holding coins from their monetary value at any given time.

Throughout below, the following conditions will be assumed:

Assumption 5.

(i) $N : [0, T] \to \mathbb{R}_+$ is increasing with $N(0) = N > 0$, and $N \in \mathscr{C}^2([0, T])$.
(ii) $\ell : \mathbb{R}_+ \to \mathbb{R}_+$ is increasing and $\ell \in \mathscr{C}^1(\mathbb{R}_+)$.
(iii) $h : \mathbb{R}_+ \to \mathbb{R}_+$ is increasing and $h \in \mathscr{C}^1(\mathbb{R}_+)$.

To lighten notation, omit the subscript k, and write

$$U(x) := \sup_{\{(v(t),b(t))\}} J(v, b) := \mathbb{E}\left\{ \int_0^{\mathcal{T}} e^{-\beta t} \left[dc(t) + \ell(X(t))dt \right] \right.$$

$$\left. + e^{-\beta \mathcal{T}} \left[b(\mathcal{T}) + h(X(\mathcal{T})) \right] \right\} \tag{7.26}$$

$$\text{subject to}\quad X'(t) = v(t) + \frac{N'(t)}{N(t)}X(t), \ X(0) = x, \tag{C0}$$

$$dc(t) = rb(t)dt - db(t) - P(t)v(t)dt, \tag{C1}$$

$$b(0) = 0, \ b(t) \geq 0 \text{ and } 0 \leq X(t) \leq N(t), \tag{C2}$$

$$|v(t)| \leq \bar{v}. \tag{C3}$$

Let

$$\tilde{P}_\beta(t) := e^{-\beta t}\mathbb{E}P(t), \quad t \in [0, T]. \tag{7.27}$$

Substituting the constraint (C1) into the objective function, and taking into account $rb(t)dt - db(t) = -e^{rt}d(e^{-rt}b(t))$, along with (7.42), we have

$$J(v,b) = (r - \beta) \int_0^{\mathscr{T}} e^{-\beta t} b(t)dt$$

$$+ \int_0^{\mathscr{T}} [-\widetilde{P}_\beta(t)v(t) + e^{-\beta t}\ell(X(t)]dt + e^{-\beta \mathscr{T}} h(X(\mathscr{T})) \qquad (7.28)$$

$$:= J_1(b) + J_2(v).$$

Hence,

$$U(x) := \sup_{\{(v,b)\}} J(v,b) = \sup_b J_1(b) + \sup_v J_2(v). \qquad (7.29)$$

Suppose $\beta \geq r$, which is analogue to (7.22)(a) in the discrete setting. Then, from the $J_1(b)$ expression in (7.28), and taking into account $b(t) \geq 0$ as constrained in (C2), we have $\sup_b J_1(b) = 0$ with the optimality binding at $b_*(t) = 0$ for all t. Therefore, the problem in (7.26) reduces to

$$U(x) = \sup_v J_2(v) \quad \text{subject to (C0), (C2'), and (C3),} \qquad (7.30)$$

where (C2') is (C2) without the constraints on $b(\cdot)$. The problem (7.26) can then be solved by dynamic programming and the Hamilton–Jacobi–Bellman (HJB) equations. The result is stated as follows.

Theorem 5. *[31] Assume that $r \leq \beta$, and $\widetilde{P}_\beta(t)$ in (7.42) satisfies the Lipschitz condition:*

$$|\widetilde{P}_\beta(t) - \widetilde{P}_\beta(s)| \leq C|t - s| \quad \text{for some } C > 0. \qquad (7.31)$$

Then, $U(x) = v(0,x)$ where $v(t,x)$ is the unique viscosity solution to the following HJB equation, where $Q := \{(t,x) : 0 \leq t < T, 0 < x < N(t)\}$:

$$\begin{cases} \partial_t v + e^{-\beta t}\ell(x) + \frac{xN'(t)}{N(t)}\partial_x v + \sup_{|v| \leq \bar{v}}\{v(\partial_x v - \widetilde{P}_\beta(t))\} = 0 & \text{in } Q, \\ v(T,x) = e^{-\beta T}h(x), \\ v(t,0) = e^{-\beta t}h(0), \ v(t,N(t)) = e^{-\beta t}h(N(t)). \end{cases} \qquad (7.32)$$

Moreover, the optimal strategy is $b_*(t) = 0$ and $v_*(t) = v_*(t,X_*(t))$ for $0 \leq t \leq \mathscr{T}_*$, where $v_*(t,x)$ achieves the supremum in (7.32), and $X_*(t)$ solves $X_*'(t) = v_*(t,X_*(t)) + \frac{N'(t)}{N(t)}X_*(t)$ with $X_*(0) = x$, and $\mathscr{T}_* := \inf\{t > 0 : X_*(t) = 0 \text{ or } N(t)\} \wedge T$.

Now specialise to linear utility $\ell(x) = \ell x$ and $h(x) = hx$, for some given (positive) constants ℓ and h. In this case, we can derive a closed-form solution to the HJB equation in (7.32), and then derive the optimal strategy $v_*(t)$ (in terms of $\widetilde{P}_\beta(t)$). Let

$$\Psi(t) := \frac{1}{N(t)}\left(he^{-\beta T}N(T) + \ell \int_t^T e^{-\beta s}N(s)ds\right). \qquad (7.33)$$

The following corollary classifies all possible optimal strategies (of the miner).

Corollary 1. *[31] Let $\ell(x) = \ell x$ and $h(x) = hx$ with $\ell, h > 0$, and $N(t)$ satisfy Assumption 5 (i). Assume that $\widetilde{P}_\beta(t)$ satisfies the Lipschitz condition in (7.31) and that $\bar{v}$ satisfies:*

$$\bar{v} \int_0^T \frac{dt}{N(t)} \le \frac{x}{N} \wedge \frac{N - x}{N}. \tag{7.34}$$

Then, the following results hold:

(i)   *Suppose $\widetilde{P}_\beta(t)$ stays constant, i.e., for all $t \in [0, T]$, $\widetilde{P}(t) = \widetilde{P}(0) = P(0)$.*
  (a)   *If $P(0) \ge \Psi(0)$, then $v_*(t) = -\bar{v}$ for all $0 \le t \le T$.*
  (b)   *If $P(0) \le \Psi(T)$, then $v_*(t) = \bar{v}$.*
  (c)   *If $\Psi(T) < P(0) < \Psi(0)$, then $v_*(t) = \bar{v}$ for $t \le t_0$, and $-\bar{v}$ for $t > t_0$, where t_0 is the unique point in $[0, T]$ such that $P(0) = \Psi(t_0)$ with $\Psi(t)$ defined in (7.33).*
(ii) *Suppose that $\widetilde{P}_\beta(t)$ is increasing in $t \in [0, T]$.*
  (a)   *If $P(0) \ge \Psi(0)$, then $v_*(t) = -\bar{v}$ for all $0 \le t \le T$.*
  (b)   *If $\widetilde{P}_\beta(T) \le \Psi(T)$, then $v_*(t) = \bar{v}$.*
  (c)   *If $P(0) < \Psi(0)$ and $\widetilde{P}_\beta(T) > \Psi(T)$, then $v_*(t) = \bar{v}$ for $t \le t_0$, and $-\bar{v}$ for $t > t_0$, where t_0 is the unique point of intersection of $\widetilde{P}_\beta(t)$ and $\Psi(t)$ on $[0, T]$.*
(iii) *Suppose that $\widetilde{P}_\beta(t)$ is decreasing in $t \in [0, T]$.*
  (a)   *If $P(0) \ge \Psi(0)$, then the miner first sells, and may then buy, etc., always at full capacity, according to the crossings of $\widetilde{P}_\beta(t)$ and $\Psi(t)$ in $[0, T]$.*
  (b)   *If $P(0) < \Psi(0)$, then the miner first buys, and may then sell, etc., always at full capacity, according to the crossings of $\widetilde{P}_\beta(t)$ and $\Psi(t)$ in $[0, T]$.*

Several remarks are in order. First note that the condition in (7.34) is to guarantee the constraint (C2') not activated prior to T, that is, to exclude the possibility of monopoly/dictatorship that will trigger a forced early exit. Second, the monotone properties of $\widetilde{P}_\beta(t)$, which classify the three parts (i)–(iii) in the corollary naturally connect to martingale pricing: $\widetilde{P}_\beta(t)$ being a constant in (i) makes the process $e^{-\beta t}P(t)$ a martingale, whereas $\widetilde{P}_\beta(t)$ increasing or decreasing, respectively in (ii) and (iii), makes $e^{-\beta t}P(t)$ a sub-martingale or a super-martingale. On the other hand, the function $\Psi(t)$ represents the rate of return of the miner's utility (from holding of coins, x); and interestingly, in the linear utility case, this return rate is independent of x while decreasing in t. Thus, the trading strategy is completely determined by comparing this return rate $\Psi(t)$ with the miner's risk-adjusted coin price $\widetilde{P}_\beta(t)$: if $\Psi(t) \ge$ (resp. $<$) $\widetilde{P}_\beta(t)$, then the miner will buy (resp. sell) coins.

Specifically, following (i) and (ii) of Corollary 1, for a constant or an increasing $\widetilde{P}_\beta(t)$ (corresponding to a risk-neutral or risk-seeking miner), there are only three possible optimal strategies: buy all the time, sell all the time, or first buy then sell. (The first-buy-then-sell strategy echoes the general investment practice that an early investment pays off in a later day.) See Figure 7.4 for an illustration.

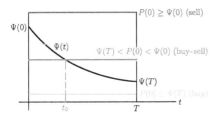
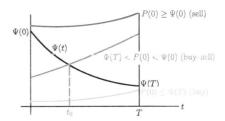

Figure 7.4   Optimal trading with linear $\ell(\,\cdot\,), h(\,\cdot\,)$ when $\widetilde{P}_\beta(t)$ is constant (left) and $\widetilde{P}_\beta(t)$ is increasing (right)

In part (iii) of Corollary 1, when $\widetilde{P}_\beta(t)$ is decreasing in t, like $\Psi(t)$, the multiple crossings between the two decreasing functions can be further pinned down when there's more model structure. Consider, for instance, when $P(t)$ follows a geometric Brownian motion (GBM):

$$\frac{dP(t)}{P(t)} = \mu dt + \sigma dB_t, \quad \text{or} \quad P(t) = P(0)e^{(\mu - \sigma^2/2)t + \sigma B_t}; \quad t \in [0, T], \qquad (7.35)$$

where $\{B_t\}$ denotes the standard Brownian motion; and $\mu > 0$ and $\sigma > 0$ are the two parameters of the GBM model, representing the rate of return and the volatility of $\{P(t)\}$. The following proposition gives the conditions under which $\Psi_\alpha(t) - \widetilde{P}_\beta(t)$ is monotone in the regime $N \to \infty$, and optimal strategies are derived accordingly.

Proposition 1. *[31] Suppose the assumptions in Proposition 1 hold, with $N(t) = N_\alpha(t)$ and $\{P(t)\}$ specified by (7.35) with $\beta > \mu$. As $N \to \infty$, we have the following results:*

1. *If for some $\varepsilon > 0$, $P(0) > \frac{1}{\beta - \mu}\left(\frac{\alpha h e^{-\mu T}(N^{\frac{1}{\alpha}} + T)^\alpha}{N^{1 + \frac{1}{\alpha}}} + \frac{\alpha\ell\beta^{-1}}{N^{\frac{1}{\alpha}}} + \ell\right) + \frac{\varepsilon}{N^{\frac{1}{\alpha}}}$, then $\Psi_\alpha(t) - \widetilde{P}_\beta(t)$ is increasing on $[0, T]$.*

2. *If for some $\varepsilon > 0$, $P(0) < \frac{1}{\beta - \mu}\left(\frac{\alpha h e^{-\beta T}}{N^{\frac{1}{\alpha}} + T} + \ell e^{-\mu T}\right) - \frac{\varepsilon}{N^{\frac{1}{\alpha}}}$, then $\Psi_\alpha(t) - \widetilde{P}_\beta(t)$ is decreasing on $[0, T]$.*

Consequently, we have:

(a) *If $P(0) > e^{(\beta - \mu)T}\Psi_\alpha(T)$ and (1) holds, or $P(0) > \Psi_\alpha(0)$ and (2) holds, then $v_*(t) = -\overline{v}$ for all t.*

(b) *If $\Psi_\alpha(0) \leq P(0) < e^{(\beta - \mu)T}\Psi_\alpha(T)$ and (1) holds, then $v_*(t) = -\overline{v}$ for $t \leq t_0$ and $v_*(t) = \overline{v}$ for $t > t_0$, where t_0 is the unique point of intersection of $\widetilde{P}_\beta(t)$ and $\Psi_\alpha(t)$ on $[0, T]$.*

(c) *If $e^{(\beta - \mu)T}\Psi_\alpha(T) \leq P(0) < \Psi_\alpha(0)$ and (2) holds, then $v_*(t) = \overline{v}$ for $t \leq t_0$ and $v_*(t) = -\overline{v}$ for $t > t_0$, where t_0 is the unique point of intersection of $\widetilde{P}_\beta(t)$ and $\Psi_\alpha(t)$ on $[0, T]$.*

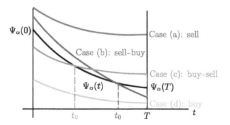

Figure 7.5   Optimal trading with linear $\ell(\cdot), h(\cdot)$ when $\widetilde{P}_\beta(t) = P(0)e^{(\mu-\beta)t}$ and $N(t) = N_\alpha(t)$

(d)   If $P(0) < e^{(\beta-\mu)T}\Psi_\alpha(T)$ and (2) holds, or $P(0) < \Psi_\alpha(0)$ and (1) holds, then $v_*(t) = v$ for all t.

See Figure 7.5 for an illustration of all four possible strategies.

7.4   PoS trading – a mean field model

We consider the question (3) in this section. In the previous sections, we study the optimal strategy for each individual miner, assuming that all other miners will 'cooperate' with her (except that no shorting is allowed). This assumption seems to be too optimistic. As mentioned in part (c) in the introduction, there are also investors or speculators participating in the PoS trading.

- In Sections 7.2–7.3, the price process (of each coin) is assumed to be exogenous. In the presence of investors and in view of their speculative nature, it is necessary to incorporate the market impact into the price formation.
- Interaction and competition among the miners and investors should play a role in each miner's decision. Thus, it is natural to formulate the PoS trading as a game building on the continuous-time control setting in Section 7.3.

With an exchange platform (e.g., Coinbase) for miner–investor tradings, we can define a notion of *equilibrium trading strategy* for a typical miner. This leads to the wealth evolution of the whole (miner) population from a mean field perspective. Refer to [32–34] for discussions on the game theoretical analysis of the PoW protocol. We would like to point out that the material in this section is preliminary (and novel), so there are many research problems in modelling, theory, and applications.

Recall that $\{N(t), 0 \leq t \leq T\}$ is the process of the volume of coins issued by the PoS blockchain. There are K miners, indexed by $k \in [K]$. For each miner k, $\{X_k(t), 0 \leq t \leq T\}$ (with $X_k(0) = x_k$) denotes the process of the number of coins that miner k holds, and $\{v_k(t), 0 \leq t \leq T\}$ denotes miner k's trading strategy.

Let $\{Z(t), t \geq 0\}$ (with $Z(0) = z$) be the process of the number of coins that investors possess, with $X_k(t), Z(t) \geq 0$ and

$$\sum_{k=1}^{K} X_k(t) + Z(t) = N(t), \quad \text{for } 0 \leq t \leq T. \tag{7.36}$$

So there are only $N(t) - Z(t)$ coins committed in the PoS election. The dynamics of miner k's coin under trading is:

$$X_k'(t) = v_k(t) + \frac{N'(t)}{N(t) - Z(t)} X_k(t) \quad \text{for} \quad 0 \le t \le \tau_k \wedge T := \mathscr{T}_k, \tag{7.37}$$

where $\tau_k := \inf\{t > 0 : X_k(t) = 0\}$. We set $X_k(t) = X_k(\mathscr{T}_k)$ for $t > \mathscr{T}_k$. If we take $Z(t) \equiv 0$ (no investors), the dynamics (7.37) reduces to (7.24). Equations (7.36)–(7.37) imply that $\sum_{k=1}^{K} v_k(t) + Z'(t) = 0$, which can be viewed as a clearing house condition. It simply yields

$$Z(t) = Z(0) - \int_0^t \sum_{k=1}^{K} v_k(s) ds. \tag{7.38}$$

Central to each miner's decision is the price process $\{P(t), t \ge 0\}$ of each (unit) of coin. The modern trading theory postulates a market impact structure underlying the price. That is, the asset price is affected by the trading volume. For ease of presentation, we adopt the linear price impact, i.e., the Almgren–Chriss model [35]:

$$P(t) = P(0) + \sigma B(t) - \eta(Z(t) - Z(0)), \tag{7.39}$$

where $\{B(t), t \ge 0\}$ is the standard Brownian motion, $\sigma > 0$ is the volatility, and $\eta > 0$ is the market impact parameter. Refer to [36, Chapter 3] for background, and [37–39] for other market impact models.

Recall that $b_k(t)$ is the (units of) risk-free asset that miner k holds at time t, and r is the risk-free rate. Here, all K miners and investors can trade coins on the exchange platform, whereas each miner can only exchange cash with an external source. For each miner k, the process of consumption $\{c_k(t), 0 \le t \le T\}$ evolves as

$$dc_k(t) = rb_k(t)dt - db_k(t) - P(t)v_k(t)dt - N'(t)L\left(\frac{v_k(t)}{N'(t)}\right)dt, \quad 0 \le t \le \mathscr{T}_k, \tag{C1}$$

where $L(\cdot)$ is an even function, increasing on $\mathbb{R}_+$, strictly convex and asymptotically super-linear. Compared to (C1) in Section 7.3, the additional term $-N'(t)L\left(\frac{v_k(t)}{N'(t)}\right)$ stands for the transaction cost which depends not only on the traded volume $v_k(t)dt$ but also the total volume $N'(t)dt$ (see [36, p. 43, (3.3)]). The quadratic cost $L(x) = \rho|x|^2$ with $\rho > 0$ corresponds to the original Almgren–Chriss model, which we will mostly stick to. We also impose the no shorting constraint:

$$b_k(0) = 0, \quad b_k(t) \ge 0 \text{ for } 0 \le t \le \mathscr{T}_k, \quad 0 \le X_k(t) \le N(t) \text{ for } 0 \le t \le \mathscr{T}_k. \tag{C2}$$

Set $b_k(t) = b_k(\mathscr{T}_k)$ and $v_k(t) = 0$ for $t > \mathscr{T}_k$.

Miner's strategy if $Z(\cdot)$ is known. It is easy to see from (7.39) that the price $P(t)$ (up to noise) only depends on the investor holdings $Z(t)$, or equivalently all the miners' holdings $\sum_{k=1}^{K} X_k(t)$. Here, suppose that each miner k 'knows' the number of coins that the investors hold. As in (7.25), the objective of miner k is:

$$
\sup_{\{(v_k(t),b_k(t))\}} J(v_k, b_k) := \mathbb{E}\bigg\{ \int_0^{\mathcal{T}_k} e^{-\beta_k t} [dc_k(t) + \ell_k(X_k(t))dt]
$$

$$
+ e^{-\beta_k \mathcal{T}_k} [b_k(\mathcal{T}_k) + h_k(X_k(\mathcal{T}_k))] \bigg\} \tag{7.40}
$$

subject to (7.37), (7.39), (C1), *and* (C2).

Assuming that all the miners are *interchangeable* (which assumes a homogenous miner population), we drop the subscript 'k' in (7.40), and the objective of a *typical* miner is:

$$
U(x) := \sup_{\{(v(t),b(t))\}} J(v, b) := \mathbb{E}\bigg\{ \int_0^{\mathcal{T}} e^{-\beta t} [dc(t) + \ell(X(t))dt]
$$

$$
+ e^{-\beta \mathcal{T}} [b(\mathcal{T}) + h(X(\mathcal{T}))] \bigg\} \tag{7.41}
$$

subject to $X'(t) = v(t) + \dfrac{N'(t)}{N(t) - Z(t)} X(t), \; X(0) = x,$ (C0)

$$
dc(t) = rb(t)dt - db(t) - P(t)v(t)dt - N'(t)L\left(\frac{v(t)}{N'(t)}\right)dt,
$$
(C1)

$$
b(0) = 0, \; b(t) \geq 0 \text{ and } 0 \leq X(t) \leq N(t), \tag{C2}
$$

$$
P(t) = P(0) + \sigma B(t) - \eta(Z(t) - Z(0)), \tag{C3}
$$

where (C0) is a repeat of the state dynamics in (7.37), and (C3) is the price dynamics in (7.39). Compared to (7.26), the volume constraint $|v(t)| \leq \bar{v}$ for $\bar{v} > 0$ is removed; instead the transaction cost $-N'(t)L\left(\frac{v(t)}{N'(t)}\right)dt$ is introduced in the budget constraint (C1). This way, the miner's strategy will no longer be a bang–bang control but depend on the specific market impact mechanism.

Let

$$
\tilde{P}_\beta(t) := e^{-\beta t}\mathbb{E}P(t) = e^{-\beta t}[P(0) - \eta(Z(t) - Z(0))] \quad \text{and} \quad \tilde{P}(t) := \tilde{P}_0(t).
$$
(7.42)

The same argument as in (7.28) and (7.29) shows that the consumption–investment problem (7.41) is separable:

$$
U(x) := \sup_{\{(v,b)\}} J(v, b) = \sup_b J_1(b) + \sup_v J_2(v),
$$

where $J_1(b) := (r - \beta) \int_0^{\mathcal{T}} e^{-\beta t} b(t) dt$ and

$$J_2(v) := \int_0^{\mathcal{T}} \left[-\widetilde{P}_\beta(t) v(t) - e^{-\beta t} N'(t) L\left(\frac{v(t)}{N'(t)}\right) + e^{-\beta t} \ell(X(t)) \right] dt + e^{-\beta \mathcal{T}} h(X(\mathcal{T})).$$

Again suppose $\beta \geq r$. Then $\sup_b J_1(b) = 0$ with the optimality binding at $b_*(t) = 0$ for all t. So the problem (7.26) is reduced to

$$U(x) = \sup_v J_2(v) \quad \text{subject to} \quad \text{(C0), (C2')}, \tag{7.43}$$

where (C2') is (C2) without the constraints on $b(\cdot)$.

Next we argue by dynamic programming, and let

$$v(t, x) := \sup_{\{v(s), s \geq t\}} \int_t^{\mathcal{T}} \left[-\widetilde{P}_\beta(s) v(s) - e^{-\beta s} N'(s) L\left(\frac{v(s)}{N'(s)}\right) + e^{-\beta s} \ell(X(s)) \right] dt$$

$$+ e^{-\beta \mathcal{T}} h(X(\mathcal{T}))$$

$$\text{subject to} \quad X'(s) = v(s) + \frac{N'(s)}{N(s) - Z(s)} X(s), \ X(t) = x,$$

$$0 \leq X(s) \leq N(s),$$

so $U(x) = v(0, x)$. Let $Q := \{(t, x) : 0 \leq t < T, \ 0 < x < N(t)\}$. Under some suitable conditions, v is the unique viscosity solution to the HJB equation:

$$\begin{cases} \partial_t v + e^{-\beta t} \ell(x) + \frac{xN'(t)}{N(t)} \partial_x v \\ \qquad + \sup_v \left\{ v(\partial_x v - \widetilde{P}_\beta(t)) - e^{-\beta t} N'(t) L\left(\frac{v}{N'(t)}\right) \right\} = 0 \quad \text{in } Q, \\ v(T, x) = e^{-\beta T} h(x), \\ v(t, 0) = e^{-\beta t} h(0), \ v(t, N(t)) = e^{-\beta t} h(N(t)). \end{cases}$$

By optimizing $v \to v(\partial_x v - \widetilde{P}_\beta(t)) - e^{-\beta t} N'(t) L\left(\frac{v}{N'(t)}\right)$, we get

$$v_* = N'(t)(L')^{-1} \left(e^{\beta t} \partial_x v - \widetilde{P}(t)\right).$$

This yields the following nonlinear PDE:

$$\begin{cases} \partial_t v + e^{-\beta t} \ell(x) + \frac{xN'(t)}{N(t) - Z(t)} \partial_x v \\ \qquad + e^{-\beta t} N'(t) \left\{ (e^{\beta t} \partial_x v - \widetilde{P}(t))(L')^{-1}(e^{\beta t} \partial_x v - \widetilde{P}(t)) \right. \\ \qquad\qquad \left. - L\left((L')^{-1}(e^{\beta t} \partial_x v - \widetilde{P}(t))\right) \right\} = 0 \quad \text{in } Q, \\ v(T, x) = e^{-\beta T} h(x), \\ v(t, 0) = e^{-\beta t} h(0), \ v(t, N(t)) = e^{-\beta t} h(N(t)). \end{cases} \tag{7.44}$$

When $L(x) = \rho x^2$, the PDE (7.44) specialises to

$$
\begin{cases}
\partial_t v + e^{-\beta t}\ell(x) + \frac{xN'(t)}{N(t)-Z(t)}\partial_x v + \frac{e^{\beta t}N'(t)}{4\rho}(\partial_x v - \widetilde{P}_\beta(t))^2 = 0 & \text{in } Q, \\
v(T,x) = e^{-\beta T}h(x), \\
v(t,0) = e^{-\beta t}h(0), \quad v(t,N(t)) = e^{-\beta t}h(N(t)),
\end{cases}
\tag{7.45}
$$

with the optimal strategy $v_*(t,x) = \frac{N'(t)}{2\rho}\left(e^{\beta t}\partial_x v(t,x) - \widetilde{P}(t)\right)$. To simplify the presentation, we assume the quadratic cost (and (7.45)) from now on.

Mean field strategy. Assume that the distribution of the miners by their coin holdings is approximated by $m_0(x)dx$ at time $t = 0$. The goal is to find an equilibrium trading strategy $v^{eq}(t \mid m_0)$, or simply $v^{eq}(t)$, which can be viewed as the averaged trading strategy among all the miners.

Now let us describe the mean field model.

1. Since there are K miners, by (7.38), the investors' equilibrium holdings are:

$$
Z^{eq}(t) = Z(0) - K\int_0^t v^{eq}(s)ds,
\tag{7.46}
$$

2. Given $Z^{eq}(\cdot)$, the miner's optimal strategy is

$$
v_*^{eq}(t,x) = \frac{N'(t)}{2\rho}(e^{\beta t}\partial_x v(t,x) - \widetilde{P}(t)),
\tag{7.47}
$$

    where v is the solution to (7.45) with $Z(t) = Z^{eq}(t)$.

3. The feedback control of a (typical) miner is $X'(t) = v_*^{eq}(t, X(t)) + \frac{N'(t)}{N(t)-Z^{eq}(t)}X(t)$. Hence, the density of the miners by their coin holdings solves the continuity equation:

$$
\partial_t m + \partial_x \left(\left(v_*^{eq}(t,x) + \frac{xN'(t)}{N(t)-Z^{eq}(t)} \right) m \right) = 0, \quad m(0,x) = m_0(x).
\tag{7.48}
$$

4. The equilibrium trading strategy $v^{eq}(t)$ satisfies the fixed point equation:

$$
\int v_*^{eq}(t,x)m(t,x)dx = v^{eq}(t).
\tag{7.49}
$$

If the mean field model (7.46)–(7.49) is well-posed (i.e., has a unique solution), then $m(t,\cdot)$ represents the wealth distribution of the whole miner population at time t. To illustrate, Figure 7.6 shows the wealth evolution of the miners with initial shares uniformly distributed on $x \in [20, 30]$. Observe that the wealth distribution spreads out and shifts to the left over the time, which implies decentralisation of the PoS protocol. While the PoS protocol alone does not lead to decentralisation, allowing trading in the PoS protocol yields decentralisation – this is a manifestation of the market power.

The problem now is to make rigorous such defined mean field model. By injecting (7.47) into (7.49), and then into (7.46), (7.45), and (7.48), we get the mean field game form:

$$
\begin{cases}
\partial_t v + H(t,x,\partial_x v, \partial_x v(\cdot,\cdot), m(\cdot,\cdot)) = 0, \\
\partial_t m + \partial_p H(t,x,\partial_x v, \partial_x v(\cdot,\cdot), m(\cdot,\cdot)) = 0 = 0, \\
m(t,0) = m_0(x), \quad v(T,x) = e^{-\beta T}h(x),
\end{cases}
\tag{7.50}
$$

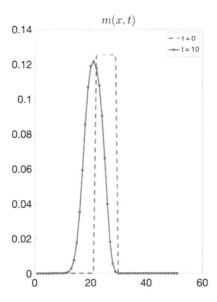

Figure 7.6   Wealth evolution of the whole miner population

with

$$H(t,x,p,Q,m) := e^{-\beta t}\ell(x) + +\frac{e^{\beta t}N'(t)}{4\rho}(p - \widetilde{P}_\beta(t))^2$$

$$+ \frac{2\rho x N'(t)}{2\rho(N(t) - Z(0)) + K\int_0^t N'(s)\int(e^{\beta s}Q(s,x) - \widetilde{P}(s))m(s,x)dxds}p, \quad (7.51)$$

where

$$\widetilde{P}_\beta(t) = e^{-\beta t}\left[P(0) + \eta K\int_0^t v^{\mathrm{eq}}(s)ds\right], \quad (7.52)$$

and $v^{\mathrm{eq}}(\cdot)$ satisfies

$$\frac{N'(t)}{2\rho}\left[e^{\beta t}\int \partial_x v(t,x)m(t,x)dx - P(0) - \eta K\int_0^t v^{\mathrm{eq}}(s)ds\right] = v^{\mathrm{eq}}(t). \quad (7.53)$$

Combining (7.52) and (7.53), we have that $\widetilde{P}_\beta(t)$ (resp. $\widetilde{P}(t)$) is a function of Q and m (i.e., $\partial_x v(\cdot, \cdot)$ and $m(\cdot, \cdot)$).

The system of equations (7.50) is a first-order mean field game with *non-local* and *non-separable* Hamiltonian. It does not seem to have been studied before. One possible idea to prove the wellposedness of (7.50) is to (1) add viscosity terms ($\varepsilon\Delta v$, $\varepsilon\Delta m$) to the equations and study the corresponding second-order mean field games (see [40]); (2) pass to the limit $\varepsilon \to 0$ by vanishing viscosity (see [41,42]). The analysis of the equations (7.50) may (probably) be very involved, and we leave it open.

7.5   Conclusion

This chapter presents and surveys recent progress on trading and wealth evolution in the PoS protocol under various settings (discrete, continuous, volume constraint, transaction cost, etc.) Below we provide a few open problems and future directions of research.

1. In Section 7.4, we present a mean field model to study the wealth distribution of the miners under the PoS protocol. This leads to a mean field game with non-local and non-separable Hamiltonian. Prove that (7.50) have a (unique) solution.
2. We have seen from Figure 7.6 that the mean field model yields decentralisation. Is it possible to prove a quantitative result to support this observation?
3. In Sections 7.2–7.4, we consider the optimal strategy of the miner assuming that $\delta_k(1 + r_{\text{free}}) \leq 1$ or $\beta \geq r$, i.e., risk-averse. What's the miner's optimal strategy if she is more risk-seeking (such that $\delta_k(1 + r_{\text{free}}) > 1$ or $\beta < r$)?
4. We assume a fixed miner population, i.e., K is fixed. In practice, some existing miners may quit, and some new miners may join at random times. What happens if there is a dynamic miner population (or K is varying over the time)?
5. We assume that the reward R_t is deterministic and is from the blockchain. But in many PoS blockchains (e.g., Ethereum), revenue for the miners comes mostly from the transaction fees. Thus, the 'reward' is from the user–miner interface (part (a)), and the users can also be the investors. What will be the miner's strategy, and the wealth evolution if we take the user–miner connection into account?
6. In Sections 7.2 and 7.4, we consider the wealth evolution of a homogenous population – that is, all the miners solve the same optimisation problem. What are the corresponding results for a heterogeneous miner population (e.g., with different risk sensitivity)?
7. We assume that the miners maximise some objective to find the best strategy. In practice, when people make decisions, they will adopt 'rational' strategy rather than the 'optimal' strategy. This leads to the idea of *bounded rationality* [43], which can be formulated in Bayesian languages. What is the miner's rational strategy?

Acknowledgements

We thank David Yao for collaborations which lead to a large part of the material presented in this chapter. We thank Erhan Bayraktar for pointing out the reference [40] on the mean field game with non-separable Hamiltonian. We also thank Siyao Jiang and Yuhang Wu for help in numerical experiments. This research is supported by

NSF Grants DMS-2113779 and DMS-2206038, and a start-up grant at Columbia University.

References

[1] Nakamoto S. Bitcoin: a peer-to-peer electronic cash system. *Decentralized Business Review*. 2008;21260.

[2] Wood G. Ethereum: a secure decentralised generalised transaction ledger. *Ethereum Project Yellow Paper*. 2014;151:1–32.

[3] McGhin T, Choo KKR, Liu CZ, *et al*. Blockchain in healthcare applications: research challenges and opportunities. *Journal of Network and Computer Applications*. 2019;135:62–75.

[4] Tanwar S, Parekh K, and Evans R. Blockchain-based electronic healthcare record system for healthcare 4.0 applications. *Journal of Information Security and Applications*. 2020;50:102407.

[5] Chod J, Trichakis N, Tsoukalas G, *et al*. On the financing benefits of supply chain transparency and blockchain adoption. *Management Science*. 2020;66(10):4378–4396.

[6] Saberi S, Kouhizadeh M, Sarkis J, *et al*. Blockchain technology and its relationships to sustainable supply chain management. *International Journal of Production Research*. 2019;57(7):2117–2135.

[7] Dowling M. Is non-fungible token pricing driven by cryptocurrencies? *Finance Research Letters*. 2022;44:102097.

[8] Wang Q, Li R, Wang Q, *et al*. Non-fungible token (NFT): overview, evaluation, opportunities and challenges. 2021. ArXiv:2105.07447.

[9] Mccrank J and Nishant N. Fidelity readies new spot bitcoin ETF filing, report says. 2023. Available at https://www.reuters.com/technology/fidelity-preparing-submit-spot-bitcoin-etf-filing-block-2023-06-27/.

[10] King S and Nadal S. Ppcoin: peer-to-peer crypto-currency with proof-of-stake. 2012. Available at https://decred.org/research/king2012.pdf.

[11] Mora C, Rollins RL, Taladay K, *et al*. Bitcoin emissions alone could push global warming above 2 C. *Nature Climate Change*. 2018;8(11):931–933.

[12] Platt M, Sedlmeir J, Platt D, *et al*. The energy footprint of blockchain consensus mechanisms beyond proof-of-work. In: *IEEE 21st International Conference on Software Quality, Reliability and Security Companion (QRS-C)*; 2021. p. 1135–1144.

[13] Chiu J and Koeppl TV. The economics of cryptocurrency: Bitcoin and beyond. *Canadian Journal of Economics*. 2022;55(4):1762–1798.

[14] Cong LW, He Z, and Li J. Decentralized mining in centralized pools. *The Review of Financial Studies*. 2021;34(3):1191–1235.

[15] Saleh F. Volatility and welfare in a crypto economy. 2019;SSRN:3235467.

[16] Wickens K. 'The Merge' to end cryptocurrency mining on gaming GPUs won't come until 2022. 2021. Available at https://www.pcgamer.com/the-merge-to-end-cryptocurrency-mining-on-gaming-gpus-wont-come-until-2022.

[17]   Brown-Cohen J, Narayanan A, Psomas A, *et al*. Formal barriers to longest-chain proof-of-stake protocols. In: *Proceedings of the 2019 ACM Conference on Economics and Computation*; 2019. p. 459–473.

[18]   Chung H and Shi E. Foundations of transaction fee mechanism design. In: *Proceedings of the 2023 Annual ACM-SIAM Symposium on Discrete Algorithms (SODA)*. SIAM, Philadelphia, PA; 2023. p. 3856–3899.

[19]   Tang W and Yao DD. Transaction fee mechanism for Proof-of-Stake protocol. 2023. ArXiv:2308.13881.

[20]   Bagaria V, Dembo A, Kannan S, *et al*. Proof-of-stake longest chain protocols: security vs predictability. 2019. ArXiv:1910.02218.

[21]   Daian P, Pass R, and Shi E. Snow white: robustly reconfigurable consensus and applications to provably secure proof of stake. In: *International Conference on Financial Cryptography and Data Security*; 2019. p. 23–41.

[22]   Kiayias A, Russell A, David B, *et al*. Ouroboros: a provably secure proof-of-stake blockchain protocol. In: *Annual International Cryptology Conference*; 2017. p. 357–388.

[23]   Saleh F. Blockchain without waste: proof-of-stake. *The Review of Financial Studies*. 2021;34(3):1156–1190.

[24]   Pemantle R. A survey of random processes with reinforcement. *Probability Surveys*. 2007;4:1–79.

[25]   Durrett R. *Probability—Theory and Examples*. Cambridge: Cambridge University Press; 2019.

[26]   Roşu I and Saleh F. Evolution of shares in a proof-of-stake cryptocurrency. *Management Science*. 2021;67(2):661–672.

[27]   Tang W. Stability of shares in the Proof of Stake protocol – concentration and phase transitions. 2022. ArXiv:2206.02227.

[28]   Tang W and Yao DD. Polynomial voting rules. 2022. ArXiv:2206.10105.

[29]   John K, Rivera TJ, and Saleh F. Equilibrium staking levels in a proof-of-stake blockchain. 2021. Available at SSRN 3965599.

[30]   Buterin V. Toward a 12-Second Block Time. 2014. Available at https://blog.ethereum.org/2014/07/11/toward-a-12-second-block-time.

[31]   Tang W and Yao DD. Trading under the Proof-of-Stake Protocol—a continuous-time control approach. *Mathematical Finance*. 2023. Available at https://onlinelibrary.wiley.com/doi/10.1111/mafi.12403. arXiv:2207.12581.

[32]   Bertucci C, Bertucci L, Lasry JM, *et al*. Mean field game approach to Bitcoin mining. 2020. ArXiv:2004.08167.

[33]   Li Z, Reppen AM, and Sircar R. A mean field games model for cryptocurrency mining. 2019. ArXiv:1912.01952.

[34]   Prat J and Walter B. An equilibrium model of the market for Bitcoin mining. *Journal of Political Economy*. 2021;129(8):2415–2452.

[35]   Almgren R and Chriss N. Optimal execution of portfolio transactions. *Journal of Risk*. 2001;3:5–40.

[36]   Guéant O. The financial mathematics of market liquidity. *Chapman & Hall/CRC Financial Mathematics Series*. London: CRC Press; 2016. From optimal execution to market making.

[37]   Donier J and Bonart J. A million metaorder analysis of market impact on the Bitcoin. *Market Microstructure and Liquidity*. 2015;1(02):1550008.

[38]   Gatheral J and Schied A. Optimal trade execution under geometric Brownian motion in the Almgren and Chriss framework. *International Journal of Theoretical and Applied Finance*. 2011;14(3):353–368.

[39]   Tóth B, Lemperiere Y, Deremble C, *et al.* Anomalous price impact and the critical nature of liquidity in financial markets. *Physical Review X*. 2011;1(2):021006.

[40]   Ambrose DM. Existence theory for non-separable mean field games in Sobolev spaces. *Indiana University Mathematics Journal*. 2022;71(2):611–647.

[41]   Cardaliaguet P, and Graber PJ. Mean field games systems of first order. *ESAIM Control, Optimisation and Calculus of Variations*. 2015;21(3):690–722.

[42]   Tang W and Zhang YP. The convergence rate of vanishing viscosity approximations for mean field games. 2023. ArXiv:2303.14560.

[43]   Simon HA. Bounded rationality. In: *Utility and Probability*, Palgrave Macmillan: London; 1990. p. 15–18.

Chapter 8
Proof-of-Stake blockchain security against quantum computing
Muhammed F. Esgin[1]

This chapter discusses the effects of quantum computing technologies on the security of blockchain systems, particularly focusing on Proof-of-Stake (PoS) blockchains. This brief discussion is then followed by a concrete protocol example that can withstand quantum computing threats. This latter part of the chapter is largely based on the work of Esgin *et al.* [1].

The goal of *quantum computing* is to exploit the rules of *quantum mechanics* to build ultra-powerful computers that have the potential to carry out certain computations exponentially faster than classical computers we use today. Such quantum computers use *qubits* that can be in a superposition of multiple values rather than simply being equal to 0 or 1.

In his seminal work [2] in 1994, Peter Shor introduced a *quantum algorithm* that can *efficiently* (i.e., in polynomial time) solve the two fundamental computational problems on which today's cryptography is built: integer factorization problem (IFP) and discrete logarithm problem (DLP). IFP- and DLP-based cryptographic schemes are used everywhere today, including to secure the Internet and various blockchain systems. PoS-based solutions are no exceptions, and prominent examples such as Algorand, Cardano, and Dfinity rely on variants of these two security assumptions that are susceptible to quantum attacks. The good news for everyone (perhaps unknowingly) relying on classical cryptography is that *large-scale* quantum computers are needed to break today's classical cryptography. Of course, nobody knows when exactly such a large-scale quantum computer would be available, but there has been significant progress in scaling up quantum computers. A particularly exciting news was recently shared by IBM where they released their goal to build a 100K qubit quantum computer by 2033 [3].

Let us try to understand the impact of quantum computing threats on the security of a PoS blockchain system that solely relies on classical cryptographic assumptions. This example is similar to what is described in the introduction of [4]. Imagine at some point in future, say time T, an adversary $\mathscr{A}$ builds a large-scale quantum computer capable of breaking classical cryptography. Then, from the public keys of the users,

[1] Faculty of Information Technology, Monash University, Australia

the adversary can compute all user secret keys by breaking classical cryptography. Note that even if *forward-security* is in play (i.e., short-lived secret keys derived from a master secret key are used at each time period), the adversary can compute the master secret key from the master public key (using a quantum computer) and then derive all individual secret keys for all time periods including those in the past. At this point, the most fundamental security assumption of PoS blockchain is broken: the adversary controls *all* parties involved in the system at all times, so there is no honest majority of stakeholders. The adversary can then create its own blockchain or fork the existing one as it desires. Note that since there is no Proof-of-Work involved, the adversary can easily outrun the honest chain and get its (adversarial) chain accepted globally.

There are various ways that can be employed to secure cryptographic algorithms against quantum computing. In fact, NIST has been running a standardization process [5] to select *post-quantum* (i.e., *quantum-safe*) algorithms for basic cryptographic functionalities, namely encryption and digital signatures. Several algorithms were selected for standardization in 2022. These post-quantum cryptography (PQC) algorithms still employ classical means of computation (i.e., using bits). However, the underlying computational security problems are different from IFP and DLP, and are believed to be secure against quantum computing attacks.

Two particularly strong candidates to achieve post-quantum security are hash-based and lattice-based cryptography. Hash-based cryptography, in particular, is widely believed to be the safest PQC approach due to its lack of mathematical structure that may be exploited by an adversary. However, this lack of mathematical structure also makes it more difficult to build advanced cryptographic tools based solely on hash functions. Lattice-based cryptography, on the other hand, exhibits a variety of algebraic properties that can be used for various reasons. Overall, a combination of these two approaches often offers the best tradeoffs in terms of security, efficiency, and functionalities. All PQC schemes selected for standardization by NIST so far are based on lattices and/or hash functions.

Let us know to start looking into the main topic of this chapter, namely realising a blockchain leader election protocol efficiently with post-quantum security using basic cryptographic tools. The main tool required for this purpose is a Verifiable Random Function (VRF) and we describe how to construct a VRF variant, called indexed VRF (iVRF), using simple cryptographic primitives in a way that suffices for blockchain leader election. The rest of this chapter is largely based on [1].

8.1   Blockchain leader election and post-quantum VRFs

A group of block creators work collectively in a blockchain system to produce and append new blocks to the blockchain. In such systems, consensus protocols are employed to agree on how blocks should be organised in sequence. A major part of a consensus protocol is to elect a leader, who determines the new block to be appended to the blockchain, and, in some cases, to additionally elects a committee, who checks the validity of the newly produced blocks. For example, in the setting of Proof-of-Stake consensus protocols, the leader is elected among the stakeholders with a probability proportional to the amount of owned stakes.

The security of a blockchain system critically relies on the property that leaders are elected to be one of the honest users that may not be easily compromised by an attacker. To accomplish such security requirements, different cryptographic mechanisms are employed by various blockchain environments, e.g., [6–10]. In the case of Algorand, that aims for an environment-friendly solution, a cryptographic sortition technique is employed, where a user self-determines if they are elected as a leader using a cryptographic tool, known as a *Verifiable Random Function (VRF)* [11]. The goal of a VRF is to introduce a method for each user to produce a *unique* lottery ticket whose validity can be publicly checked via a cryptographic proof provided by the user. If a user has a winning ticket, they publish the ticket along with a certifying proof, which together constitute the VRF output. Such a VRF use in consensus protocols supports high performance and scalability, and allows the Algorand ecosystem to support millions of users. VRFs are also used as a core cryptographic tool in other blockchain systems including Dfinity [9], Ouroboros Praos [6] (used in Cardano), Filecoin [12], and Rangers Protocol [13].

The VRF and signature schemes employed by Algorand, namely ECVRF [14] and Ed25519 [15], rely on the difficulty of the discrete logarithm problem (DLP), which is vulnerable against quantum attacks as discussed before. In light of the catastrophic potential attacks described earlier in the chapter, it is security critical to migrate to post-quantum solutions, particularly for the consensus protocol part, to make sure at least that the security of prior rounds cannot be compromised. In fact, in recognition of the importance of post-quantum security, Algorand has recently introduced *post-quantum secure* state proofs.*

A major bottleneck against making Algorand-like consensus protocols post-quantum is the lack of an *efficient* post-quantum replacement of its VRF. Prior attempts [4,16,17] to construct practically efficient post-quantum VRFs have significant disadvantages compared to our solution as we discuss next.

Esgin *et al.* [4] introduced the first practical post-quantum VRF proposal, named LB-VRF. This scheme is based on (module) lattices and is relatively efficient for the lattice setting. More concretely, an LB-VRF proof costs about 5 KB, which is somewhat larger than an ordinary signature based on the same computational assumptions (at around 2.5–3 KB). A significant limitation of LB-VRF is being *few-time*, meaning that each VRF key pair may only be used to generate a few VRF outputs, particularly just one output for the most efficient instantiation. This limitation leads to practical issues because one has to come up with custom-designed methods to handle frequent key refreshing almost every round (i.e., every 5 s). Furthermore, the actual communication cost rises by the public key size to more than 8.3 KB as the new key needs to be communicated almost every round. Another lattice-based VRF proposal, named LaV, was recently introduced by Esgin *et al.* in [16]. Even though LaV is a standard

---

*See https://developer.algorand.org/docs/get-details/algorand_consensus/#state-proof-keys (accessed on July 26, 2022).

*Table 8.1   Performance comparison of our iVRF in Section 8.3.1 (with $N = 2^{18}$
evaluations) to other quantum-safe VRF proposals and
(non-quantum-safe) ECVRF. The sizes are given in bytes and the times
are in milliseconds. For ECVRF, we take the results reported in [17]. For
our iVRF, the VRF value can be computed from the proof and hence its
size is given as zero.*

	Sizes of			Runtimes of			Number of evaluations	Security basis
Scheme	**PK**	**Proof**	**VRF**	**Keygen**	**Eval**	**Verify**		
SL-VRF [17]	48	40,000	32	0.38	765.00	475.00	Unlimited block cipher	LowMC [19]
LaV [16]	6420	11,980	124	–	–	–	Unlimited	Lattices
LB-VRF [4]	3320	4940	84	0.33	3.10	1.30	1	Lattices
X-VRF [17]	64	2720	32	426,000	0.74	0.90	$N = 2^{18}$	Hash
iVRF [1]	32	608	0	<3087	0.01	0.02	$N = 2^{18}$	Hash
ECVRF [14]	32	80	32	0.05	0.10	0.10	Unlimited	Discrete log. (quantum-insecure)

VRF (i.e., can directly replace ECVRF used in Algorand in terms of functionality), its main drawback is the proof size of about 10 KB.

By employing hash functions, Buser *et al.* [17] introduced X-VRF, a post-quantum VRF construction based on the XMSS signature [18]. Like XMSS, this VRF proposal is stateful, but this limitation may not be a significant concern for blockchain applications (at least for its use in Algorand). The main drawback of X-VRF (compared to the iVRF solution to be described) is a significant communication overhead at about 3 KB. In [17], the authors also develop a standard VRF proposal, named SL-VRF, but the communication cost of SL-VRF is significantly larger, at about 40 KB. A performance summary of these existing VRF proposals is provided in Table 8.1.

In light of the above state of affairs for post-quantum VRFs, a natural question one can ask is as follows.

Do we really need a full VRF to realize an Algorand-like consensus? If not, what is precisely the tool needed for that purpose and how can we construct it from the most basic cryptographic primitives?

The simplicity, efficiency, sustainability, and (long-term) reliability properties are of significant importance as we are interested in a solution that (i) can be readily deployed into Algorand's network, (ii) does not require wasting natural resources, and (iii) offers the strongest security in the post-quantum era. As a result, the VRF solution, called iVRF, described in this chapter is based solely on hash functions.

Before going into more details of the solution, we present independent views on Bitcoin's, Algorand's, and our approaches to solving the leader election[†]/lottery problem on blockchain. These will be helpful in understanding our high-level approach without getting into technical details.

A view of Bitcoin's approach: A common feature of all three approaches that we discuss now is that the blockchain protocol generates a random "magic" number, say Q_n, at each protocol round n. In Bitcoin's approach, this magic number is used to select a random one-way function H_{Q_n} from a large family of hash functions. Then, the idea of Bitcoin's Proof-of-Work (PoW) approach is to have users race *real-time* to find a "lucky" input, x, that maps under H_{Q_n} to one of the target values such as $H_{Q_n}(x) < v$ for some threshold v. The main drawback, well-known in the community, is the tremendous energy consumption and the waste of resources due to the real-time racing as the more computational power one spends, the more chance they have in winning the race.

A view of Algorand's approach: Algorand aims to solve the unsustainability issue of Bitcoin's PoW by moving to a Proof-of-Stake (PoS)-based approach. In Algorand, users fix their key pairs in advance of participating in the consensus, say $(\mathsf{pk}_i, \mathsf{sk}_i)$ for user i. Effectively, fixing the keys seals everyone's fate in that now each user has an internal secret function H_{sk_i}, which they cannot change since the corresponding public key pk_i acts as its commitment. When the blockchain protocol generates the random magic number Q_n for round n, each user locally computes $H_{\mathsf{sk}_i}(Q_n)$ and checks whether the result is a "winning ticket." The probability of success in the latter check is based on the amount of stake one has. If the check is successful, they can generate a (zero-knowledge) proof to show that they are indeed a winner of the lottery for round n.

Views of our approach: Our approach in a way is a new look at a combination of the above two approaches. In particular, we first want to deviate from real-time racing in Bitcoin while still making use of the magic number Q_n to choose a random function H_{Q_n} at each block generation round. Since we have these functions chosen at each round without a particular user's control,[‡] what we do is simply ask every user (participating in the consensus) to commit to an input of their choice *in advance* of that round. In particular, at some round $t < n$ (or earlier), each user i commits to their input x_i on blockchain and simply wins the lottery if $H_{Q_n}(x_i) = v$ for a target value v. To prove that user i indeed won the lottery, they simply publish x_i and everyone

---

[†]We note that the high-level approaches we discuss (Bitcoin's, Algorand's, and ours) do not guarantee a *single* leader election (and hence, the term "leader election" is not used to mean "single leader election"). Thanks to the flexibility of the iVRF approach, if multiple potential leaders arise in our protocol, one can employ, for example, the techniques in Algorand (discussed in Section 8.5) to recognise one of them as the true leader.

[‡]Here, we are assuming the ideal case where Q_n is generated truly at random by some means. Of course, this is not possible to achieve in practice, but this issue is outside of our simplified discussion here. In the actual consensus protocol, the magic number can be generated similar to Algorand and our approach is flexible enough to support different ways to generate Q_n.

can straightforwardly check the claim by calculating $H_{Q_n}(x_i)$. Overall, for improved efficiency, we ask users to commit to a set of inputs $x_{i,j}$'s early on and use the nth value $x_{i,n}$ at round n, where the use of the nth value can be verified so that users do not get to choose between multiple $x_{i,j}$'s.

A "dual" view of our approach is that each user i commits to a one-time function $H_{x_{i,n}}$ for each round n in advance, and just evaluates $H_{x_{i,n}}(Q_n)$ to check lottery winning similar to Algorand. However, the major difference of our approach from Algorand's is that we do not require a (zero-knowledge) proof to show the validity of computation and simply ask users to publish $H_{x_{i,n}}$. The latter approach of ours significantly simplifies the functionality required from the cryptographic tool to accomplish leader election and enables a very efficient instantiation from the most basic primitives. We discuss our approach in more detail in Section 8.1.2.

Forward security: Many blockchain systems such as Algorand and Ouroboros Praos [6] employ *forward-secure* digital signatures to maintain the security of prior rounds in case some stored user key is compromised at some point. Existing *generic* approaches to achieving forward security can be straightforwardly realized in the post-quantum setting by instantiating the underlying ordinary signatures using post-quantum ones.

One such generic approach is known as the MMM approach [20]. In the MMM "sum" composition, a user creates N key pairs $(pk_1, sk_1), \ldots, (pk_N, sk_N)$ of an ordinary signature and constructs a Merkle tree using the public keys as the tree leaves. To sign a message at a particular time i, the user communicates pk_i and an authentication path in addition to a signature on the actual message.

An alternative generic approach, adopted by Algorand, works as follows. A user first generates a key pair (mpk, msk) of an ordinary signature, and similarly round key pairs $(pk_1, sk_1), \ldots, (pk_N, sk_N)$. Then, each round public key is signed with msk, denoted as σ_i', and, at a round i, the user communicates (σ_i', pk_i) in addition to the signature on the actual message. Therefore, the communication difference between the Algorand's approach vs the MMM approach is the cost of a signature (σ_i') vs an authentication path. The smallest signature length among the schemes selected for standardization by NIST for Post-Quantum Cryptography[§] is at about 700 bytes, which means even an authentication path for a Merkle tree with 2^{20} leaves is cheaper than such a post-quantum signature. Note that the latter Algorand approach also incurs more computation due to signing of round public keys.

Another alternative approach to constructing forward-secure post-quantum signature could be to use a post-quantum Identity-Based Signature (IBS) scheme. In this case, the IBS master secret key is used to derive signing keys for the round keys, where each round is assigned a different ID. The master secret key is deleted and round keys are stored and used to sign messages, and then each one is deleted as the corresponding round period expires. It is well known that such IBS can be constructed from a two-level Hierarchical Identity-Based Encryption (HIBE) scheme. An improved variant of the post-quantum lattice-based LATTE HIBE scheme [21] and

---

[§] https://csrc.nist.gov/Projects/post-quantum-cryptography/

its practical implementation are reported in a recent work [22]. However, the user private keys in the latter scheme are already longer than 3 KB (even for a one-level HIBE), and signatures will be even longer. This approach to forward security, therefore, leads to a longer communication cost compared to an MMM-based solution, which can be instantiated with communication of less than 2.2 KB for each message signed using the Falcon signature scheme [23]. We further note that Algorand's approach described earlier is an application of a folklore generic IBS construction via certification described, e.g., in [24]. Overall, in the post-quantum setting, the MMM approach already stands out as one of the best options and we can efficiently combine it with iVRF.

8.1.1 Summary of results

Our main result covered in this chapter is a simple, efficient, sustainable, and post-quantum solution to blockchain leader election problem. Although this solution is based on simple cryptographic tools, the insights to develop this solution are not obvious as they require a new formal treatment of VRFs. Hence, we start by formalizing the concrete VRF requirements for the leader election problem, specifically tailored to the blockchain setting. This leads to notions of (many-time) indexed VRF (iVRF) and authenticated iVRF with forward security ("authenticated MT-iVRF" or "authenticated iVRF," in short). The former is targeted at the blockchain leader election problem alone, while the latter combines all requirements to accomplish an Algorand-like consensus, where a forward-secure signature is needed. We believe these definitions capture the requirements in a real-life blockchain setting more closely, particularly matching the sequential (i.e., "indexed") nature of blockchain protocols.

Then, we describe our solutions for (many-time) iVRF and authenticated iVRF that build on a cryptographic hash function, ordinary (t-time) signature (for a parameter t), and pseudorandom generator (PRG), which can be built from a hash function. The security of these instantiations is proven (in [1]) assuming the existence of a secure hash function, digital signature, and PRG satisfying natural security requirements in the standard model (without random oracles). Since we do not require a random oracle, there is no complicated quantum random oracle model (QROM) analysis needed to argue security against (full) quantum adversaries.

iVRF constructions are implemented in C language on a standard computer with two different post-quantum signature schemes Falcon [23] and XMSS [18] (see Section 8.4 for more details). The performance results of iVRF together with a comparison with other practical post-quantum VRF proposals are provided in Table 8.1. In the table, we also include ECVRF (used by Algorand) performance results as a reference point even though ECVRF is not quantum-safe. We can see from the table that our iVRF enjoys the smallest sizes across all components compared to other post-quantum schemes. Its evaluation and verification times also outperform all proposals in the table, including ECVRF. The only downside of the iVRF approach is its key generation time linear in the total number of allowed evaluations N (arising due to a Merkle hash tree computation).

iVRF key generation is only a one-time computation per N evaluations that can be straightforwardly parallelized. Note that blockchain applications typically do not require very frequent such evaluations. Particularly, each evaluation (out of N) of iVRF is for one Algorand round, which takes about 4.5 s. Therefore, $N = 2^{23}$ evaluations suffice for $4.5 \cdot 2^{23}$ s, which is more than a year. As discussed in Section 8.4, for $N = 2^{23}$, even our full authenticated iVRF key generation (including the signature scheme's costs) takes about 10 h on a *single* core. This computation can be easily completed within a year by progressively running it whenever the device is turned on. Therefore, we believe the key generation time is not a significant limitation for blockchain applications of our approach, especially considering the significant gains of our solution in all other performance metrics. Note also that Algorand already requires a similar $O(N)$ key generation time as discussed further in Section 8.5.3. We now provide an overview of iVRF-based leader election solution and then discuss its advantages.

8.1.2   Overview of iVRF-based leader election

This section discusses an overview of how our final authenticated many-time iVRF (MT-iVRF) with forward security construction works in the Algorand setting. As mentioned earlier, our solution relies on having users commit to an ordered set of inputs (i.e., random strings), where the index of each input can be verified. We already know an excellent tool for this purpose: Merkle tree! More generally, we can use any (static) vector commitment.

Let us set N (a power of two) as a parameter that defines the number of rounds before a user key is refreshed. This parameter can be adjusted as desired, but users' (local) key generation time is linear in N due to the Merkle tree construction (see Table 8.1 for a concrete key generation time). We envision that key refreshments of all users are synchronized in the following sense. The time periods are split into *epochs*, composed of N consecutive rounds, and d rounds before an epoch starts, for a delay parameter d, nodes wanting to get involved in consensus in that epoch are expected to commit to their Merkle tree root on blockchain. If a user performs this commitment at a later time, they still need to wait for d rounds before being able to join the consensus and their Merkle tree still needs to have N leaves.[‖]

Let us now see how the key generation is done. A user, Alice, generates N pseudorandom values $x_{0,0}, \ldots, x_{N-1,0}$ from a random seed s using a PRG and computes $x_{i,j} = H^j(x_{i,0})$ (i.e., j recursive application of H on $x_{i,0}$) for $j = 1, \ldots, t - 1$ and $i = 0, \ldots, N - 1$, where t is a parameter denoting the number of iterations needed to reach agreement within a round (with high probability). She also generates N key pairs $(\mathsf{pk}_0, \mathsf{sk}_0), \ldots, (\mathsf{pk}_{N-1}, \mathsf{sk}_{N-1})$ of an ordinary (t-time) signature Σ using another random seed s' with the PRG. With these values, Alice now computes $x_{i,t} = H(x_{i,t-1}, \mathsf{pk}_i)$

[‖] If a user joins late, they can actually leave a bottom left sub-tree "empty" as that part will not be needed. For example, if a user joins 16 rounds late, then they can just pick the left-most tree node at level 4 (from the bottom) and $N - 16$ leaves to construct the Merkle tree. The sub-tree consisting of the first 16 leaves will not be needed.

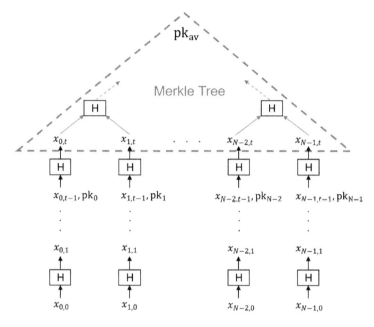

Figure 8.1   *Overall structure of our authenticated MT-iVRF with forward security.*
The term $x_{i,0}$'s are pseudorandom strings generated from a seed. The
pk_i's are (independent) public keys of an ordinary (t-time) signature.

and constructs a Merkle tree with $(x_{0,t}, \ldots, x_{N-1,t})$ as the leaves (depicted in Figure
8.1). Alice publishes the Merkle tree root on blockchain as her public key[¶] (or commitment) and keeps the seeds (s, s') and the intermediate Merkle tree nodes as her
secret key.

Now suppose we are at the jth iteration of the ith round of consensus in an epoch
that Alice is able to participate. Let n denote the actual block round number with
a "magic number" Q_n (note that $i \equiv n \bmod N$). To generate an authenticated iVRF
output on an input message μ to be authenticated/signed, she outputs $v = \mathsf{H}(x_{i,j}, Q_n)$
as the VRF value, $\sigma = \Sigma.\mathsf{Sign}_{\mathsf{sk}_i}(\mu)$ as the signature and $\pi = (x_{i,j}, \mathsf{pk}_i, \mathsf{AP}_i)$ as the
proof where AP_i denotes the Merkle tree authentication path w.r.t. the index i.[**]

Upon receiving an authenticated iVRF output $(v, \sigma, (x, \mathsf{pk}, \mathsf{AP}))$, the verification of iVRF works by first checking if $v = \mathsf{H}(x, Q_n)$ and v is below a threshold.
Furthermore, it checks that σ is a valid signature on μ under pk. Finally, for

---

[¶]To prevent Alice from publishing multiple Merkle roots, we can simply have a flag bit in each account
that states whether a user has published their Merkle root for that epoch. If that is the case, the verifiers
would reject subsequent Merkle root commitments on blockchain.
[**]In the actual protocol, Alice in fact does not need to communicate v since it can be computed from $x_{i,j}$
and the public Q_n.

$x' := \mathsf{H}(\mathsf{H}^j(x), \mathsf{pk})$, it checks that the Merkle tree root computed via x' and AP is equal to Alice's public key (or commitment) on blockchain for that epoch.

The intuition behind security is quite simple. Alice generated and committed to $x_{i,j}$'s before seeing Q_n. So, she cannot choose them to bias the output of $\mathsf{H}_{Q_n}(x_{i,n}) := \mathsf{H}(x_{i,j}, Q_n)$. Merkle tree commitment also ensures (computationally) that there is only a single valid $x_{i,j}$ that Alice can use at round n. Hence, assuming the randomness of Q_n, no user has a better advantage of winning the lottery. Of course, as in Algorand, we can adjust the winning condition based on the amount of stake to establish a PoS-based setting or the adjustment can be w.r.t. any publicly available information.

The forward security of our approach is inherited from the "sum" composition in the MMM paper [20]. As in Algorand, we assume that the adversary cannot corrupt a user within a round (i.e., in 4–5 s). To allow such corruption, we can simply ask users to build a Merkle tree with $N \cdot t$ leaves in the first place and consume t leaves at each round (even if the actual number of iterations in a round is less than t).

As mentioned earlier, our approach in general can work with any (static) vector commitment, which would replace the role of Merkle tree in our description. Therefore, our approach can benefit from further improvements in the context of vector commitments.

8.1.3   Advantages of iVRF-based leader election

Simplicity and flexibility: Our approach supports the use of any ordinary signature and any hash function (satisfying natural properties), which are already supported by almost all blockchain applications. These tools have been studied for a long time, and their post-quantum variants are either already standardized or in standardization. Thanks to its simplicity and flexibility, we believe our approach can be easily adapted to work for a range of blockchain systems, for example, Cardano, Dfinity, and Rangers Protocol. Note that our approach does not necessarily require the consensus protocol to be based on Proof-of-Stake, and it may be possible, for example, to adapt it to the Proof-of-Storage setting in Filecoin [12].

Confidence in (post-quantum) security: Hash functions (and symmetric primitives in general) are considered to be the most reliable solution to building quantum-safe cryptosystems. Therefore, our leader election solution is built on the safest alternative. For our full solution with authentication (using digital signatures), one can choose the best tradeoff between security and efficiency for a specific system thanks to the flexibility of our approach.

Sustainability: Our approach does not have any racing conditions and, therefore, does not lead to a tremendous waste of natural resources like Bitcoin.

Efficiency: Combined with one of the best solutions (i.e., the MMM approach) to achieving forward security in the post-quantum setting, the only additional communication cost of our iVRF-based approach is 32 bytes (i.e. the cost of sending the relevant round's $x_{i,j}$), which is a minimal cost one could expect to have. In comparison, combining an MMM-style forward-secure post-quantum signature with X-VRF [17], the smallest post-quantum VRF proposal, (under a common hash tree) would give an additional overhead due to the VRF functionality of about 2100 bytes. This overhead is almost two orders of magnitude more than the 32 byte overhead in our iVRF-based construction. We discuss the computational efficiency in Section 8.4 after introducing more details about the concrete digital signature.

We refer to the reader to [1] for formal definitions of iVRF and authenticated iVRF (that additionally employs a digital signature).

Outline of the rest of the chapter: We formally define the iVRF notions in Section 8.2, followed by their instantiations in Section 8.3. We analyze the performance of these schemes and provide implementation results in Section 8.4. Then, we discuss an application of our iVRF-based approach in Algorand in Section 8.5. We refer the reader to [1] for security analyses, and standard definitions of hash functions, Merkle tree, PRGs, and digital signatures.

8.2   Formal definitions of Many-Time Indexed VRF

In this section, we discuss the formal definitions of a Many-Time Indexed VRF (MT-iVRF) and authenticated MT-iVRF with forward security. Particularly, we discuss the definitions of an authenticated MT-iVRF with forward security, and an MT-iVRF is simply a special case of that. For simplicity, we refer to our constructions as MT-iVRF and authenticated MT-iVRF (omitting "with forward security" or even "MT-" sometimes).

Our definitions are adapted from those of an ordinary VRF [11] and a forward-secure (or key-evolving) signature [25]. We also adapt the unbiasability definition of [4] into our setting. An important feature of our definitions is that we capture more closely the real-life setting in blockchain, where the protocol is inherently stateful and indexed (by round/iteration numbers). Our modifications over the prior definitions allow us to construct the desired tool efficiently from simple cryptographic primitives.

In an Algorand-like consensus setting (see Section 8.5 for details), we want to enable parties to run a cryptographic sortition where a set of users *secretly* determine their eligibility to participate in consensus. This should be done in a way that no selected party is known to the outside world until they reveal this information. To realise this functionality, VRF is used in Algorand where the VRF uniqueness property ensures that users cannot increase their chance of being selected by producing multiple outputs. Furthermore, the VRF pseudorandomness property prevents an adversary from identifying potential leaders (even if it knows the magic number Q_n) because each user's VRF output looks random to the outside parties, implying that the adversary cannot predict their output. The main insights in modifying the formal VRF requirements are as follows. First, in the inherently stateful blockchain ecosystem, we introduce an index (corresponding, e.g., to the round number) to capture time for VRF evaluation and verification to enable index-based properties. Second, we observe that pseudorandomness property is *not* required for past rounds as consensus protocol has already finished for them. As a result, thanks to the formally captured indexing, we can remove the pseudorandomness requirement for previously queried indices. With the above high-level intuition in mind, let us now move to the rigorous definitions.

8.2.1   Syntax

Let N be the parameter denoting the maximum number of time periods (i.e., "rounds") allowed (i.e., the iVRF is N-time), and t be the parameter denoting the maximum number of "iterations" allowed within any given time period/round. In particular, we are here assuming a more generalized setting where each time period is split into further "iterations," where the forward security will be required w.r.t. to the time periods (not iterations). Note that fixing $t = 1$ leads to the standard forward security setting in [25]. In our definitions of the authenticated MT-iVRF, we let **iAV.Eval** take two input messages μ_1, μ_2 to allow verifiable VRF evaluation on one message (μ_1) and authentication of another message (μ_2). The above two generalizations to the formal definitions are done to properly capture an Algorand-like blockchain setting.

In the functions below, we do not index the secret key in order not to clutter the presentation and the key update function **iAV.KeyUpd** simply periodically updates the secret key. The time period index i is clear from the descriptions of **iAV.Eval** and **iAV.Verify** functions as it is part of the input. An authenticated many-time indexed VRF, **iAV**, is given by the following five algorithms (**iAV.ParamGen, iAV.Keygen, iAV.KeyUpd, iAV.Eval, iAV.Verify**):

pp $\leftarrow$ **iAV.ParamGen**(1^λ) : Given the security parameter λ, set up and return public parameters **pp** containing N. We assume that **pp** is an implicit input to the other algorithms.

$(\text{pk}_{\text{av}}, \text{sk}_{\text{av}}) \leftarrow$ **iAV.Keygen**(**pp**) : Given the public parameters **pp**, return a public-secret key pair $(\text{pk}_{\text{av}}, \text{sk}_{\text{av}})$.

$\text{sk}_{\text{av}} \leftarrow$ **iAV.KeyUpd**(sk_{av}) : Given the given secret key sk_{av} for the previous period, update (overwrite) sk_{av} for the current time period.

$(v, \sigma, \pi) \leftarrow$ **iAV.Eval**$_{\text{sk}_{\text{av}}}(\mu_1, \mu_2, (i,j))$: Given input messages $\mu_1, \mu_2 \in \{0,1\}^{\ell(\lambda)}$ and a pair of indices (i,j) with $0 \leq i < N$ and $0 \leq j < t$, return a VRF value $v \in \{0,1\}^{m(\lambda)}$ w.r.t. μ_1, a signature σ w.r.t. μ_2 and an accompanying proof π.

$0/1 \leftarrow$ **iAV.Verify**$_{\text{pk}_{\text{av}}}(\mu_1, \mu_2, (i,j), v, \sigma, \pi)$: Given input messages μ_1, μ_2, a pair of indices (i,j) with $0 \leq i < N$ and $0 \leq j < t$, a VRF value v, a signature σ and a purported proof π, check using π if (v, σ) is correctly generated for the given $(\mu_1, \mu_2, (i,j))$ and pk_{av}.

The (non-authenticated) MT-iVRF construction (in Section 8.3.1) does not have a signature σ and a second message μ_2. Hence, it only serves the VRF functionality without any authentication. The purpose of the parameters t and j is to formally match our application setting to Algorand. For applications not requiring them, one may simply fix $(t, j) = (1, 0)$.

8.2.2   Correctness and security definitions

Compared to an ordinary VRF, there are two main distinctions of our security definitions. First, uniqueness holds in the case of any (arbitrarily generated) fixed input–index pair $(\mu_1, (i,j))$, rather than just any (arbitrarily-generated) fixed input μ_1. Second, pseudorandomness is satisfied against any challenge input–index pair (μ_1, i), where the index i is never queried to the iAV.Eval oracle $\mathscr{O}_{\text{iAV.Eval}}$. In the case of ordinary VRFs, the adversary is not allowed to query the $\mathscr{O}_{\text{iAV.Eval}}$ oracle on the challenge *input* μ_1.

Provability : For any $(v, \sigma, \pi) \leftarrow \text{iAV.Eval}_{\text{sk}_{\text{av}}}(\mu_1, \mu_2, (i,j))$ with $(\text{pk}_{\text{av}}, \text{sk}_{\text{av}}) \leftarrow$ iAV.Keygen(pp), $\text{sk}_{\text{av}} \leftarrow \text{iAV.KeyUpd}^i(\text{sk}_{\text{av}})$ and $\text{pp} \leftarrow \text{iAV.ParamGen}(1^\lambda)$, the algorithm $\text{iAV.Verify}_{\text{pk}_{\text{av}}}(\mu_1, \mu_2, (i,j), v, \sigma, \pi)$ outputs 1.

Computational full uniqueness (CFU) : Let $\mathscr{A}$ be a polynomial-time adversary playing the following experiment Exp-CFU:

1. $\text{pp} \leftarrow \text{iAV.ParamGen}(1^\lambda)$.
2. $(\mu_1, i, j, \text{pk}_{\text{av}}, \mu_2, v, \sigma, \pi, \hat{\mu}_2, \hat{v}, \hat{\sigma}, \hat{\pi}) \leftarrow \mathscr{A}(\text{pp})$.

The adversary $\mathscr{A}$ wins the game if $\text{iAV.Verify}_{\text{pk}_{\text{av}}}(\mu_1, \mu_2, (i,j), v, \sigma, \pi) = \text{iAV.Verify}_{\text{pk}_{\text{av}}}(\mu_1, \hat{\mu}_2, (i,j), \hat{v}, \hat{\sigma}, \hat{\pi}) = 1$ and $v \neq \hat{v}$, with $0 \leq i < N$ and $0 \leq j < t$. An (N-time) authenticated MT-iVRF with forward security is said to satisfy *computational full uniqueness*, if the adversary $\mathscr{A}$ wins the above game with at most $\text{negl}(\lambda)$ probability.

Pseudorandomness : Let $\mathscr{A} = (\mathscr{A}_1, \mathscr{A}_2)$ be a polynomial-time adversary playing the following experiment Exp-PRand:

1. $\text{pp} \leftarrow \text{iAV.ParamGen}(1^\lambda)$,
2. $(\text{pk}_{\text{av}}, \text{sk}_{\text{av}}) \leftarrow \text{iAV.Keygen}(\text{pp})$,
3. $(\mu_1^*, \mu_2^*, i^*, j^*, \text{st}) \leftarrow \mathscr{A}_1^{\mathscr{O}_{\text{iAV.Eval}}(\cdot)}(\text{pk}_{\text{av}})$,
4. $\text{sk}_{\text{av}} \leftarrow \text{iAV.KeyUpd}^{i^*}(\text{sk}_{\text{av}})$,
5. $(v_0, \sigma_0, \pi_0) \leftarrow \text{iAV.Eval}_{\text{sk}_{\text{av}}}(\mu_1^*, \mu_2^*, (i^*, j^*))$,
6. $v_1 \xleftarrow{\$} \{0,1\}^{m(\lambda)}$,
7. $b \xleftarrow{\$} \{0,1\}$,
8. $b' \leftarrow \mathscr{A}_2^{\mathscr{O}_{\text{iAV.Eval}}(\cdot)}(v_b, \text{st})$,

where $\mathscr{O}_{\text{iAV.Eval}}(\cdot)$ is an oracle that on input a message-index tuple $(\mu_1, \mu_2, (i,j))$ outputs a VRF value v, a signature σ, and a corresponding proof of correctness π. The adversary is restricted querying $\mathscr{O}_{\text{iAV.Eval}}(\cdot)$ on index pairs (i,j) for j sequentially incrementing (i.e., $\mathscr{A}$ must query (i,j) first before being able to query $(i, j+1)$). Let $\mathscr{I}$ be the set of all index pairs queried by the adversary. The adversary wins the game if $b = b'$ and $(i^*, j^*) \notin \mathscr{I}$.

We say that an authenticated MT-iVRF with forward security is *pseudorandom* if any PPT adversary $\mathscr{A}$ wins Exp-PRand with probability at most $\frac{1}{2} + \text{negl}(\lambda)$.

Forward-secure unforgeability : Let $\mathscr{A} = (\mathscr{A}_1, \mathscr{A}_2)$ be a polynomial-time adversary playing the following experiment Exp-Forge:

1. $\text{pp} \leftarrow \text{iAV.ParamGen}(1^\lambda)$,
2. $(\text{pk}_{\text{av}}, \text{sk}_{\text{av}}) \leftarrow \text{iAV.Keygen}(\text{pp})$,
3. Set $i = 0$,
4. Until $\mathscr{A}$ stops or i reaches $N - 1$: increment i by 1; set $\text{sk}_{\text{av}} \leftarrow \text{iAV.KeyUpd}(\text{sk}_{\text{av}})$ and $\text{st}_i \leftarrow \mathscr{A}_1^{\mathscr{O}_{\text{iAV.Eval}}(i;\cdot)}(\text{pp}, \text{pk}_{\text{av}})$,

5. $(\mu_1, \mu_2, k, j, v, \sigma, \pi) \leftarrow \mathscr{A}_2(\mathsf{pp}, \mathsf{pk}_{\mathsf{av}}, \mathsf{sk}_{\mathsf{av}}, \mathsf{st}_1, \dots, \mathsf{st}_i)$,
6. $b \leftarrow \mathsf{iAV.Verify}_{\mathsf{pk}_{\mathsf{av}}}(\mu_1, \mu_2, (k, j), v, \sigma, \pi)$,

where $\mathscr{O}_{\mathsf{iAV.Eval}}(i; \cdot)$ is an oracle that returns an $\mathsf{iAV.Eval}$ output w.r.t. the ith secret key $\mathsf{sk}_{\mathsf{av}}$ and time period i. $\mathscr{A}$ wins if $b = 1$, $1 \le k < i$, $0 \le j < t$ and μ_2 was not queried to $\mathscr{O}_{\mathsf{iAV.Eval}}$. We say that an indexed VRF is *forward-secure unforgeable* if

$$\Pr[\mathscr{A} \text{ wins } \mathsf{Exp\text{-}Forge}] \le \mathsf{negl}(\lambda).$$

Unbiasability : Let $\mathscr{A} = (\mathscr{A}_1, \mathscr{A}_2)$ be a polynomial-time adversary playing the following experiment $\mathsf{Exp\text{-}Bias}$:

1. $\mathsf{pp} \leftarrow \mathsf{iAV.ParamGen}(1^{\lambda})$,
2. $(\mathsf{pk}_{\mathsf{av}}, \mu_2, v, i, j, \mathsf{st}) \leftarrow \mathscr{A}_1(\mathsf{pp})$,
3. $\mu_1 \xleftarrow{\$} \{0, 1\}^{\ell(\lambda)}$,
4. $(\sigma, \pi) \leftarrow \mathscr{A}_2(\mu_1, \mathsf{st})$,
5. $b \leftarrow \mathsf{iAV.Verify}_{\mathsf{pk}_{\mathsf{av}}}(\mu_1, \mu_2, (i, j), v, \sigma, \pi)$.

$\mathscr{A}$ wins if $b = 1$. We say that an authenticated MT-iVRF with forward security is *unbiasable* if

$$\Pr[\mathscr{A} \text{ wins } \mathsf{Exp\text{-}Bias}] \le 2^{-\ell(\lambda)} + \mathsf{negl}(\lambda).$$

8.3 iVRF constructions

We first introduce our MT-iVRF which is constructed from a secure Merkle hash tree and which can evaluate up to N time periods (i.e., rounds). This scheme allows multiple iterations within a single round, matching the Algorand setting. After that, we present our final MT-iVRF scheme which also provides authentication and forward security.

8.3.1 MT-iVRF

As discussed, the index has two parts as (i, j), where $i = 0, \dots, N - 1$ and $j = 0, \dots, t$ for some public parameters $t, N \ge 1$. This construction is the setting depicted in Figure 8.1 with no pk_i's. We use a cryptographic hash family $\mathscr{H}$ and a PRG $\mathsf{G} : \{0, 1\}^{\lambda} \to (\{0, 1\}^{\lambda})^N$ with functions $(\mathsf{G.Key}, \mathsf{G.Next})$ to generate an initial state and a pair of next state and randomness, respectively (see [1] for more details).

$\mathsf{iVRF.ParamGen}(1^{\lambda})$: Pick a hash function $\mathsf{H} \xleftarrow{\$} \mathscr{H}$. Set parameters t and N for a power-of-2 N. Return $\mathsf{pp} = (\mathsf{H}, \mathsf{G}, N, t)$.

$\mathsf{iVRF.Keygen}(\mathsf{pp})$:

1. Set up $s \leftarrow \mathsf{G.Key}(1^{\lambda})$.
2. Derive pseudorandom values $(x_{0,0}, \dots, x_{N-1,0})$ by running $\mathsf{G.Next}$ iteratively on s.
3. Compute $x_{i,j+1} = \mathsf{H}(x_{i,j})$ for $i = 0, \dots, N - 1$ and $j = 0, \dots, t - 1$.
4. Construct a Merkle tree using $(x_{0,t}, \dots, x_{N-1,t})$. Let **root** be the root of the tree.
    Return $(\mathsf{pk}_{\mathsf{v}}, \mathsf{sk}_{\mathsf{v}}) = (\mathsf{root}, s)$.

iVRF.Eval$_{\mathsf{sk}_v}(\mu, (i,j))$:
1. Derive $x_{i,0}$ from $s = \mathsf{sk}_v$ and update the state of the PRG G.
2. Compute $y = \mathsf{H}^{t-1-j}(x_{i,0})$.
3. Compute $v - \mathsf{II}(y, \mu)$.
4. Compute an authentication path AP_i w.r.t. the leaf index i.
Return v as the VRF value along with a proof $\pi = (y, \mathsf{AP}_i)$.

iVRF.Verify$_{\mathsf{pk}_v}(\mu, (i,j), v, \pi)$:
1. Parse $\pi = (y, \mathsf{AP})$.
2. If $v \neq \mathsf{H}(y, \mu)$, return 0.
3. Compute $x_{i,t} = \mathsf{H}^{j+1}(y)$.
4. Compute a Merkle root, root', using $x_{i,t}$ and AP w.r.t. the leaf index i.
If $\mathsf{root}' = \mathsf{pk}_v$, return 1. Otherwise, return 0.

8.3.2 *Authenticated MT-iVRF with forward security*

In the MMM (recursive) sum composition approach [20], described in [1] in more detail, to construct a forward-secure (FS) signature for N time periods, one makes use of a Merkle tree with N leaves, where each leaf corresponds to a random (one-time) signature key pair with the public keys used to construct the Merkle tree. Therefore, our MT-iVRF instantiation can be naturally combined with the MMM approach. The advantage in this case is that we will have a *single* Merkle tree (and a single tool) to realize both the VRF functionality and the forward-secure signature. This means that it is sufficient to communicate a *single* authentication path to authenticate both the keys for the FS signature and the evaluator's committed values y used to compute the VRF value $v = \mathsf{H}(y, \mu)$ (where μ is the VRF input/message). As a result, the additional communication overhead of our final authenticated MT-iVRF construction over the MMM approach is minimal at just 32 bytes (recall that $v = \mathsf{H}(y, \mu)$ can be computed in the Algorand application, so need not be communicated).

Concretely, when constructing the Merkle tree, we set $x_{i,t} = \mathsf{H}(x_{i,t-1}, \mathsf{pk}_i)$ (instead of $x_{i,t} = \mathsf{H}(x_{i,t-1})$) in key generation, where $\mathsf{pk}_0, \ldots, \mathsf{pk}_{N-1}$ are independent public keys of a (t-time) signature scheme Σ with standard ($\Sigma.\mathsf{Keygen}, \Sigma.\mathsf{Sign}, \Sigma.\mathsf{Verify}$) functions. As with the previous construction, we use a cryptographic hash family $\mathscr{H}$ of functions $\mathsf{H} : \{0, 1\}^* \rightarrow \{0, 1\}^{2\lambda}$ and a PRG $\mathsf{G} : \{0, 1\}^\lambda \rightarrow (\{0, 1\}^\lambda)^N$ with functions ($\mathsf{G.Key}, \mathsf{G.Next}$).

iAV.ParamGen(1^λ) : Pick hash function $\mathsf{H} \xleftarrow{\$} \mathscr{H}$. Set parameters $t = \mathsf{poly}(\lambda)$ and $N = \mathsf{poly}(\lambda)$ for a power-of-2 N. Return $\mathsf{pp} = (\mathsf{H}, \mathsf{G}, N, t)$.

iAV.Keygen(pp) :
1. Set up seeds $s, s' \leftarrow \mathsf{G.Key}(1^\lambda)$.
2. Derive pseudorandom values $(x_{0,0}, \ldots, x_{N-1,0})$ by running $\mathsf{G.Next}$ iteratively on s.
3. Compute $x_{i,j+1} = \mathsf{H}(x_{i,j})$ for $i = 0, \ldots, N-1$ and $j = 0, \ldots, t-2$.
4. Derive pseudorandom values $(r_0, \ldots, r_{N-1})$ by running $\mathsf{G.Next}$ iteratively on s'.
5. $(\mathsf{pk}_i, \mathsf{sk}_i) \leftarrow \Sigma.\mathsf{Keygen}(\mathsf{pp}; r_i)$ for $i = 0, \ldots, N-1$.

6. Compute $x_{i,t} = \mathsf{H}(x_{i,t-1}, \mathsf{pk}_i)$ for $i = 0, \ldots, N - 1$.
7. Construct a Merkle tree using $(x_{0,t}, \ldots, x_{N-1,t})$. Let **root** be the root of the tree.

Return $(\mathsf{pk}_{\mathsf{av}}, \mathsf{sk}_{\mathsf{av}}) = (\mathsf{root}, (s, 0, s', 0))$.

iAV.KeyUpd($\mathsf{sk}_{\mathsf{av}}$) : Parse $\mathsf{sk}_{\mathsf{av}} = (s, x, s', r)$ and update $\mathsf{sk}_{\mathsf{av}}$ as $(\mathsf{G.Next}(s), \mathsf{G.Next}(s'))$.

iAV.Eval$_{\mathsf{sk}_{\mathsf{av}}}(\mu_1, \mu_2, (i,j))$:
1. Parse $\mathsf{sk}_{\mathsf{av}} = (s_i, x_{i,0}, s_i', r_i)$.
2. Compute $y = \mathsf{H}^{t-1-j}(x_{i,0})$
3. Compute $v = \mathsf{H}(y, \mu_1)$.
4. Compute $\mathsf{pk} \leftarrow \Sigma.\mathsf{Keygen}(\mathsf{pp}; r_i)$
5. Compute $\sigma \leftarrow \Sigma.\mathsf{Sign}_{\mathsf{sk}}(\mu_2)$
6. Compute an authentication path AP_i w.r.t. the leaf index i.

Return v as the VRF value, σ as the signature, and $\pi = (y, \mathsf{pk}, \mathsf{AP}_i)$ as the accompanying proof.

iAV.Verify$_{\mathsf{pk}_{\mathsf{av}}}(\mu_1, \mu_2, (i,j), v, \sigma, \pi)$:
1. Parse $\pi = (y, \mathsf{pk}, \mathsf{AP})$.
2. If $v \neq \mathsf{H}(y, \mu_1)$, return 0.
3. If $\Sigma.\mathsf{Verify}_{\mathsf{pk}}(\sigma, \mu_2) = 0$, return 0.
4. Compute $y' = \mathsf{H}^j(y)$
5. Compute $x_i = \mathsf{H}(y', \mathsf{pk})$
6. Compute a Merkle root, root', using x_i and AP w.r.t. the leaf index i.

If $\mathsf{root}' = \mathsf{pk}_{\mathsf{av}}$, return 1. Otherwise, return 0.

8.4   Performance analysis and implementation

Thanks to the simplicity of our scheme, the performance analysis can straightforwardly be done by counting the number of operations. For the hash operations, we look at the amount of bytes to be hashed rather than how many $\mathsf{H}(\,\cdot\,)$ operations appear in the description to capture a more accurate result, and consider 32-byte values for $x_{i,j}$'s, μ_i's and the hash output. We write $|\sigma|_B$ and $|\mathsf{pk}|_B$ to denote the byte-lengths of the ordinary signature and its public key.

iAV.Keygen consists of the following main operations:

1. $2N$ PRG iterations,
2. less than $(t + 2) \cdot N \cdot 32 + N \cdot |\mathsf{pk}|_B$ bytes of hash calculations, and
3. N (ordinary) signature key generations.

Therefore, iAV.Keygen runtime is likely to be dominated by N (ordinary) signature key generations (for reasonable values of t), which is consistent with our implementation results discussed further below in this section. Note that key generation of Algorand's approach to forward security (as discussed in the introduction) involves invoking ordinary signature key generation *and* signing algorithms N times each. Hence, our iAV.Keygen runtime is likely to closely match (or may even be faster than) Algorand's approach. Note also that in the context of Algorand, keys for the next epoch can be generated progressively in the current epoch so that the key generation runtime is amortized.

Next, **iAV.Eval** consists of the following main operations:

1. at most $(t + 1) \cdot 32$ bytes of hash calculations,
2. 1 (ordinary) signature key generation, and
3. 1 (ordinary) signing.

Note that the authentication path in **iAV.Eval** can simply be retrieved when the Merkle tree is stored.

Finally, **iAV.Verify** consists of the following main operations:

1. at most $(2 \log N + t + 2) \cdot 32 + |\textbf{pk}|_B$ bytes of hash calculations, and
2. 1 (ordinary) signature verification.

In terms of communication, **iAV.Eval** requires transmission of an ordinary signature σ, an ordinary signature public key **pk**, an authentication path ($\log N$ 32-byte strings), and a 32-byte string (and another 32-byte string if v needs to be communicated). So, in total, $|\sigma|_B + |\textbf{pk}|_B + (\log N + 1) \cdot 32$ bytes of communication is needed.

The storage requirement by the evaluator is heavily dominated by the storage of the Merkle tree nodes (if they are stored). If the whole tree is stored, then about $32 \cdot 2N = 64N$ bytes of storage is needed. However, standard optimizations such as partial tree storage (together with progressive computation of missing nodes and deletion of used nodes) can be adopted. For example, by computing the two sibling leaf nodes together every two time periods, we can avoid storage of leaf nodes and reduce the storage requirement to $32N$ bytes.

We implemented our authenticated MT-iVRF with forward security (from Section 8.3.2) in C language[††] (on a single Intel i7-7700K core at 4.2 GHz). We used Falcon-512 [23] to instantiate the post-quantum signature, SHA-256 for the hash function **H**, and AES-256 with the CTR-DRBG mode [26] (implemented by using the AES-NI hardware instructions [27]) for the PRG **G**. Falcon-512 has a public key of 897 bytes and a signature of 666 bytes. We used the Falcon variant with the ChaCha20 [28] seed expander provided by the latest Falcon reference implementation,[‡‡] with both AVX2 and FMA instructions enabled. Clang 14.0.6 compiler was used to compile the code, with optimization flags `-O3 -march=native`. We disabled Hyper-threading and Turbo Boost during the benchmarks.

In Tables 8.2 and 8.3, we summarize the concrete performance results of our authenticated MT-iVRF with forward security proposal and our execution of Falcon-512 signature, respectively. When computing the proof sizes in Table 8.2, we remove the costs due to the signature scheme to clearly show the impact of varying parameters since the cost due to the signature is fixed and arises from authentication, not the VRF

[††]Source code available at https://gitlab.com/raykzhao/ivrf
[‡‡]https://falcon-sign.info/Falcon-impl-20211101.zip (this reference implementation is also adopted in Algorand)

Table 8.2   Performance of our authenticated MT-iVRF with forward security in Section 8.3.2 for different parameters using Falcon-512

(N,t)	Proof size	Keygen	Eval	Verify	Key Lifetime in Algorand
$(2^{18}, 16)$	608 bytes	19.44 min	4.63 ms	0.046 ms	2 weeks
$(2^{18}, 100)$	608 bytes	19.82 min	4.72 ms	0.088 ms	2 weeks
$(2^{23}, 16)$	768 bytes	10.40 h	4.63 ms	0.049 ms	> 1 year
$(2^{23}, 100)$	768 bytes	10.45 h	4.67 ms	0.092 ms	> 1 year

Table 8.3   Runtimes of our execution of signature algorithms

Scheme	Keygen time	Signing time	Verify time
Falcon-512	4.45 ms	0.18 ms	0.023 ms
XMSS-128	290.51 ms	290.98 ms	1.23 ms

functionality. We also note that when running iAV.Eval and iAV.Verify, we set $j = 0$ and $j = t - 1$, respectively, to capture the *worst-case* running times.

Let us first analyze the impact of the parameter t. It is easy to see that the proof size is independent of t (as also evident from the theoretical analysis above) and that iAV.Keygen runtime increases very little even when t is increased to a large value like 100. The parameter t has also little impact on the iAV.Eval runtime, and iAV.Verify is still very fast even in the worst case with $t = 100$. Therefore, we believe there is a lot of freedom for the choice of t.

Using the results of Tables 8.2 and 8.3, it is easy to derive that the vast majority of iAV.Keygen time is spent on Falcon key generations. Similarly, the vast majority of iAV.Eval time is spent of Falcon key generation and signing. In fact, the slight variations in iAV.Eval for different N values are mainly due to the variations in the Falcon signature runtimes as iAV.Eval runtime is (almost) independent of N (neglecting the minor cost of retrieving $\log N$ tree nodes).

The runtimes of our execution of Falcon-512 (see Table 8.3) are close to the reported runtimes on the official Falcon website.[§§] Note that some of our runtimes in Table 8.3 are faster, due to the ChaCha20 seed expander (up to 8% faster for Keygen on Intel CPUs, as reported by the latest Falcon reference implementation) and higher CPU frequency in our benchmark platform (4.2 GHz vs 2.3 GHz).

We also measured the performance of the XMSS signature [18] as a choice of signature based on symmetric-key primitives. We added the parameter set XMSS-128 with 128 leaves (greater than our choices of $t \in \{16, 100\}$) using SHA-256 in the

---

[§§]https://falcon-sign.info/

XMSS reference implementation.[III] XMSS-128 has a public key of 64 bytes and a signature of 2404 bytes. The runtimes of our execution of XMSS-128 are summarised in Table 8.3. Note that we did not use the "fast" variant in the XMSS reference implementation with the BDS algorithm [29], since the BDS algorithm needs to be iterated j times in iAV.Eval. This becomes more than $2\times$ slower than the iAV.Eval without the BDS algorithm when $j = 99$ in our experiment. Compared to Falcon-512, the Keygen and Verify times of XMSS-128 are more than $50\times$ slower, and the signing time is more than $1000\times$ slower. In addition, the signature size of XMSS-128 is also $3.6\times$ bigger than Falcon-512. Therefore, Falcon-512 is a better choice as the signature algorithm due to its advantages in the runtimes and the signature size.

8.5 Application to Algorand

The Algorand protocol is a fork-free PoS protocol in which consensus is achieved using a Byzantine Agreement (BA) protocol [30,31]. To prevent the adversary from adaptively corrupting parties who participate in the protocol, the parties who are actively running the protocol change after every step[¶] of the protocol. This is achieved using a VRF that takes into account parties' stakes. The security of the signature primitives (including the VRF), and, by extension, of the BA protocol, rely on computational assumptions that are known to be broken in the context of a quantum adversary. Hence, to attain post-quantum security for this protocol, it is necessary to shift to alternate constructions for these primitives. The purpose of this section is to provide a high-level explanation of the relevant aspects of Algorand's BA protocol that should be replaced with post-quantum secure alternatives.

We begin by explaining how parties register their keys to the Algorand blockchain [32]. To create an account, a party registers its public account key *apk* to the blockchain using a registration transaction that includes the spending public key and the amount of coins belonging to the account owner. At each step of the BA protocol, parties individually run the sortition algorithm to check if they are eligible to participate in the consensus protocol. The sortition is implemented using a VRF (see below for how parties register their VRF keys).

At round n, a party computes the output of their VRF on input their VRF secret key *vsk* and a special quantity Q_n, which is derived from the blockchain. The main idea is that Q_n will be unpredictable to any party at the time of registering its public key to the blockchain. Therefore, it also should not be able to predict if it will be eligible to participate in the consensus protocol at round n. We elide a detailed description

---

[III] https://github.com/XMSS/xmss-reference

[¶] Note that a *round* of the Algorand protocol may include several *periods*, each consisting of a constant number of *steps*, namely 5 steps [30]. In our iVRF formal model, we use two indices (for rounds and iterations), and each step of a period in Algorand increments one iteration in our iVRF model (i.e., there is no need to introduce a third index in the formal model, which would unnecessarily complicate its presentation).

of how the protocol computes Q_n, as it is not relevant for explaining the sortition mechanism.

The initial quantity Q_0 is assumed to be randomly generated (as part of the genesis block). At round n, the previous round's magic number Q_{n-1} is used. Particularly, the *leader* of period j of round n is elected as the party P_i with the lowest VRF value (proportional to its stakes) satisfying,*** ,†††

$$\mathsf{H}(\Sigma.\mathsf{Sign}_i(n, j, 1, Q_{n-1})) \leq p \cdot stake(P_i), \tag{8.1}$$

where p is a predefined threshold value and $stake(P_i)$ denotes the amount of stakes owned by P_i. More generally, parties determine their eligibility to participate in the protocol for a given step $s > 1$ (of period j) of the BA protocol by checking whether

$$\mathsf{H}(\Sigma.\mathsf{Sign}_i(n, j, s, Q_{n-1})) \leq p' \cdot stake(P_i), \tag{8.2}$$

where $p' \gg p$ is a predefined value.

Every period of the protocol is associated with a leader who is also elected via VRF. The BA protocol may have several periods (each consisting of a constant number of steps with rotating participants). Each potential round leader in round n proposes a block including new valid transactions together with its VRF proof for round n and broadcasts them to the network. After the blocks are proposed by the potential leaders, all participants of the protocol verify the correctness of the VRF outputs and choose the candidate block with the lowest VRF value. Once a block is accepted by collecting a strong majority of votes (2/3 of the votes) from the active protocol participants, parties move on to the next round.

8.5.1 Key management in Algorand

In Algorand, there are four types of keys: *spending keys*, *VRF (selection) keys*, *voting keys*, and (recently introduced) *state proof keys* [32]. Spending keys, also known as root keys, are used for sending and receiving coins by an account. An account is identified with the root public key *apk* of the spending key. Also, later on, the VRF, voting and state proof keys of the account are validated via the spending keys.

VRF keys are used to check if an account is selected for participation in the voting phase as the leader or, more generally, as an active participant in the BA protocol. Hence, all protocol messages are validated with a VRF proof.

Voting keys are used to authenticate participation during the voting phase of the BA agreement protocol. To achieve *forward security*, voting keys are periodically updated. This simple update works as follows: parties delete the latest used private key, and move to the next one. To avoid registering a new voting key each time, per epoch, a batch of ephemeral voting keys $(epk_1, esk_1), (epk_2, esk_2), \ldots$ (10,000 as the default value) are generated. These keys are authenticated using a signature relative to the root voting key *apk*, which is validated by the signature of the spending key.

***The signature used in Algorand's VRF (given in 8.1) has the uniqueness property.

†††Note that in the Algorand protocol given in [30], the period parameter j is omitted since each round is described over one period, whereas the current implementation of the protocol explained in [32] may include several periods per round.

Thus, a batch of keys are committed and (partially) validated as follows whenever a new epoch begins. First, the user registers a new root key *epk*, which it validates by signing with the spending key of the root public key *apk* of the previous epoch. Each ephemeral voting key *epk_i* is later validated using *epk*.

In theory (to ensure full forward security), voting keys should be updated immediately after their use in a step of the BA protocol. However, in practice, they are updated every round [32]. This results in a slightly weaker form of security where a fully adaptive adversary may indefinitely stall progress of the protocol. However, such a strong adversary appears somewhat unrealistic in practice.

Recently, Algorand introduced state proof keys used to generate post-quantum secure state proofs. Similar to voting keys, state proof keys consist of ephemeral keys that are renewed in epochs.

8.5.2 *Modifications to the Algorand protocol*

We aim to achieve a post-quantum version of Algorand protocol by replacing cryptographic algorithms that are vulnerable to quantum attacks. In March 2022, Algorand added *state proofs* to the protocol to improve its resilience against quantum attacks. In state proofs, a subset-sum-based hash function [33] and the Falcon signature algorithm [23] are used. However, the rest of the protocol mainly utilizes prequantum algorithms. Algorand uses SHA-512/256 and EdDSA [34,35] as primary hash function and signature scheme, respectively.

The security of the Algorand protocol relies on a strong honest majority among each of the BA committees that actively run the protocol. With the above choices, the Algorand protocol achieves its desired security properties with overwhelming probability ($1 - 10^{-18}$ given appropriate network conditions) [7]. The committee and leader elections for the BA protocol are done via the VRF function. However, since the VRF function is instantiated with the pre-quantum algorithms, these election protocols are not post-quantum secure.[‡‡‡] In our protocol, we can replace the signature scheme EdDSA with any post-quantum signature, and particularly propose to use Falcon signature since it has the minimal total size for a public key and a signature among those selected by the NIST for post-quantum signature standardization. Also, we replace the VRF function with MT-iVRF, which is defined in Section 8.3. In fact, as discussed before, we can realize both VRF and signature functionalities by a single tool, our authenticated MT-iVRF from Section 8.3.2.

As mentioned earlier, the election in the BA protocol is done via a VRF with the input of Q_n value, which should satisfy *uniqueness*, *pseudorandomness*, and *unbiasability* (see Section 5.6 and proof of Lemma 5.11 in [30]). Our iVRF construction satisfies somewhat different notions of uniqueness, pseudorandomness, and unbiasability than the ones stated in [30]. First of all, the iVRF formal model defined in

---

[‡‡‡]We note here that the uniqueness property of ECVRF used in Algorand does not rely on any computational assumption [14] and, therefore, is plausibly post-quantum (in ROM). However, the pseudorandomness property requires DDH assumption [14] and, therefore, ECVRF as a whole is not post-quantum.

Section 8.2 is designed to collectively capture the VRF and forward secure signature requirements in an Algorand-like blockchain setting, where the protocol is inherently indexed (or timed). Particularly, we assume the protocol operates in rounds (indexed by i), periods within rounds (indexed by j), and each period consists of a constant number of steps. We require in an Algorand-like blockchain setting that at any particular step of a period of any round, each (computationally bounded) user can only produce a single valid VRF value, as captured by the formal iVRF uniqueness model. Similarly, we need pseudorandomness to hold against indices that have not been queried before. That is, it is fine for the outputs from previous steps/rounds to not satisfy pseudorandomness, as the past unique VRF values have already served their purpose and are no longer relevant. Moreover, by combining the forward-secure signature with iVRF, our construction given in Section 8.3.2 reduces the validation costs. More specifically, we require only one Merkle Tree authentication path, rather than two in the separate construction case.

Thanks to the blockchain-oriented design of our formal definitions, the security properties achieved by our iVRF are sufficient to ensure the required properties on the BA committee elections leveraged in Algorand's proofs. As shown in [1], iVRF satisfies the aforementioned properties, and thereby can be substituted in the original Algorand protocol without impacting its security.

Finally, recall that our MT-iVRF construction includes t pseudorandom strings $(x_{i,j})$ per round. Here, the iteration parameter t can be chosen based on the network and security assumptions. The BA protocol of Algorand is expected to terminate within at most 2.5 periods (which corresponds to 16 steps in total) [31]. As discussed in Section 8.4, the parameter t has little impact on the computation (and no impact on the communication) performance and, hence, can be safely adjusted without a significant compromise in performance.

8.5.3   Interpreting iVRF performance for Algorand

It is easy to see that the **iAV.Keygen** runtime is heavily dominated by Falcon key generations, which are needed anyway for forward security. As discussed earlier, this key generation process can be amortized over time or parallelized. For example, for $N = 2^{23}$, splitting the computation into four cores (and using four random seeds instead of one to generate signature keys) reduces the required *once-a-year* computation time to just 2.6 h. Alternatively, whenever the user's device is turned on, the signature keys can be progressively computed (and hashed to avoid storing the whole key). Therefore, in terms of keygen procedure, there is effectively no computational overhead over what already needs to be done to achieve forward security. Note that the ephemeral key generation process that already exists in Algorand together with a little more of effort for the generation of $x_{i,j}$'s and the Merkle tree can serve as **iAV.Keygen**.

From Table 8.2, we can see that an evaluation (including signing) can be done under 5 ms, which is well below the Algorand's round time at 4.5 s. Therefore, a committee member's local authenticated iVRF evaluations are not expected to lead to any slowdown. We can also conclude that 50,000 or more **iAV.Verify** executions can be performed within the time period of a round. In fact, as seen in Tables 8.1 and 8.2, our verification (including signature validation) runs even faster than ECVRF verification used by Algorand. Therefore, we also do not expect any slowdown due to verification.

As discussed in Section 8.4, for the storage of the Merkle tree nodes, we need about $32N$ bytes, meaning only 256 MB is needed even for $N = 2^{23}$. Note that the existing Algorand protocol already has a similar storage requirement where N pairs of an ephemeral key and a signature (each pair of size about 96 bytes) are stored.

Perhaps the only significant cost introduced with the use of our authenticated MT-iVRF in the Algorand setting is the increased communication. As discussed earlier, the vast majority of the increased communication cost stems from the use of a post-quantum forward-secure signature and there is only a 32-byte additional cost due to the VRF functionality. Such an additional cost of increased communication appears unavoidable in the current state of affairs when post-quantum security is desired as evidenced by the increased sizes of all schemes standardized by NIST.[§§§]

8.6   Conclusion

In this chapter, we described a simple and efficient method to realize the VRF functionality required in the blockchain setting for the leader election problem. Our solution does not involve a racing condition as in Bitcoin and can be instantiated from well-known basic (post-quantum) primitives. We believe that our iVRF-based approach can be readily deployed in the Algorand blockchain system as only minor modifications are needed.

References

[1]   Esgin MF, Ersoy O, Kuchta V, *et al.* A new look at blockchain leader election: simple, efficient, sustainable and post-quantum. In: *ACM Asia Conference on Computer and Communications Security (ACM AsiaCCS)*. ACM; 2023. Full version at https://eprint.iacr.org/2022/993.pdf.

[2]   Shor PW. Algorithms for quantum computation: discrete logarithms and factoring. In: *35th Annual Symposium on Foundations of Computer Science*, Santa Fe, New Mexico, USA, 20–22 November 1994. IEEE Computer Society; 1994. p. 124–134. Available from: https://doi.org/10.1109/SFCS.1994.365700.

[3]   Gambetta J and Steffen M. Charting the course to 100,000 qubits; 2023. Available at https://research.ibm.com/blog/100k-qubit-supercomputer (accessed: 2023-06-07).

[4]   Esgin MF, Kuchta V, Sakzad A, *et al.* Practical post-quantum few-time verifiable random function with applications to Algorand. In: *Financial Cryptography (2)*, vol. 12675 of LNCS. Springer; 2021. p. 560–578.

[§§§]csrc.nist.gov/Projects/post-quantum-cryptography/selected-algorithms-2022

[5]   NIST. Post-Quantum Cryptography; 2017. https://csrc.nist.gov/projects/post-quantum-cryptography.

[6]   David B, Gazi P, Kiayias A, *et al*. Ouroboros Praos: an adaptively-secure, semi-synchronous proof-of-stake blockchain. In: *EUROCRYPT (2)*, vol. 10821 of LNCS. Springer; 2018. p. 66–98.

[7]   Gilad Y, Hemo R, Micali S, *et al*. Algorand: scaling Byzantine agreements for cryptocurrencies. In: *Symposium on Operating Systems Principles (SOSP)*. ACM; 2017. p. 51–68.

[8]   Gorbunov S. Algorand Releases First Open-Source Code: Verifiable Random Function; 2018. Available at https://medium.com/algorand/algorand-releases-first-open-source-code-of-verifiable-random-function-93c2960abd61.

[9]   Hanke T, Movahedi M, and Williams D. DFINITY Technology Overview Series, Consensus System. CoRR. 2018;abs/1805.04548. Available from: http://arxiv.org/abs/1805.04548.

[10]   Chia Documentation; 2018. Available at https://docs.chia.net/docs/ 03consensus/consensus_intro.

[11]   Micali S, Rabin MO, and Vadhan SP. Verifiable random functions. In: *FOCS*. IEEE Computer Society; 1999. p. 120–130.

[12]   What Sets It Apart: Filecoin's Proof System; 2020. Available at https://spec.filecoin.io/algorithms/expected_consensus/.

[13]   RangersProtocol Whitepaper; 2022. Available at https://www.rangersprotocol.com/pdf/RangersProtocolWhitepaper.pdf.

[14]   Papadopoulos D, Wessels D, Huque S, *et al*. Making NSEC5 Practical for DNSSEC; 2017. https://ia.cr/2017/099. Cryptology ePrint Archive, Report 2017/099.

[15]   Bernstein DJ, Duif N, Lange T, *et al*. High-speed high-security signatures. In: *CHES*, vol. 6917 of LNCS. Springer; 2011. p. 124–142.

[16]   Esgin MF, Steinfeld R, Liu D, *et al*. Efficient hybrid exact/relaxed lattice proofs and applications to rounding and VRFs. In: *CRYPTO*. Lecture Notes in Computer Science. Springer; 2023 (Full version at ia.cr/2022/141).

[17]   Buser M, Dowsley R, Esgin MF, *et al*. Post-quantum verifiable random function from symmetric primitives in PoS blockchain. In: *ESORICS*, vol. 13554 of LNCS. Springer; 2022. p. 25–45.

[18]   Buchmann J, Dahmen E, and Hülsing A. XMSS – a practical forward secure signature scheme based on minimal security assumptions. In: *PQCrypto*, vol. 7071 of LNCS. Springer; 2011. p. 117–129.

[19]   Albrecht MR, Rechberger C, Schneider T, *et al*. Ciphers for MPC and FHE. In: *EUROCRYPT (1)*, vol. 9056 of LNCS. Springer; 2015. p. 430–454.

[20]   Malkin T, Micciancio D, and Miner SK. Efficient generic forward-secure signatures with an unbounded number of time periods. In: *EUROCRYPT*, vol. 2332 of LNCS. Springer; 2002. p. 400–417.

[21]   *Quantum-Safe Identity-Based Encryption*. Sophia-Antipolis, France: The European Telecommunications Standards Institute; 2019.

[22]   Zhao RK, McCarthy S, Steinfeld R, *et al*. Quantum-safe HIBE: does it cost a Latte?; 2021. https://eprint.iacr.org/2021/222. Cryptology ePrint Archive, Paper 2021/222.

[23] Fouque PA, Hoffstein J, Kirchner P, *et al.* Falcon: fast-Fourier lattice-based compact signatures over NTRU. Submission to the NIST's PQC Standardization Process. 2018;36(5).

[24] Bellare M, Namprempre C, and Neven G. Security proofs for identity-based identification and signature schemes. In: *EUROCRYPT*, vol. 3027 of LNCS. Springer; 2004. p. 268–286.

[25] Bellare M and Miner SK. A forward-secure digital signature scheme. In: *CRYPTO*, vol. 1666 of LNCS. Springer; 1999. p. 431–448.

[26] NIST. Recommendation for Random Number Generation Using Deterministic Random Bit Generators; 2015. https://doi.org/10.6028/NIST.SP.800-90Ar1.

[27] Gueron S. Intel's new AES instructions for enhanced performance and security. In: *FSE*, vol. 5665 of LNCS. Springer; 2009. p. 51–66.

[28] Bernstein DJ. ChaCha, a variant of Salsa20; 2008. https://cr.yp.to/chacha/chacha-20080128.pdf.

[29] Buchmann J, Dahmen E, and Schneider M. Merkle tree traversal revisited. In: *PQCrypto*, vol. 5299 of LNCS. Springer; 2008. p. 63–78.

[30] Chen J and Micali S. Algorand: a secure and efficient distributed ledger. *Theor Comput Sci*. 2019;777:155–183.

[31] Chen J, Gorbunov S, Micali S, *et al.* ALGORAND AGREEMENT: super fast and partition resilient Byzantine agreement. *IACR Cryptol ePrint Arch*. 2018; 377.

[32] Foundation A. Algorand Key Specification; 2022. Available at: https://github.com/algorandfoundation/specs/blob/master/dev/partkey.md.

[33] Gilad Y, Lazar D, and Peikert C. Subset-Sum Hash Specification; 2021. Available at: https://github.com/algorandfoundation/specs/blob/master/dev/cryptographic-specs/sumhash-spec.pdf.

[34] Josefsson S and Liusvaara I. Edwards-Curve Digital Signature Algorithm (EdDSA). *RFC*. 2017;8032:1–60.

[35] Bernstein DJ. Curve25519: new Diffie–Hellman speed records. In: *Public Key Cryptography*, vol. 3958 of LNCS. Springer; 2006. p. 207–228.

Chapter 9

Summarizing Proof-of-Stake mechanisms and their practical deployments: applications, attacks, solutions, and future directions

Cong T. Nguyen[1,2] Dinh Thai Hoang[3], Diep N. Nguyen[3], Van-Dinh Nguyen[4] and Eryk Dutkiewicz[3]

The concept of Proof-of-Stake (PoS) first emerged in Peercoin [1] as an approach to reduce the demanding energy consumption of the Proof-of-Work (PoW) mechanism, where the mining difficulty of the PoW can be reduced by burning stakes, i.e., consuming digital tokens. Since then, PoS has gradually evolved to become a standalone consensus mechanism with significant advantages over the PoW mechanism, including negligible energy consumption and higher transaction processing capability. These advantages have shifted the research focus from PoW to PoS in academia, and, in turn, given rise to numerous PoS-based real-world applications. For example, Ethereum, the cryptocurrency with the second highest market capitalization (more than $200 billion [2]), has recently switched from PoW to pure PoS [3]. Cardano, another pure PoS cryptocurrency, has a market capitalization of more than $10 billion [2]. Besides their monetary values, these cryptocurrencies also support numerous decentralized applications in diverse areas such as finance, web browsing, gaming, advertising, identity management, and supply chain management [4].

Although the PoS mechanisms offer significant advantages, they still face various security threats. Particularly, there are many attacks targeting the PoS mechanisms, including double-spending, Sybil, race, bribery, transaction denial, grinding, desynchronization, eclipse, long-range, nothing-at-stakes, past majority, and 51% attacks. Some of these attacks can be completely prevented by most PoS-based blockchain networks. However, for some attacks (e.g., 51% attacks), there is no effective solution to mitigate. Besides these attacks, the formation of stake pools also poses a threat to PoS networks where stakeholders might delegate too much voting power to the stake pools, leading to centralization problems [4]. Additionally, in federated-blockchain systems where users can transfer their assets among different blockchains, there is also the risk of centralization where users may shift their assets to a single blockchain, leaving the

[1] Institute of Fundamental and Applied Sciences, Duy Tan University, Vietnam
[2] Faculty of Information Technology, Duy Tan University, Vietnam
[3] School of Electrical and Data Engineering, University of Technology Sydney, Australia
[4] College of Engineering and Computer Science, VinUniversity, Vietnam

others vulnerable to attacks [5]. Additionally, in PoS-based blockchain networks with shardings, the vulnerability to attacks increases significantly as the number of shards increases [6,7]. Given their potentially significant impact, attention to these security threats has grown continuously, as evidenced by the increasing number of research works on these topics in recent years. Nevertheless, more efforts are still needed to develop effective solutions to effectively address those fast-evolving issues.

In this chapter, we first provide a quick recap on the PoS consensus mechanisms including their consensus processes and advantages. Then, we introduce several advanced PoS mechanisms and their real-world applications. Moreover, we discuss potential attacks targeting PoS networks as well as potential approaches to mitigate them. We also present challenges and related potential research directions, such as the stake pools formation, federated-blockchain systems, and PoS shardings.

9.1   Summarizing the PoS consensus mechanisms

9.1.1   Fundamental background

A PoS consensus mechanism was created as a more energy-efficient alternative to the PoW mechanism. In PoS, leaders are chosen based on their contributions to the blockchain network, rather than their computational power. Specifically, a node's stake is determined by the number of digital tokens it holds or deposits, such as coins in a cryptocurrency. This means that instead of using large amounts of energy to search for a solution as in PoW, a leader is selected based on its stakes to perform the mining process and add a new block to the chain. To this end, the Follow-the-Satoshi (FTS) algorithm is often employed to simulate the stake-based leader selection process as illustrated in Figure 9.1. Specifically, all tokens in the blockchain are indexed and the FTS algorithm uses a hash function that takes a seed (such as the previous block's header or a random string created by other selected nodes) as input. The algorithm then outputs a token index, which is used to search the transaction history and find the current owner of that token. This owner is then selected as the leader to create a new block to add to the chain [4,8]. As a result, the more tokens a node possesses, the higher the chance it is selected as the leader.

9.1.2   Advantages of PoS

The PoS consensus mechanism has several advantages over other consensus mechanisms such as PoW. Some of the key advantages of PoS include:

- *Energy efficiency:* Since the leader is not determined by computing power, PoS is much more energy-efficient compared to PoW. Although there is still a need for computing and communication resources to participate in the consensus process, e.g., to validate transactions and broadcast messages, this resource consumption is negligible compared to that of the PoW mechanism [4,8].
- *Lower entry requirements:* Compared to PoW, PoS does not require the nodes to have expensive hardware to participate in the consensus process. This can reduce the centralization risk as more nodes can join the network [4,8].

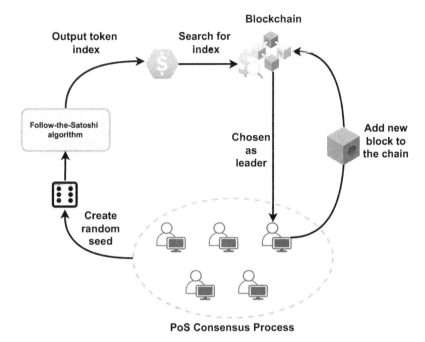

Figure 9.1   An illustration of the PoS consensus process. Typically, the consensus participants first create a random seed. This seed is then used by the FTS algorithm to output a token index. The current owner of that token is chosen as the leader who will add a new block to the chain.

- *More secure against 51% attacks:* In PoS, the adversary who wants to conduct 51% attacks needs to acquire more than 50% of the network tokens. In this case, when the adversary attacks, the network tokens might quickly lose their monetary value. As a result, the adversary also suffers the loss from its action. In contrast, in PoW networks, the adversary can use its computing power to attack a network and then continue to join another network where the token value is not affected. Consequently, the cost of 51% attacks in PoW networks is much lower than that in the PoS networks [4,8].

9.2   Emerging PoS mechanisms and their applications

9.2.1   *Ethereum*

Initially, Ethereum [3], the current second largest cryptocurrency employed PoW, similar to Bitcoin. However, to improve its security, reduce energy consumption, and pave the way to implement scaling solutions (e.g., shardings), Ethereum switched to PoS in September 2022. Particularly, Ethereum now employs a PoS-based consensus mechanism where validators lock up specific amounts of cryptocurrency or crypto

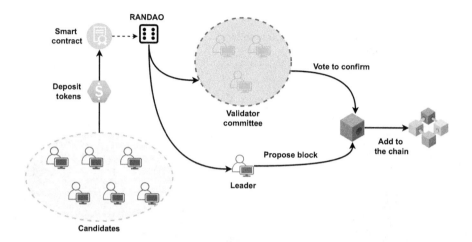

Figure 9.2   An illustration of the Ethereum's consensus process. The consensus
participants first make deposits to a smart contract. Among them, a
leader and committee of validators are randomly selected. The leader
then creates a new block, and the validators vote to confirm that block
and add it to the chain.

tokens, essentially staking their assets within a blockchain-based smart contract. In return for this commitment, they gain the opportunity to validate new transactions and earn rewards. However, if they incorrectly validate fraudulent or erroneous data, they face the risk of losing a portion or the entirety of their staked assets as a penalty [9].

In Ethereum, time is segmented into units called slots, each lasting for 12 s, and these slots are grouped into epochs, with each epoch consisting of 32 slots. As illustrated in Figure 9.2, within each slot, a single validator is chosen at random (using RANDAO [3], a smart-contract-based random number generator) to serve as the block proposer. Its role is to craft a new block and transmit it to other nodes within the network. Simultaneously, during each slot, another random selection process identifies a committee of validators. The votes from this committee are crucial in determining the validity of the proposed block. The division of the validator set into committees holds significance in maintaining a manageable network load. These committees effectively partition the validator set, ensuring that every active validator participates in the network's operations during each epoch but not necessarily during every individual slot [10].

Ethereum's PoS mechanism establishes its cryptographic security by implementing a system of rewards and penalties for the capital staked by participants. This incentive structure motivates individual users to operate as honest validators while penalizing those who deviate from the rules. It also imposes a substantial cost on potential attackers, discouraging network attacks. Furthermore, Ethereum has a protocol that governs the selection of honest validators for proposing or validating blocks, processing transactions, and casting their votes regarding the state of the blockchain's head.

Moreover, Ethereum also employs a mechanism called "checkpoint blocks." In each epoch, the initial block serves as a checkpoint. Validators cast their votes for checkpoint pairs they deem valid. When a pair of checkpoints gain sufficient votes, i.e., at least two-thirds of the total staked tokens, these checkpoints receive an upgrade. Particularly, after receiving enough votes, the older checkpoint is considered "finalized," whereas the latest checkpoint becomes "justified" [10].

Furthermore, in rare instances where multiple blocks are in the same position near the head of the blockchain (e.g., due to bad network conditions), a fork-choice mechanism comes into play. This mechanism selects blocks that contribute to the "heaviest" chain, determined by the number of validators who have cast their votes for these blocks, with the weighting based on their staked tokens balance [11–13].

Due to the recent switch to PoS and the ability to create user-defined smart contracts, Ethereum has many real-world applications [14], including:

- *Ethereum cryptocurrency* is a platform based on blockchain technology that allows for the development of smart contracts and decentralized applications. Its influence on the blockchain and cryptocurrency industries has been significant, as it has enabled the creation of a wide variety of innovative applications that go beyond simple digital currency transactions. Moreover, it is currently the second-largest cryptocurrency with a market capitalization of more than $200 billion.
- *Uniswap* [15] is a decentralized exchange built on the Ethereum network, enabling the exchange of ERC20 tokens for any user. It holds the distinction of being the largest decentralized exchange operating within the Ethereum blockchain [16]. Different from other exchange platforms, Uniswap has novel functionalities such as concentrated liquidity and multiple fee levels [17]. In contrast to the typical exchange model, which aims to generate fees, Uniswap is conceived as a public resource, serving as a tool for the community to trade tokens devoid of platform fees or intermediaries.
- *MakerDAO* [18] operates as a decentralized autonomous organization (DAO) built upon the Ethereum blockchain. It is one of the prominent DApps within the Ethereum ecosystem and was the pioneer in achieving significant adoption within the realm of decentralized finance (DeFi) [19]. MakerDAO developed a protocol that permits users to make loans in the form of a stablecoin known as DAI. This process is executed by locking a portion of their Ethereum tokens within MakerDAO's smart contracts, yielding a corresponding amount of DAI. When users decide to pay back the loans, the smart contract will automatically return the Ethereum tokens to the users [20].
- *The Sandbox* is a Metaverse application, i.e., a virtual world, built upon the Ethereum blockchain [21]. In The Sandbox, players have the capacity to construct, possess, and profit from their gaming ventures [22]. In 2018, it made a strategic move to transition into the blockchain environment, thereby granting players genuine ownership of their creations in the form of non-fungible tokens (NFTs) and offering incentives for their active involvement within the ecosystem.

- *Decentraland* is another Metaverse application based on Ethereum. Decentraland forms an expansive open-world metaverse that seamlessly integrates virtual reality, augmented reality, and the internet. Within Decentraland, participants can engage in various activities, including gaming, collectible trading, the buying and selling of virtual properties and avatar wearables, social interaction, and collaborative engagement. Moreover, users have the ability to govern and oversee their personally crafted virtual worlds via a DAO framework [23,24].
- *Brave* is a cost-free, open-source web browser based on Ethereum. This browser prioritizes user privacy by automatically blocking specific advertisements and website trackers by default [25]. Additionally, users have the option to enable ads that compensate them with Basic Attention Tokens for their attention [26]. These tokens and wallets are based on Ethereum, and they serve as a cryptocurrency and can also be employed for transactions with registered websites and content creators. As of August 2022, Brave reported an impressive user base, with over 57.42 million monthly active users, 19.3 million daily active users, and more than 1.6 million content creators [27].

9.2.2   Ouroboros

Ouroboros [28] is a family of pure PoS-based consensus mechanisms (including Ouroboros classic [28], Ouroboros Genesis [29], Ouroboros Praos [30], Ouroboros Chronos [31], and Ouroboros Crypsinous [32]) that operates by forming a dynamic committee determined by the distribution of stakes [28–33]. The protocol organizes time into epochs, during which committee members engage in a Publicly Verifiable Secret Sharing (PVSS) protocol to generate seeds for the FTS algorithm, as illustrated in Figure 9.3. This algorithm produces specific coin indices, and the individuals currently possessing those coins are chosen as leaders and subsequently become the committee members for the next epoch. Unlike PoW protocols, Ouroboros leaders exclusively produce empty blocks. The responsibility for confirming and adding transactions to the blocks lies with input endorsers. To encourage participation in the consensus process, block rewards are distributed among committee members, leaders, and input endorsers. Furthermore, Ouroboros integrates a stake delegation mechanism, allowing stakeholders to delegate their committee participation rights. This inclusion aims to incentivize smaller stakeholders to contribute to the consensus procedures.

   Ouroboros is a protocol that has been proven to be safe under a partially synchronous network assumption, as long as the adversary controls less than 51% of the total stake. In practice, partial synchrony cannot be guaranteed, so Ouroboros considers asynchronous nodes to be part of the adversary nodes. The dynamic stake distribution is also taken into account and incorporated into the adversary's stake. The seed creation process cannot be biased by the adversary, which mitigates grinding attacks where block proposers may try different block hashes in an attempt to influence the next leader selection round. Attacks where the adversary secretly builds alternative forks to later overtake the main chain, such as nothing-at-stake attacks and long-range attacks, are mitigated by having only one designated leader in each round.

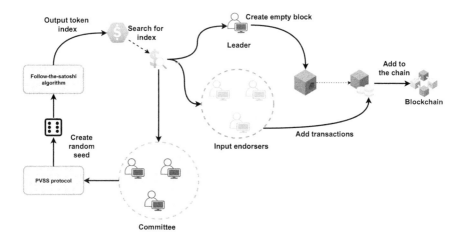

Figure 9.3   An illustration of the Ouroboros consensus process. In Ouroboros, the committee participates in the PVSS protocol to generate seeds for the FTS algorithm. Based on that, the leader and input endorsers for the current epoch and the committee for the next epoch are chosen. The leader will create empty block, and the input endorsers will add transactions to that block before it is added to the chain.

The incentive mechanism is also analyzed in the paper, and being honest is proven to be a δ-equilibrium strategy for participants.

Ouroboros offers several benefits, including swift transaction confirmation times (e.g., 2 min) and high transaction throughput (around 257 transactions per second). Furthermore, due to its unique approach where only selected leaders create blocks, Ouroboros consumes minimal energy when compared to PoW-based networks.

Cardano (https://www.cardano.org), the cryptocurrency that Ouroboros was developed for, has a current market capitalization of more than $10 billion. Beyond cryptocurrencies, Ouroboros is also employed by Sp8de (https://sp8de.com), which is a blockchain-based platform designed for interactive gaming. It provides a range of services customized to meet the specific requirements of the gaming sector. These services include a verifiable random number generator called CHAOS, marketing assistance in the form of Marketing-as-a-Service, and SPX, a digital utility token (digital utility tokens are only used to gain access to services) supported by publicly verifiable randomness.

9.2.3   Algorand

Similar to Ouroboros, the Algorand [34,35] protocol functions through the involvement of a committee. As illustrated in Figure 9.4, Algorand takes a different approach by employing a cryptographic sortition mechanism rather than the FTS algorithm to choose leaders and committee members based on stake distribution. This cryptographic sortition is essentially a Verifiable Random Function (VRF). It takes as inputs

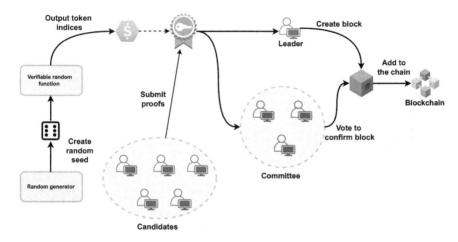

Figure 9.4   An illustration of the Algorand consensus process. Random seeds from random number generators are used by a VRF to output tokens' indices. Owner of these tokens can submit proofs to become leader and committee members. The leader then creates a new block, and the committee members vote to add that block to the chain.

a consensus node's private key and a seed and produces both a hash and a proof that can be publicly verified. Each consensus node is allocated a range of hash values proportional to its stake in the network. If the hash falls within a node's designated range, that node is selected. Consequently, a node's likelihood of being chosen is directly linked to its stake amount. The key distinction between the cryptographic sortition mechanism and the FTS algorithm lies in the fact that, with cryptographic sortition, the identity of the selected node is not revealed until it presents the proof. This means that adversaries cannot target a node in advance. Initially, the seed for the VRF is generated at the start of the process using a distributed random number generator. Subsequently, this seed is used to create a new seed via the VRF for the next round. Furthermore, the Algorand protocol does not solely rely on the leader selection process for security. The committee takes on the responsibility of voting on blocks to be added to the blockchain in each round, resulting in immediate block finalization.

Algorand has the capacity to function through an asynchronous period, provided that it is succeeded by a synchronous period. Under this assumption, Algorand has been proven to maintain its security as long as at least 51% of the total stake is under the control of honest participants. This security is assured because the committee votes to finalize every block, eliminating the occurrence of forks. Consequently, numerous attacks commonly associated with forks, such as double-spending, long-range, nothing-at-stakes, and bribery attacks, are effectively mitigated. To further enhance security, Algorand employs a method where a node's private key and the seed are used as inputs, with the private key being distributed ahead of the seed. This approach serves to mitigate grinding attacks, as potential adversaries would need to manipulate the leader selection process simultaneously to mount an attack.

While Algorand generates more than one block in each round, the quantity of blocks remains relatively small, and participants do not engage in hash rate competition to produce blocks. Consequently, the energy consumption associated with the Algorand protocol is notably lower in comparison to PoW mechanisms. Furthermore, Algorand can achieve a substantial transaction throughput, reaching up to 875 transactions per second. Notably, the protocol holds a significant advantage over many other PoS and PoW protocols due to its provision of immediate finality, meaning that blocks and transactions are immediately confirmed. As a result, transaction confirmation times are considerably faster, approximately 20 s, in contrast to protocols that rely on the longest chain rule, such as Ouroboros and PoW protocols.

Currently, Algorand has been adopted by several blockchain networks. Among them, Algorand (https://www.algorand.com) is a cryptocurrency with a market cap of more than $750 million. Arcblock (https://www.arcblock.io), a blockchain platform for Decentralized Applications (DApps), is also employing Algorand. The main characteristics and applications of Ethereum, Ouroboros, and Algorand are summarized in Table 9.1.

Table 9.1   Summary of Ethereum, Ouroboros, and Algorand consensus mechanisms

	Ethereum	Ouroboros	Algorand	DPoS
Time	Epochs and slots	Epochs and slots	No	Epochs and slots
Committee	Create random seeds	Vote to confirm checkpoints blocks	Vote to confirm blocks	Select leaders by round-robin
Random seeds	Participants vote	Participants vote	Random generator	None
Random algorithm	RANDAO	FTS	VRF	None
Block creation	Leader creates block with transactions	Leader creates empty block. Input endorsers add transactions	Leader creates block with transactions	Leaders create blocks and transactions
Finality	Probabilistic	Probabilistic	Immediate	Immediate
Applications	Ethereum cryptocurrency, Uniswap, MakerDAO, The Sandbox, Decentraland, Brave	Cardano, Sp8de	Algorand cryptocurrency, Arcblock	Bitshares, EOS, Steem

9.2.4   Delegated Proof-of-Stake

Delegated Proof of Stake (DPoS) was first introduced as the core consensus mechanism of the BitShares blockchain project [36]. DPoS aims to address the scalability issues associated with traditional PoW and PoS mechanisms. The core idea of DPoS is to elect a small number of trusted nodes, known as delegates or witnesses, by the stakeholders to validate transactions and produce new blocks. These delegates play a crucial role in maintaining the integrity of the blockchain.

Particularly, stakeholders in DPoS also have stakes similar to the stakeholders in PoS, as illustrated in Figure 9.5. However, instead of directly participating the consensus process by staking, the stakeholders in DPoS use their stakes to delegate their voting rights to the delegates. The more voting rights a delegate received, the higher chance it is selected to be the committee member. Once a fixed number of delegates has been elected, the take turns to validate transactions and produce new blocks in a round-robin manner until the epoch ends.

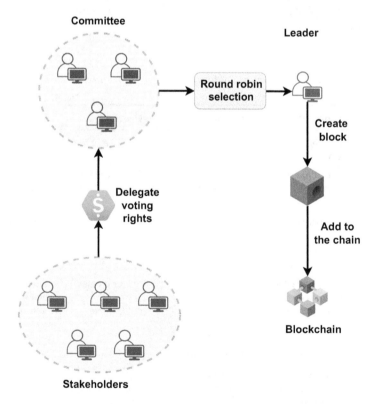

Figure 9.5   An illustration of the DPoS consensus process. Stakeholders can delegate their voting rights to choose committee members, i.e., delegates. The delegates are then chosen in a round-robin manner to be leaders. The leader then creates a new block to add to the chain.

Security in DPoS is primarily maintained through economic incentives and reputation. Specifically, delegates tend to act honestly since any malicious activity could lead to a loss of community support and, consequently, a decrease in their chances of being elected as delegates in the future. This ties with the loss of block reward, and thus delegates are disincentivized from acting maliciously. Additionally, stakeholders can also vote to remove underperforming or dishonest delegates, providing a self-regulating mechanism for the network [37].

Since the number of delegates is often small, e.g., around 30 delegates per epoch, the communication complexity is smaller compared to that of other PoS mechanisms. Moreover, due to the deterministic round-robin selection, the latency of DPoS can be very low. However, this comes as a trade-off for security, as delegates can be easily targeted by attackers and are prone to corruption (e.g., bribes). Furthermore, this might lead to high level of centralization as delegate with high reputation can be repeatedly voted for multiple consecutive epochs [37].

To overcome those issues, various frameworks and schemes have been proposed in the literature. For example, a downgrade mechanism is developed in [38] to quickly remove malicious delegates, thereby improving efficiency, fairness, and decentralization in the consensus process. Moreover, a delegate assessment scheme is proposed in [39] to categorize the delegates based on their performance, thereby facilitating countermeasures when a delegate becomes malicious. A similar dynamic trust scheme is presented in [40] to improve the reliability of delegates via frequent trust assessment.

With the advantages of higher scalability, energy efficiency, and faster transaction processing, DPoS has been employed in several real-world blockchain network. Among them, Steem is a blockchain-based social media platform that was designed to incentivize content creation, curation, and community engagement [41]. Moreover, EOS [2] is a cryptocurrency with more than $800 million in total market capitalization. Furthermore, Bitshares [36] is a blockchain network that has a cryptocurrency as well as an integrated decentralized exchange, with a market capitalization of more than $32 million [2].

9.3   Security properties and potential attacks on PoS

9.3.1   Security properties

Before discussing attacks, it is important to introduce the security properties, as they are the foundation for attacks mitigation. Particularly, to maintain the blockchain's security, a consensus mechanism must satisfy the following properties [42]:

- **Persistence:** Once a transaction is more than κ blocks deep in the chain of an honest user, all other honest users will have that transaction in the same position in their chains.
- **Liveness:** After a sufficient period, a valid transaction will be confirmed by all the honest users.

Persistence guarantees that once a transaction has been validated, meaning it has reached a depth of more than κ blocks in the blockchain, it becomes irreversible.

Without *persistence*, a malicious actor could execute a double-spending attack by initially sending a transaction to use some tokens. After that transaction is confirmed, the attacker could create a fork in the blockchain to remove the transaction. If this fork is accepted by honest users, the attacker can essentially reclaim the tokens they had previously spent. In contrast, while *persistence* ensures that data remains unchangeable, the liveness property ensures that all valid transactions will eventually find their way into the blockchain. Without *liveness*, an attacker could obstruct every transaction within a blockchain. Both *persistence* and *liveness* can be guaranteed if the consensus mechanism can ensure that the following probabilities are overwhelmingly low, e.g., <0.01% [42]:

- **Common prefix (CP) with parameter** $\kappa \in \mathbb{N}$: For any pair of honest users, their versions of the chain $\mathscr{C}_1, \mathscr{C}_2$ must share a common prefix. Specifically, assuming that $\mathscr{C}_2$ is longer than $\mathscr{C}_1$, removing κ last blocks of $\mathscr{C}_1$ results in the prefix of $\mathscr{C}_2$.
- **Chain growth (CG) with parameter** $\varsigma \in \mathbb{N}$ **and** $\tau \in (0, 1]$: A chain possessed by an honest user at time $t + \varsigma$ will be at least $\varsigma\tau$ blocks longer than the chain it possesses at time t.
- **Chain quality (CQ) with parameter** $l \in \mathbb{N}$ **and** $\mu \in (0, 1]$: Consider any part of the chain that has at least l blocks, the ratio of blocks created by the adversary is at most $1 - \mu$. In the ideal case, $1 - \mu$ equals the adversarial ratio $1 - \gamma$.

9.3.2 Attacks and mitigation

9.3.2.1 Double-spending attacks

Double spending [43,44] has been a central issue that blockchain technologies have aimed to address since their inception. In fact, most, if not all, attacks related to the blockchain ultimately seek to execute a double spend at some point during their operation. In this attack scenario, the perpetrator endeavors to spend the same digital currency on at least two separate occasions, hence, the term "double-spend." In the blockchain context, the attacker tries to carry out a transaction, waits for approval from the merchant, and subsequently reverses that transaction in order to spend the same digital currency in another transaction. This can be accomplished in blockchain systems by introducing a conflicting transaction, potentially within a different fork of the blockchain, as illustrated in Figure 9.6.

It is straightforward to see that with *persistence*, or equivalently CP, guaranteed, this attack cannot succeed. In the previous example, the merchant only needs to wait until the transaction is κ blocks deep in the chain to approve it. At this point, it is intractable for the attacker to revert the transaction [45]. Moreover, in some PoS consensus mechanisms with immediate finality such as Algorand, the transaction is immediately confirmed and irreversible once it is included in the blockchain. Therefore, double-spending attacks are prevented.

9.3.2.2 Sybil attacks

In a Sybil attack [28,43], an adversary creates multiple identities to disrupt or misguide a network decision or opinion. This attack is particularly dangerous in peer-to-peer networks where the state of the network depends on the majority vote. For example,

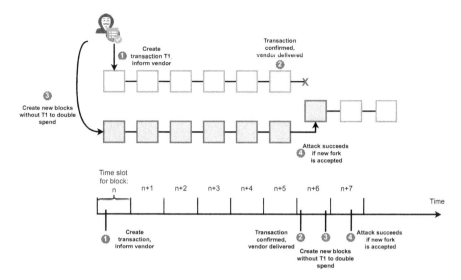

Figure 9.6   *An illustration of a double-spending attack. The attacker first creates a transaction to purchase goods from a vendor, while secretly building a fork. When the vendor confirms the transaction and delivers goods to the attacker, the attacker replaces a part of the chain with the secret fork, thereby gaining back the tokens it spent.*

in BFT voting protocols, the adversary can create numerous participants to unfairly influence the vote. In blockchains, this could create many issues such as finalizing a block, branching the blockchain, and electing validators [46–48].

To prevent this attack, PoS consensus mechanisms do not select leaders and/or committee members based on the number of participants. Instead, they are selected based on their stakes. As a result, even if the adversary creates many accounts and splits their stakes accordingly, their combined chance to be selected is the same as in the case when the adversary only uses one account. Therefore, this attack can be effectively prevented.

9.3.2.3   Race attacks

A race attack [43] only occurs in blockchains with probabilistic finality. In these blockchains, a certain number of blocks are typically required before considering a transaction to be finalized. While the network usually has a recommended confirmation count, users or merchants might not always follow the recommendation. Transactions involving significant amounts of funds might need a higher number of confirmations before they are deemed valid. Sometimes, a service may be improperly configured and not wait for the recommended number of confirmations on a particular blockchain. In such cases, a double-spending attack becomes possible.

In this attack, an adversary mines a fork of the blockchain until it meets the minimal requirements of that service. It then claims the goods associated with the transaction and quickly submits another conflicting transaction to revert the spent tokens. Since the original transaction might not be finalized, there is a chance that it is eventually replaced by a later transaction [49]. This attack can be straightforwardly prevented by the consensus mechanisms with immediate finality. In other cases, merchants/users are encouraged to wait for more blocks to be appended to the chain before confirming the transaction.

9.3.2.4 Bribery attacks

A bribery attack [50–52], also known as a Short-Range attack, revolves around the act of bribing leaders to focus on specific blocks or forks within the blockchain. Through this manipulation, the attacker can produce conflicting blocks or transactions, thereby significantly increasing the chance to successfully perform other attacks. For example, consider the case where the adversary is elected the leader of Block k. The adversary then makes a transaction at Block k to purchase goods from a vendor. Next, the adversary bribes the leaders of blocks $k + 1$ to $k + 6$, and thus essentially becomes the creators of those blocks. After Block $k + 6$ is appended to the chain, the vendor confirms this transaction and sends the goods to the adversary. The adversary then orders the bribed leaders to change their blocks, creating a fork that erases the original transaction in Block k, thereby gaining back the tokens spent in that transaction.

It is worth noting that bribery attacks can happen outside of the blockchain, e.g., by paying real-world money. Consequently, it is impossible to completely prevent this attack in probabilistic finality blockchain. To mitigate this attack, an approach is to increase the penalty for malicious behaviors, thereby increasing the costs of bribery attacks. Another approach is using a checkpoint blocks mechanism, similar to Ethereum. Since the checkpoint blocks are unchangeable, the attacker cannot revert any transaction that appears before the checkpoint blocks. However, these checkpoint blocks need to appear in sufficiently short intervals, otherwise, the attacker can successfully perform bribe attacks in between two checkpoint blocks. The only on-chain way to fully prevent bribery attacks is voting to finalize every block, i.e., immediate finality, as in Algorand.

9.3.2.5 Transaction denial attacks

In a transaction denial attack [28,43,53], the attacker aims to hinder the confirmation of a particular transaction or all transactions. For example, the attacker might aim to block outgoing transactions from a certain account or block all transactions to reduce the throughput of the blockchain. To this end, however, the adversary must be the leader or control the block creation of every slot. Otherwise, under the guarantee of *liveness* (or equivalently CQ and CG properties), any transaction will eventually be included in the chain. Moreover, an approach to mitigate transaction denial attacks that block all transactions, i.e., produce empty blocks, is to increase the penalty for malicious behaviors.

It is worth noting that the other type of transaction denial attacks (censorship attacks), which block transactions from certain users, cannot be fully prevented as the block creator can freely choose which transactions to include in the block. Nevertheless, as long as *liveness* is guaranteed, the transaction will eventually be included in the chain.

9.3.2.6   Grinding attacks

In grinding attacks [43,54], the attacker attempts to manipulate the process of selecting slot leaders to increase their chances of being chosen to create blocks. This can be used as a stepping stone for other attacks, such as double-spending. Particularly, the attacker can execute a trial-and-error process to test various block headers and content variations to find the combination that maximizes the chance for it to be selected as a slot leader in future rounds.

This type of attack impacts PoS mechanisms that derive randomness for the slot leader selection process from raw data within the blockchain itself, specifically from block headers and content. Due to this weakness, in contemporary PoS mechanisms, the randomness seed is not derived from the block raw data anymore. For example, the seeds are created by the committee via a PVSS scheme in Ouroboros or RANDAO in Ethereum.

9.3.2.7   Desynchronization and eclipse attacks

In most PoS consensus mechanisms, consensus participants need to participate in message exchange rounds to cast their votes, e.g., committee members vote to choose leaders for each slot. These communications require the participants to be online and able to send/receive messages. Desynchronization and eclipse attacks [55–57] are the attacks that attempt to block the communications of consensus participants by targeting them on the network level, e.g., blocking access to the time server to desynchronize. Moreover, in some cases, network failures (not necessarily because of the attackers) can also cause these issues.

Although these network issues are beyond the reach of the blockchain, they still pose severe threats to the consensus process. In most PoS mechanisms, the participants that are affected by these issues are taken into account when assessing security, and in some cases even incorporated as part of the adversary. For example, Ouroboros's security model considers these participants as adversarial and can tolerate up to 50% of participants to be desynchronized. Another approach is presented in Algorand where the consensus process can function properly for a short asynchronous duration.

9.3.2.8   Long-range attacks

An attacker aiming to carry out a double spending attack in the future may employ a long-range attack [58]. In this attack, the attacker computes a longer valid blockchain that commences right after the genesis block. In this new chain, the attacker is the sole stakeholder actively participating in the protocol. Even if the attacker only owns a small fraction of the total stake, they can construct this chain locally, producing blocks only for the slots where they are elected as the slot leader. They continue generating blocks ahead of the current time until their alternative chain surpasses the main chain in terms of block count.

Subsequently, the attacker can execute a transaction on the main chain, waiting for it to be confirmed (and for goods or services to be provided in exchange for the transaction). Afterward, they present the longer alternative chain to nullify their previously confirmed transaction.

In PoS mechanisms that employ a committee, long-range attacks can be easily prevented. Particularly, in these mechanisms, the leaders are selected by the committee via votes. Moreover, the committee of the next epoch is selected using seeds created by the current committee. Therefore, the fork presented by the attackers will be rejected by honest participants.

9.3.2.9   Nothing-at-Stake Attacks

The Nothing-at-Stake attacks [59], in a broader sense, refer to vulnerabilities in PoS blockchain systems where participants can produce multiple chains simultaneously with little effort. This is possible because PoS blockchains require relatively little computational effort to construct. Based on this, the attacker can build long forks to attempt other types of attacks such as double-spending attacks.

However, it is worth noting that the act of creating long forks by itself is not a threat. In fact, creating long forks is just a step in an attack, and thus as long as the original attack is mitigated, then the forks pose no threat. Moreover, as long as *persistence* and CP are guaranteed, then the fork will not be accepted by honest users. Furthermore, with the additional security from the committee voting and mechanisms such as VRF and PVSS, it is intractable to have a long fork to be accepted, unless the attacker controls more than 51% of the total network stakes.

9.3.2.10   Past majority attacks

PoS mechanisms often make the assumption that only the current majority of stake-holders are honest in their threat models. This implies that previous users, which may not currently hold any stake, could be compromised. This introduces a potential vulnerability for any PoS system because a group of malicious stakeholders from the past can construct an alternative blockchain by exploiting these old accounts [60]. This is facilitated by the negligible computation needed to create a PoS fork.

However, this attack [28] can only affect users who have not been online for a long time. Even in such cases, these users can quickly realize that the fork is not valid because their transactions (based on the fork) will not be accepted by the majority of users. Frequently active users will not accept the fork as long as *persistence* and CP hold. Moreover, mechanisms such as checkpoint blocks can also mitigate this type of attack.

9.3.2.11   51% Attacks

51% attacks [4,43,61] pose a risk to any consensus mechanism. In the case of the PoW mechanism, if an entity gains control of the majority of the hashing power within a specific time frame, it can exert full control over the blockchain. For example, the adversary can create a fork from the main chain and start mining on their own branch. Gradually, the attacker can outpace the main chain with their branch taking its place. In PoW protocols, where block generation relies on probability, there are numerous opportunities for conflicting branches, but these decrease as we exceed the 51% threshold. Consequently, the attacker may dominate the main chain, but branch reversions tend to occur frequently beyond this point.

A 51% attack in PoS networks operates under a similar principle as in PoW networks but with a few key differences due to the nature of PoS consensus. Particularly, in PoS mechanisms with committees, the committee members are often the ones who will (indirectly) decide the leaders and committee members for the next epoch via voting. With the majority of stakes, the adversary can dominate and unfairly influence the voting process, thereby exerting their influence on the next epoch's committees and leaders. As a result, *persistence* and *liveness* can no longer be guaranteed, and consequently, many types of attacks can be successfully performed. In the PoS networks without committees, an attacker with more than 51% stakes can be elected to be a leader for many consecutive blocks. As a result, the attacker can easily perform double-spending attacks.

Although up to date there is no solution to prevent 51% attacks, it is worth noting that 51% attacks in PoS networks can be much more challenging to execute compared to PoW networks. The reason is that acquiring a majority stake in a PoS network often requires significant financial investment, and it may be difficult to accumulate such a large amount of cryptocurrency without driving up the price significantly.

Moreover, in the case of PoW, the attacker can attack a network and then use the computing power to participate in another network. The cost in this case is only the energy consumption during the attack. However, in the case of PoS, the attacker needs to buy at least 51% stakes of the network. As the attack occurs, the price will plummet, and it is very hard for the attacker to regain the money used to purchase the stakes. The cost in this case is therefore much higher than that of the PoW case. The main characteristics and mitigation approaches of the attacks discussed earlier are summarized in Table 9.2.

9.4 Other challenges and future research directions

9.4.1 Stake pools formation

In PoS networks, the chances of an individual stakeholder with a small stake amount being chosen as a leader are insignificant. Additionally, active participation in the consensus process necessitates a constant network connection, which comes with operational expenses. Consequently, small stakeholders often pool their stakes together to increase their odds of winning the right to create blocks and to collectively manage operational costs [4]. This practice leads to the establishment of stake pools, which, similar to mining pools in PoW networks, are regarded as single entities. This aggregation of stakes in stake pools presents a potential risk of centralization within PoS networks. Particularly, when a large number of stakeholders join a single stake pool, the pool can become too powerful and control a

Table 9.2   Summary of attacks on PoS and their mitigation approaches.

Attacks	Aim	Procedure	Mitigation
Double-spending	Gain back spent tokens	Create forks and transactions to revert original transaction	Guarantee *persistence* and CP, immediate finality
Sybil	Gain unfair advantage in voting	Create numerous fake identities	Select based on stakes instead of the number of identities
Race	Gain back spent tokens	Users/vendors confirm transactions before recommended counts	Wait for transactions to be deep enough in the chain
Bribery	Support other attacks	Bribe leaders to create blocks with malicious intent	Immediate finality, slash deposits, checkpoint blocks
Transaction denial	Block transactions from certain or all users	Creates empty block. Ignore transactions from certain users	Guarantee *liveness*, CG, and CQ, slash deposits
Grinding	Unfairly influence the leader selection process	Try different block headers and contents	Use different randomness source
Desynchronization and eclipse	Block communications of consensus participants	Target network connections	Take network failures into account in security models
Long-range	Erase/replace transactions history	Use long forks to replace the main chain	Have designated leaders, broadcast voting results
Nothing-at-Stake	Support other attacks	Create multiple long forks	Guarantee *persistence* and CP, immediate finality, checkpoint blocks
Past majority	Erase/replace transactions history	Create long forks	Can only affect offline users, Guarantee *persistence* and CP, immediate finality, checkpoint blocks
51%	Gain full control of the chain	Dominate and unfairly influence the voting process	No complete solution. Attract more users to the network to increase the cost of attack

significant portion of the network's total stake. This can lead to a situation where the pool can manipulate the network's consensus mechanism and potentially compromise the security of the network. Additionally, if a stake pool operator is malicious, they can use their position to carry out attacks on the network or steal funds from the stakeholders.

The authors in [4] apply the non-cooperative game theory to analyze the formation of stake pools and their effects on the decentralization of the PoS blockchain network. Non-cooperative game theory is a branch of game theory that models situations of conflicting interests among the players, where each player acts independently to maximize their profit, which is affected by the actions of all players. In the considered game, the network users can freely choose to invest in a number of stake pools in the network. Moreover, when more users invest in the pools, the reward of individual users will decrease. Therefore, non-cooperative game theory is applied to analyze the stake pools and the behaviors of the stakeholders.

The authors then prove that there exists at least one Nash equilibrium in the game, and they also prove that the best strategy for users is to invest all of their budget in the pools. The uniqueness of the Nash equilibrium is also proven, and an iterative algorithm is developed to find the Nash equilibrium. The simulation results in the paper show that the formation of stake pools can lead to centralization in PoS blockchain networks. The authors also simulate the ratio between the block reward and the total network stake to determine its impact on the decentralization of the network, and the results show that a higher block reward can lead to a more decentralized network, while a lower block reward can lead to a more centralized network.

Another game theoretic approach is presented in [62] to analyze the stake pool formation. However, unlike [4], the game considered in [62] is a Stackelberg game. In this Stackelberg game, certain players called leaders make their moves first. Based on that, the remaining players, called followers, will make their moves accordingly. In practice, the stake pools often announce their costs and fees first, and the users will choose to invest accordingly. Therefore, this situation is modeled as a Stackelberg game with one leader (a stake pool) and multiple followers (users).

The authors analyze the game and show that the users' best actions are to either invest in the pool or self-mine (participate in the consensus process individually). The followers' sub-game equilibrium is then proven to exist and is unique. As a result, for every action of a leader (every amount of fee and cost), there is a unique way that the users will respond, and thus a unique equilibrium state will occur. Then, the authors formulate a Mixed-Integer Programming model to find the optimal action for the leader and prove that there exists a unique Stackelberg equilibrium in the game. Simulation results show that if the stake pool is properly managed, it can enhance network security and performance.

9.4.2 Federated-blockchain Systems

Despite its widespread use and potential, blockchain technology is encountering several challenges. The rapid growth of blockchain and the immense popularity of cryptocurrencies have led to the emergence of numerous blockchain networks.

For instance, in just one year, the number of cryptocurrency networks has surged more than threefold (from 2,000 cryptocurrencies in 2019 to 7,400 as of December 2020 [5]). These blockchain networks employ various consensus mechanisms, resulting in significant fragmentation because they are unable to communicate with each other.

However, there are numerous applications based on blockchain technology where the capability to transfer assets across different blockchains is crucial. Examples include coalition loyalty programs [63] and retail payments [5]. In coalition loyalty programs, users need to exchange their loyalty points among different programs, each stored on distinct blockchains in the form of blockchain tokens. Similarly, in retail payments, vendors may only accept a specific type of token, necessitating users to convert their tokens to another type.

Nevertheless, within single blockchain networks, users seeking to exchange tokens often have to rely on centralized exchange platforms, such as Binance [64] and Kraken [65]. This reliance on centralized exchanges contradicts the decentralized nature of blockchain technology and introduces significant security risks. Notably, these exchanges have suffered numerous attacks, resulting in a cumulative loss of over $1 billion [5] in recent years. Furthermore, the trade-off between performance and security in consensus mechanism designs typically results in high latency and limited processing capacity. For example, Bitcoin requires approximately one hour to validate a transaction and can handle fewer than seven transactions per second [4]. These limitations pose challenges to the widespread utility of blockchain technology in various scenarios. To address this issue of low transaction processing capacity, sharding mechanisms [66] can be employed. Sharding involves dividing the blockchain network into multiple sub-networks to enhance throughput. However, a significant limitation of sharding is that these sub-networks remain under the control of the same network operator and continue to utilize the same type of tokens. Consequently, sharding alone does not facilitate the transfer of assets between distinct blockchains. Therefore, there is a need for an effective framework that not only enables interoperability among blockchain networks but also ensures the security and performance of each individual network.

To tackle these challenges, sidechain technology [67] has been developed to enable the creation of a federated blockchain system. In such a federated blockchain system, there exist multiple blockchains, and users within the system can move their assets between any of these blockchains. The concept of sidechain technology was initially introduced in [67] as an innovative approach to facilitate cross-chain transactions. Specifically, the mechanisms of sidechain technology, including two-way peg and Simplified Payment Verification (SPV) proof [67], enable a group of validators to authenticate and validate transactions between different blockchains. While this development has paved the way for numerous research endeavors and applications, it is worth noting that the security and performance aspects of sidechains were only briefly mentioned and not thoroughly explored in [67]. Subsequently, following the introduction of sidechain technology, several noteworthy real-world applications have emerged, including PoA [68] and Liquid [69]. However, these networks are all built upon the foundation of PoW, which requires significant energy consumption.

Due to its significant advantages, recent research efforts in the field of sidechain technology have shifted their focus toward the PoS mechanism. In [70], a protocol has been developed to enable cross-chain transfers between a primary blockchain (referred to as the main chain) and a secondary chain (known as the sidechain). This protocol relies on a group of certifiers selected by the main chain to validate cross-chain trans-actions. One notable advantage of this proposed protocol lies in the separation of the sidechain and main chain in terms of security and operational independence. In [71], the authors introduce a sidechain system where both the sidechain and the main chain employ a PoS mechanism, specifically Ouroboros [28]. Unlike previous works, this research places a stronger emphasis on the security aspects of sidechain technology, offering formal definitions and robust security analyses. Similarly, in [72], the authors present a cross-chain transfer protocol designed to facilitate interoperability between a main chain and a sidechain. This protocol comes with formal definitions, and a consensus mechanism is detailed in a manner similar to [71].

In [73], a PoS-based framework is introduced for a federated blockchain system. In this framework, cross-chain transactions are managed by a group of validators selected based on their stakes once a day, and they receive rewards for their valida-tion efforts. However, the framework demands that over 66% of the network stakes be under the control of honest users. In [74], a federated blockchain framework is developed using the Tendermint consensus mechanism [75]. In this setup, cross-chain transactions are handled by a fixed group of validators. This arrangement carries a higher risk of centralization since these validators are predetermined and publicly known within the entire network. In [76], an innovative method for cross-chain trans-fers is proposed. This method enables the exchange of assets among different parties on various blockchain networks by requiring both the sender and receiver of a trans-action to vote on it. In [77], a cross-chain commitment protocol is created to facilitate asset transfers between different blockchains. Unlike previous work, this protocol addresses scenarios where users need to send their transactions to a specific smart contract within a specified time frame to complete their asset transfers.

It is worth noting that a common limitation of the above works is that they do not address the risk of centralization. Specifically, the capability to transfer assets across multiple chains raises the risk of centralization towards a single chain, e.g., the chain with the highest block reward. This centralization poses security threats to the other chains within the same federation because they will have fewer stakes and thus be more vulnerable to attacks, as illustrated in Figure 9.7. To address this issue, the authors in [5] formulate a multiple-leaders–multiple-followers game where the users are followers and the chains are leaders. In this game, the chains set their block rewards and the users will move their assets to the chains to participate in the consensus process accordingly. The authors then analyze the game and prove the existence and uniqueness of the Stackelberg equilibrium. Interestingly, the exact formula for the equilibrium can also be determined. Simulation results show that the game analysis can help to determine the centralization risk in terms of CP, CQ, and CG violation probabilities, as well as enhance the system's security and performance.

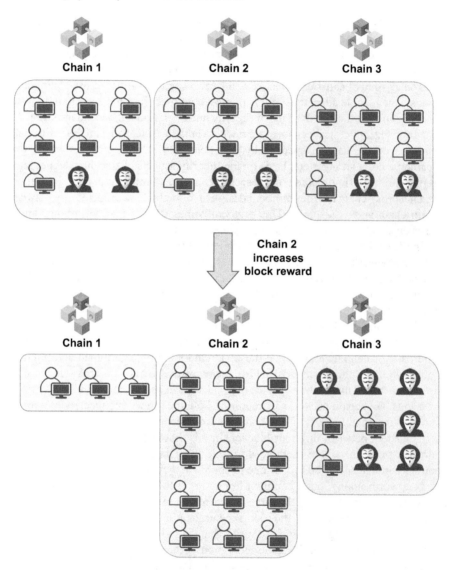

Figure 9.7   *An illustration of the centralization risk in Federated-blockchain systems. Initially, the adversary only controls 22.2% of Chain 3. Then, Chain 2 increases its block rewards and attracts more users there. Consequently, the adversary moves its stakes to Chain 3, thereby controlling more than 66.6% of Chain 3.*

9.4.3   PoS shardings

Although the PoS mechanism's transaction processing capability is a massive improvement over that of the PoW, it is still inadequate for applications with millions of users

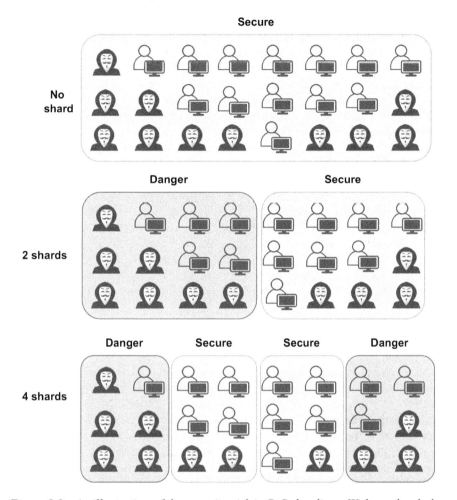

Figure 9.8 An illustration of the security risk in PoS shardings. With no shard, the adversary only controls nearly 46% of the network stakes. With 2 shards, the adversary controls 58.3% of a shard. With 4 shards, the adversary controls 83.3% of one shard and 50% of another shard.

such as Metaverse or Web 3.0. To tackle this challenge and enhance the scalability of the solution, a recent approach called the sharding mechanism [66,78] has been proposed. This mechanism aims to partition the blockchain network into multiple sub-networks known as shards. Each shard operates its own independent consensus process for transaction validation and generates a new block during each time slot. With multiple shards operating in parallel, it becomes possible to create and add multiple new blocks to the blockchain within the same time slot. Consequently, this significantly boosts the transaction processing speed.

However, there are trade-offs to consider between security and speed in this approach. Essentially, the more shards a network is divided into, the lower its overall security. This division makes it easier for potential adversaries to carry out 51% attacks, as illustrated in Figure 9.8. For instance, if a PoS-based blockchain network is divided into 10 shards, an adversary might only need control over 6% of the total network stakes (coins) to successfully execute a 51% attack, compared to the requirement of at least 51% of the stakes when there are no shards in the network. Therefore, it is essential to carefully determine the number of shards and how user stakes are allocated within each shard to prevent any vulnerability that could be exploited by an adversary. To address this issue, an optimization problem is formulated in [6] that aims to maximize the number of shards while ensuring that the risk of 51% attack in each shard is minimal. To this end, authors first derive the probability that a shard is overwhelmed by the adversary under uncertainties, i.e., which user is adversarial is not known. Then, using Hoeffding bound [79], the required stakes allocation threshold can be deduced. Finally, the authors formulate the optimization problem as a Mixed-Integer Nonlinear Programming problem. To solve this problem, a decomposition technique and a Lagrangian-based approach are proposed. Simulation results show that the proposed approach can achieve up to 66.6% higher throughput in a very short running time.

9.5 Conclusion

In this chapter, we have first provided a concise summary of the PoS consensus mechanism, covering its key concepts and benefits. Then, we have presented notable advanced PoS mechanisms and their real-world applications. Moreover, we have reviewed PoS security properties and introduced potential attacks targeting PoS networks as well as potential approaches to mitigate them, including double-spending, Sybil, race, bribery, transaction denial, grinding, desynchronization, eclipse, long-range, nothing-at-stakes, past majority, and 51% attacks. Furthermore, we discussed the challenges faced in PoS networks and potential research directions, including stake pool formation, federated blockchain systems, and PoS shardings.

References

[1] King S and Nadal S. Ppcoin: Peer-to-peer crypto-currency with proof-of-stake. Self-Published Paper, August 2012;19(1).

[2] Today's Cryptocurrency Prices by Market Cap [homepage on the Internet]. CoinMarketCap; 2023 [updated 2023 Aug 23; cited 2023 Aug 23]. Available from: https://coinmarketcap.com/.

[3] PROOF-OF-STAKE (POS) [homepage on the Internet]. Ethereum; 2023 [updated 2023 Aug 23; cited 2023 Aug 23]. Available from: https://ethereum.org/en/developers/docs/consensus-mechanisms/pos/.

[4] Nguyen CT, Hoang DT, Nguyen DN, *et al.* Proof-of-stake consensus mechanisms for future blockchain networks: fundamentals, applications and opportunities. *IEEE Access.* 2019;7:85727–85745.

[5]   Nguyen CT, Hoang DT, Nguyen DN, *et al*. Fedchain: secure proof-of-stake-based framework for federated-blockchain systems. *IEEE Transactions on Services Computing*. 2023;16(4):2642–2656.

[6]   Nguyen CT, Hoang DT, Nguyen DN, Xiao Y, Niyato D and Dutkiewicz E, MetaShard: a novel sharding blockchain platform for metaverse applications, *IEEE Transactions on Mobile Computing*, doi: 10.1109/TMC.2023.3290955.

[7]   Nguyen CT, Hoang DT, Nguyen DN, *et al*. Metachain: a novel blockchain-based framework for metaverse applications. In: *2022 IEEE 95th Vehicular Technology Conference: (VTC2022-Spring)*. IEEE; 2022. p. 1–5.

[8]   Wang W, Hoang DT, Hu P, *et al*. A survey on consensus mechanisms and mining strategy management in blockchain networks. *IEEE Access*. 2019;7: 22328–22370.

[9]   Zhang W and Anand T. Ethereum architecture and overview. In: *Blockchain and Ethereum Smart Contract Solution Development: Dapp Programming with Solidity*. Springer; 2022. p. 209–244.

[10] Kushwaha SS, Joshi S, Singh D, *et al*. Systematic review of security vulnerabilities in Ethereum blockchain smart contract. *IEEE Access*. 2022;10:6605–6621.

[11] Schwarz-Schilling C, Neu J, Monnot B, *et al*. Three attacks on proof-of-stake Ethereum. In: *International Conference on Financial Cryptography and Data Security*. Springer; 2022. p. 560–576.

[12] Neu J, Tas EN, and Tse D. Two more attacks on proof-of-stake GHOST/Ethereum. In: *Proceedings of the 2022 ACM Workshop on Developments in Consensus*; 2022. p. 43–52.

[13] D'Amato F, Neu J, Tas EN, *et al*. *Goldfish: No More Attacks on Proof-of-Stake Ethereum*. Cryptology ePrint Archive. 2022.

[14] Ethereum: Top 10 Biggest Projects [homepage on the Internet]. CoinMarketCap; 2023 [updated 2022 Aug 23; cited 2023 Aug 23]. Available from: https://coinmarketcap.com/alexandria/article/ethereum-top-10-biggest-projects.

[15] Ottina M, Steffensen PJ, and Kristensen J. Uniswap v3. In: *Automated Market Makers: A Practical Guide to Decentralized Exchanges and Cryptocurrency Trading*. Springer; 2023. p. 159–279.

[16] Heimbach L, Schertenleib E, and Wattenhofer R. Risks and returns of uniswap v3 liquidity providers. 2022. arXiv preprint arXiv:220508904.

[17] Fan Z, Marmolejo-Cossío FJ, Altschuler B, *et al*. Differential liquidity provision in Uniswap v3 and implications for contract design. In: *Proceedings of the Third ACM International Conference on AI in Finance*; 2022. p. 9–17.

[18] Ellinger EW, Mini T, Gregory RW, *et al*. Decentralized Autonomous Organization (DAO): the case of MakerDAO. *Journal of Information Technology Teaching Cases*. 2023;p. 20438869231181151.

[19] Brennecke M, Guggenberger T, Schellinger B, *et al*. The de-central bank in decentralized finance: a case study of MakerDAO. *55th Hawaii International Conference on System Sciences*; 2022, pp. 4–7.

[20] Kozhan R and Viswanath-Natraj G. Fundamentals of the MakerDAO governance token. In: *3rd International Conference on Blockchain Economics,*

Security and Protocols (Tokenomics 2021). Schloss Dagstuhl-Leibniz-Zentrum für Informatik; 2022.

[21]   Nakavachara V and Saengchote K. Is Metaverse LAND a good investment? It depends on your unit of account! 2022. arXiv preprint arXiv:220203081.

[22]   Huynh-The T, Gadekallu TR, Wang W, *et al*. Blockchain for the metaverse: a review. *Future Generation Computer Systems*. 2023;143:401–419.

[23]   Guidi B and Michienzi A. Social games and Blockchain: exploring the Metaverse of Decentraland. In: *2022 IEEE 42nd International Conference on Distributed Computing Systems Workshops (ICDCSW)*. IEEE; 2022. p. 199–204.

[24]   Nnamonu O, Hammoudeh M, and Dargahi T. Digital forensic investigation of web-based virtual reality worlds: decentraland as a case study. *IEEE Communications Magazine*. 2023;61(9):72–78.

[25]   Madhusudhan R and Surashe SV. Privacy and security comparison of web browsers: a review. In: *International Conference on Advanced Information Networking and Applications*. Springer; 2022. p. 459–470.

[26]   Serada A, Grym J, and Sihvonen T. The economy of attention on blockchain in the Brave browser. In: *Futures of Journalism: Technology-stimulated Evolution in the Audience-News Media Relationship*. Springer; 2022. p. 49–62.

[27]   Mohamed A and Ismail I. A performance comparative on most popular Internet Web Browsers. *Procedia Computer Science*. 2022;215:589–597.

[28]   Kiayias A, Russell A, David B, *et al*. Ouroboros: a provably secure proof-of-stake blockchain protocol. In: *Annual International Cryptology Conference*. Springer; 2017. p. 357–388.

[29]   Badertscher C, Gaži P, Kiayias A, *et al*. Ouroboros genesis: composable proof-of-stake blockchains with dynamic availability. In: *Proceedings of the 2018 ACM SIGSAC Conference on Computer and Communications Security*; 2018. p. 913–930.

[30]   David B, Gaži P, Kiayias A, *et al*. Ouroboros praos: an adaptively-secure, semi-synchronous proof-of-stake blockchain. In: *Advances in Cryptology—EUROCRYPT 2018: 37th Annual International Conference on the Theory and Applications of Cryptographic Techniques*, Tel Aviv, Israel, April 29–May 3, 2018 Proceedings, Part II 37. Springer; 2018. p. 66–98.

[31]   Badertscher C, Gaži P, Kiayias A, *et al*. Ouroboros chronos: permissionless clock synchronization via proof-of-stake. Cryptology ePrint Archive. 2019.

[32]   Kerber T, Kiayias A, Kohlweiss M, *et al*. Ouroboros crypsinous: privacy-preserving proof-of-stake. In: *2019 IEEE Symposium on Security and Privacy (SP)*. IEEE; 2019. p. 157–174.

[33]   Aragon N, Blazy O, Deneuville JC, *et al*. Ouroboros: an efficient and provably secure KEM family. *IEEE Transactions on Information Theory*. 2022;68(9):6233–6244.

[34]   Chen J and Micali S. Algorand: a secure and efficient distributed ledger. *Theoretical Computer Science*. 2019;777:155–183.

[35]   Gilad Y, Hemo R, Micali S, *et al*. Algorand: scaling byzantine agreements for cryptocurrencies. In: *Proceedings of the 26th Symposium on Operating Systems Principles*; 2017. p. 51–68.

[36]   Schuh F and Larimer D. Bitshares 2.0: General Overview. 2017. Accessed June 2017. Available: http://docs bitshares org/downloads/bitshares-general pdf.

[37]   Saad SMS and Radzi RZRM. Comparative review of the blockchain consensus algorithm between proof of stake (pos) and delegated proof of stake (dpos). *International Journal of Innovative Computing*. 2020;10(2).

[38]   Yang F, Zhou W, Wu Q, *et al*. Delegated proof of stake with downgrade: a secure and efficient blockchain consensus algorithm with downgrade mechanism. *IEEE Access*. 2019;7:118541–118555.

[39]   Hu Q, Yan D, Han Y, *et al*. An improved delegated proof of stake consensus algorithm. *Procedia Computer Science*. 2021;187:341–346.

[40]   Sun Y, Yan B, Yao Y, *et al*. DT-DPoS: a delegated proof of stake consensus algorithm with dynamic trust. *Procedia Computer Science*. 2021;187: 371–376.

[41]   Building better communities, creating rewarding opportunities and empowering entrepreneurs [homepage on the Internet]. Steem; 2023 [updated 2023 Aug 23; cited 2023 Aug 23]. Available from: https://steem.com/about/.

[42]   Garay J, Kiayias A, and Leonardos N. The bitcoin backbone protocol: analysis and applications. In: *Annual International Conference on the Theory and Applications of Cryptographic Techniques*. Springer; 2015. p. 281–310.

[43]   Deirmentzoglou E, Papakyriakopoulos G, and Patsakis C. A survey on long-range attacks for proof of stake protocols. *IEEE Access*. 2019;7: 28712–28725.

[44]   Zhang S and Lee JH. Double-spending with a sybil attack in the bitcoin decentralized network. *IEEE Transactions on Industrial Informatics*. 2019;15(10):5715–5722.

[45]   Nicolas K, Wang Y, and Giakos GC. Comprehensive overview of selfish mining and double spending attack countermeasures. In: *2019 IEEE 40th Sarnoff Symposium*. IEEE; 2019. p. 1–6.

[46]   Swathi P, Modi C, and Patel D. Preventing Sybil attack in blockchain using distributed behavior monitoring of miners. In: *2019 10th International Conference on Computing, Communication and Networking Technologies (ICCCNT)*. IEEE; 2019. p. 1–6.

[47]   Platt M and McBurney P. Sybil in the haystack: a comprehensive review of blockchain consensus mechanisms in search of strong sybil attack resistance. *Algorithms*. 2023;16(1):34.

[48]   Platt M and McBurney P. Sybil attacks on identity-augmented Proof-of-Stake. *Computer Networks*. 2021;199:108424.

[49]   Aggarwal S and Kumar N. Attacks on blockchain. In: *Advances in Computers*, vol. 121. New York, NY: Elsevier; 2021. p. 399–410.

[50]   Sun H, Ruan N, and Su C. How to model the bribery attack: a practical quantification method in blockchain. In: *Computer Security–ESORICS 2020: 25th European Symposium on Research in Computer Security, ESORICS 2020,*

Guildford, UK, September 14–18, 2020, Proceedings, Part II 25. Springer; 2020. p. 569–589.

[51]   Bonneau J. Why buy when you can rent? Bribery attacks on bitcoin-style consensus. In: *International Conference on Financial Cryptography and Data Security*. Springer; 2016. p. 19–26.

[52]   Judmayer A, Stifter N, Zamyatin A, *et al*. Pay to win: cheap, cross-chain bribing attacks on pow cryptocurrencies. In: *Financial Cryptography and Data Security. FC 2021 International Workshops: CoDecFin, DeFi, VOTING, and WTSC*, Virtual Event, March 5, 2021, Revised Selected Papers 25. Springer; 2021. p. 533–549.

[53]   Chaganti R, Boppana RV, Ravi V, *et al*. A comprehensive review of denial of service attacks in blockchain ecosystem and open challenges. *IEEE Access*. 2022;10:96538–96555.

[54]   Chepurnoy A. Interactive proof-of-stake. 2016. arXiv preprint arXiv: 160100275.

[55]   Xu G, Guo B, Su C, *et al*. Am I eclipsed? A smart detector of eclipse attacks for Ethereum. *Computers & Security*. 2020;88:101604.

[56]   Zhang S and Lee JH. Eclipse-based stake-bleeding attacks in PoS blockchain systems. In: *Proceedings of the 2019 ACM International Symposium on Blockchain and Secure Critical Infrastructure*; 2019. p. 67–72.

[57]   Shihab S and AlTawy R. Lightweight authentication scheme for healthcare with robustness to desynchronization attacks. *IEEE Internet of Things Journal*. 2023;10:18140–18153.

[58]   Sanda O, Pavlidis M, Seraj S, *et al*. Long-range attack detection on permissionless blockchains using deep learning. *Expert Systems with Applications*. 2023;218:119606.

[59]   Lys L, Forestier S, Vodenicarevic D, *et al*. Defending against the nothing-at-stake problem in multi-threaded blockchains. 2023. arXiv preprint arXiv:230210009.

[60]   Cilloni T, Cai X, Fleming C, *et al*. Understanding and detecting majority attacks. In: *2020 IEEE International Conference on Decentralized Applications and Infrastructures (DAPPS)*. IEEE; 2020. p. 11–21.

[61]   Aponte-Novoa FA, Orozco ALS, Villanueva-Polanco R, *et al*. The 51% attack on blockchains: a mining behavior study. *IEEE Access*. 2021;9: 140549–140564.

[62]   Nguyen CT, Nguyen DN, Hoang DT, *et al*. Blockroam: blockchain-based roaming management system for future mobile networks. *IEEE Transactions on Mobile Computing*. 2021;21(11):3880–3894.

[63]   Nguyen CT, Hoang DT, Nguyen DN, *et al*. Blockchain-based secure platform for coalition loyalty program management. In: *2021 IEEE Wireless Communications and Networking Conference (WCNC)*. IEEE; 2021. p. 1–6.

[64]   Binance Official Website [homepage on the Internet]. Binance; 2023 [updated 2023 Aug 23; cited 2023 Aug 23]. Available from: https://www.binance.com/en.

[65] Kraken Crypto Exchange [homepage on the Internet]. Kraken; 2023 [updated 2023 Aug 23; cited 2023 Aug 23]. Available from: https://www.kraken.com/.

[66] Yu G, Wang X, Yu K, *et al*. Survey: sharding in blockchains. *IEEE Access*. 2020;8:14155–14181.

[67] Back A, Corallo M, Dashjr L, *et al*. Enabling blockchain innovations with pegged sidechains. 2014;72:201–224. URL: http://www opensciencereview-com/ papers/123/enablingblockchain-innovations-with-pegged-sidechains.

[68] Barinov I, Baranov V, and Khahulin P. POA Network White Paper. 2018. URL: https://github com/poanetwork/wiki/wiki/POA-Network-Whitepaper.

[69] Dilley J, Poelstra A, Wilkins J, *et al*. Strong federations: an interoperable blockchain solution to centralized third-party risks. 2016. arXiv preprint arXiv:161205491.

[70] Garoffolo A and Viglione R. Sidechains: decoupled consensus between chains. 2018. arXiv preprint arXiv:181205441.

[71] Gaži P, Kiayias A, and Zindros D. Proof-of-stake sidechains. In: *2019 IEEE Symposium on Security and Privacy (SP)*. IEEE; 2019. p. 139–156.

[72] Garoffolo A, Kaidalov D, and Oliynykov R. Zendoo: a zk-SNARK verifiable cross-chain transfer protocol enabling decoupled and decentralized sidechains. In: *2020 IEEE 40th International Conference on Distributed Computing Systems (ICDCS)*. IEEE; 2020. p. 1257–1262.

[73] Wood G. Polkadot: vision for a heterogeneous multi-chain framework. *White Paper*. 2016;21(2327):4662.

[74] Kwon J and Buchman E. Cosmos whitepaper. *A Networks Distributed Ledgers*. 2019;27.

[75] Amoussou-Guenou Y, Del Pozzo A, Potop-Butucaru M, *et al*. Dissecting tendermint. In: *International Conference on Networked Systems*. Springer; 2019. p. 166–182.

[76] Herlihy M, Liskov B, and Shrira L. Cross-chain deals and adversarial commerce. 2019. arXiv preprint arXiv:190509743.

[77] Zakhary V, Agrawal D, and Abbadi AE. Atomic commitment across blockchains. 2019. arXiv preprint arXiv:190502847.

[78] Xie J, Yu FR, Huang T, *et al*. A survey on the scalability of blockchain systems. *IEEE Network*. 2019;33(5):166–173.

[79] Mitzenmacher M and Upfal E. *Probability and Computing: Randomization and Probabilistic Techniques in Algorithms and Data Analysis*. Cambridge: Cambridge University Press; 2017.

Index

Printed in the USA
CPSIA information can be obtained
at www.ICGtesting.com
JSHW011507221024
72173JS00005B/1227